Learning from Baby P

of related interest

Whistleblowing and Ethics in Health and Social Care
Speaking Out
Angie Ash
ISBN 978 1 84905 632 8
eIBSN 978 1 78450 108 2

Hidden Cameras
Everything You Need to Know About Covert Recording,
Undercover Cameras and Secret Filming
Joe Plomin
ISBN 978 1 84905 643 4
eISBN 978 1 78450 136 5

Tackling Child Neglect
Research, Policy and Evidence-Based Practice
Edited by Ruth Gardner
ISBN 978 1 84905 662 5
eISBN 978 1 78450 165 5

Practical Guide to Child Protection
The Challenges, Pitfalls and Practical Solutions
Joanna Nicolas
ISBN 978 1 84905 586 4
eISBN 978 1 78450 032 0

Risk in Child Protection
Assessment Challenges and Frameworks for Practice
Martin C. Calder with Julie Archer
ISBN 978 1 84905 479 9
eISBN 978 0 85700 858 9

Challenging Child Protection
New Directions in Safeguarding Children
Edited by Lorraine Waterhouse and Janice McGhee
ISBN 978 1 84905 395 2
eISBN 978 0 85700 760 5

How We Treat the Sick
Neglect and Abuse in Our Health Services
Michael Mandelstam
ISBN 978 1 84905 160 6
eISBN 978 0 85700 355 3

LEARNING FROM BABY P

The Politics of blame, fear and denial

Sharon Shoesmith

Jessica Kingsley *Publishers*
London and Philadelphia

First published in 2016
by Jessica Kingsley Publishers
73 Collier Street
London N1 9BE, UK
and
400 Market Street, Suite 400
Philadelphia, PA 19106, USA

www.jkp.com

Library of Congress Cataloging in Publication Data
Names: Shoesmith, Sharon, author. Title: Learning from Baby
P : the politics of blame, fear and denial / Sharon
Shoesmith. Description: London ; Philadelphia : Jessica Kingsley Publishers, 2016. |
Includes bibliographical references and index. Identifiers: LCCN
2016012750 | ISBN 9781785920035 (alk. paper) Subjects: LCSH:
Child abuse--Great Britain--Case studies. | Child
welfare--Great Britain--Case studies. | Social service--Great
Britain--Case studies. | Social work administration--Great Britain--Case
studies. Classification: LCC HV6626.54.G7 S56 2016 | DDC 362.760941--dc23 LC
record available at https://urldefense.proofpoint.com/v2/url?u=https- 3A__lccn.
loc.gov_2016012750&d=BQIFAg&c=euGZstcaTDllvimEN8b7jXrwqOf-
v5A_CdpgnVfiiMM&r=1v35CMXDPq9tusP6l-
19m3h61RNMvLridzO13DRUbWg&m=moP0M3Rn0J8FfyOJH-
Og1fHpfPfeY1JHAgnRad5TSP4&s=aNFllgJTiwKuzsfoeDfCEuVyG0F_
BvqG-wT9rNr_B3s&e=

British Library Cataloguing in Publication Data
A CIP catalogue record for this book is available from the British Library

ISBN 978 1 78592 003 5
eISBN 978 1 78450 238 6

Printed and bound in Great Britain

This book is dedicated to the memory of Peter Connelly
and to all those who loved him and miss him.

Acknowledgements

I want to acknowledge four groups of people. First, my colleagues in social care and health who were blamed for Peter's death and the courage they have needed to live with it; second, my legal team, especially James Maurici QC and solicitors Tony Child and Ros Foster; third, the professors and lecturers at Birkbeck University who encouraged me to complete my doctorate on which this book is based; and finally the staff at Jessica Kingsley Publishers for a very efficient process.

Contents

Preface   11

Introduction   13
Responses to the news of Baby P's death   15
The impact of Peter Connelly's death on children's social care   18
The context of this book   19
The approach of this study   20
Documents used in the research for this book   21
Considering the ethics   22
Structure of the book   24

1. **The Background to the Familial Homicide of Peter Connelly**   **26**
Introduction   26
The nature and prevalence of familial child homicide   26
Familial child homicide (1997–2010)   28
The history and perceptions of the London Borough of Haringey and its Council   29
    Haringey's population   29
    Haringey's children   30
    Haringey's child protection services   31
    Haringey Council and its past   32

      Haringey Council's improvement and decline   36

      Conclusion   38

2. **The Denial of Crimes Against Children**   **40**

      Introduction   40

      Childhood, the family and social care services   41

      Sequestration of information about child death   45

        The effects of sequestration   46

      Growing awareness of 'child abuse'   50

      Contemporary knowledge of familial child homicide   51

      Six high-profile inquiries into familial child abuse
and homicide   53

        Maria Colwell   54

        Jasmine Beckford   56

        Events in Cleveland, North-East England   60

        The aftermath of the death of James Bulger   64

        Satanic abuse   66

        Victoria Climbié   66

      Conclusion   69

3. **Exploring Processes of Blame, Fear and Denial from a
Psychosocial Perspective**   **72**

      Introduction   72

      The place of psychoanalytic concepts in the psychosocial   73

        'Othering'   77

        Denial   79

        The dynamics of denial   80

        Blaming and scapegoating   83

        The effects of social media   84

      'The circulation of affect'   86

      The interaction of the media, politicians and the public   89

        The impact of relationships between the media and politicians   89

        The media's role in holding power to account   91

        Engagement with the public   94

      Two research studies   97

      Conclusion   99

4. **The Socio-Political and Cultural Context of the Death of
Peter Connelly**   **102**

Introduction   102

The impact of Labour policies on families and children's
social care   103
    New Labour policies for children and families   103
    Labour and social care policies in Every Child Matters (ECM)   108
    The delivery of social care   109
    Systems of governance, partnership and accountability   111
    Inspection of Children's Services   112

The impact of Labour's Every Child Matters (ECM) initiative   113
    The science of child abuse and its effects   113
    Risk management   116
    Serious Case Reviews (SCRs)   118
    The impact of models of public accountability   119

The political context preceding public knowledge of the
familial homicide of Peter Connelly   123

Conclusion   128

5. **The Narrative about Baby P Emerges**   **130**

Introduction   130

Tuesday 11 November 2008   131

Wednesday 12 November 2008   138
    The exchange at Prime Minister's Question Time   140
    Ed Balls reacted   142
    David Cameron's article in the Evening Standard   143
    The responses of members of the public on day 2   148

Thursday 13 November 2008   150
    David Cameron's letter published in the Sun   151
    Ed Balls changed his position   155
    Haringey Council politicians   158
    The responses of members of the public on day 3   159

Friday 14 November 2008   162
    The responses of members of the public on day 4   165

Saturday 15 and Sunday 16 November 2008   167
    The responses of members of the public on day 5   172

From virtual to actual presence on the streets   176

Uncertainty, power and familial child homicide   177

Conclusion   179

6. **The Identification of a Cultural Trope that Blames Social Workers for Harm to Children**   181

Introduction   181

Mediated populist engagement   182

Distortions of 'public accountability'   185

Bringing closure   187

Identifying and defining the cultural trope   194

The potency of the cultural trope   197

   Ofsted's accusation of deceit   *197*

   Presentations in court   *198*

   The 'official' Serious Case Review (SCR2)   *199*

How far-reaching is the cultural trope?   203

The inquest for Peter Connelly   206

7. **Transcending Blame, Fear and Denial**   **208**

The crime of familial child homicide   211

The cultural trope and the proposed crime of 'wilful neglect'   213

New opportunities   218

Where next?   221

Who's Who?   *225*

Glossary   *228*

The Research Materials and Their Uses   *231*

Bibliography   *238*

Notes   *259*

Subject Index   *263*

Author Index   *269*

Preface

The death of Peter Connelly, known to the public as 'Baby P', was a tragic loss of young life. The convictions of his mother, her boyfriend and his brother for 'causing or allowing' Peter's death were a shock to the nation. One can only assume that the events were an enormous trauma for Peter's young siblings. Peter had been known to social workers who worked for the London Borough of Haringey, many health professionals including paediatricians from London's world-renowned Great Ormond Street Hospital, and to police from London's Metropolitan Police Service. Those professionals who knew Peter and his family shared that sense of shock and disbelief.

But it was the blaming, mainly of social workers but also of the paediatrician, that followed the news of Peter's death that had far-reaching consequences for children and their families, for the social work profession, and for the individual professionals 'named and shamed' by politicians and the media. Following the responses to Peter's death, social workers reacted spontaneously to bring many more children into the care of local authorities; and the social work profession, which has achieved so much over many decades, became driven by a fear of failure greater than anything that had gone before.

This book draws upon doctoral research that I undertook over a period of four years at the University of London culminating in the award of a PhD in 2015. The book is not about me or my colleagues who were sacked from our jobs following Peter's death. It is not about seeking retribution or pursuing restoration. The research and this book are about *understanding* the responses to the familial homicide of Peter Connelly. Given the seriousness of the impact on children and on the social work profession understanding these responses is vitally important. It is not simply about *my* understanding of the responses, but is an attempt to improve my understanding and that of others of how, and to some extent why, events took place as they did. In particular, the book seeks to understand the processes of blame, fear and denial that were so prominent in the responses to Peter's death, which might now with some degree of understanding provide opportunities to learn.

Introduction

Peter Connelly, known to the public as 'Baby P', was found dead at his home in Tottenham in the north London Borough of Haringey, on 3 August 2007 when he was aged 17 months. The public became aware of his death 15 months after he died when his mother Tracey Connelly, her boyfriend Steven Barker, and his brother Jason Owen (previously Barker) were convicted on 11 November 2008. All three had been charged with Peter's murder and all three pleaded not guilty. Tracey Connelly pleaded guilty to 'causing or allowing' Peter's death. No one was convicted of murder but instead each was convicted of 'causing or allowing' Peter's death under the Domestic Violence Crime and Victims Act (DVCVA 2004).

The DVCVA puts a clear legal responsibility on adults who have frequent contact with a child to take reasonable steps to protect that child from serious physical harm from others in the household. The Act introduced a crime of familial homicide of children or vulnerable adults. Peter had been a victim of familial child homicide. Familial child abuse or homicide describes harm to children by family members or others in the household and in this book the term is used to include murder, manslaughter and the act of 'causing or allowing' harm or death.

The sentencing of Connelly, Barker and Owen for 'causing or allowing' Peter's death was to take place on 15 December 2008, but was delayed to allow for a second trial to be heard against Tracey Connelly and Steven Barker for the rape of a child. The second trial was carried out under strict instructions of no press coverage and concluded in May 2009. Sentencing for both cases took place on 22 May 2009 (discussed further in Chapter 6). 'Causing or allowing' a death carries a maximum prison sentence of 14 years but none received the maximum sentence for Peter's death. Tracey Connelly and Jason Owen each received indeterminate periods of imprisonment, Connelly for a minimum term of five years and Owen for three years. Steven Barker received 12 years for causing or allowing Peter's death to run concurrently with a life sentence for the rape of a two-year-old child. The minimum term was 20 years with 10 years before he could be considered for parole.

An inquest into Peter's death had been opened on 10 August 2007 and, after several hearings and adjournments, eventually a decision was made on 30 November 2010 not to proceed with the inquest. Peter was the youngest of four siblings at the time of his death and another 'half-sibling' was born to Tracey Connelly, Peter's mother, while she was in prison on remand charged with Peter's murder. Peter and his family were of English and Irish heritage and Peter was the only boy.

At the time of Peter's death I was Haringey Council's Director of Education and Children's Social Care Services. Peter had been known to social workers in my department, to several health professionals including paediatricians mainly from Great Ormond Street Hospital (GOSH), and to police officers in the Child Abuse Investigation Team (CAIT) of London's Metropolitan Police. Peter's death brought shock and devastation to those professionals who had known him, many of whom had seen him only days before he died. It also brought devastation to Peter's family. Peter and his siblings had spent the weekend before he died with their father and maternal grandmother. Peter's death was a tragic loss of life in unexplained circumstances.

Responses to the news of Baby P's death

Within hours of the convictions of Tracey Connelly, Steven Barker and Jason Owen being reported in the press, responses to the news of Peter's death came from multiple sources. These included: the print and broadcast media; politicians from the three main parties including the Prime Minister and the leader of the Conservative Opposition; social and health care professionals; police officers; employees and elected members of Haringey Council; the regulators Ofsted, the Health Care Commission (later renamed the Care Quality Commission [CQC]) and Her Majesty's Inspectorate of Constabulary (HMIC); and also the public.

Within two days of the news of Peter's homicide the *Sun* tabloid newspaper set up a petition calling for me, Peter's social workers and a paediatrician from GOSH to be sacked. Two weeks later the petition was delivered to the Prime Minister, Gordon Brown. The *Sun* claimed that 1.4 million people had signed the e-petition, organised under the banner 'Beautiful Baby P; Campaign for Justice' (*Sun* 15/11/08, p.6). At the same time a large number of social networking groups were set up either in memory of Peter Connelly or seeking to avenge his death. In the weeks after the news of Peter's death, social networking groups on Facebook that focused on the death of Baby P were estimated to have over 1.6 million members (Parton 2011).

The media coverage was extensive. Using the search term 'Baby P', the Nexis online database of UK newspapers and journals shows that in the year from November 2008 to November 2009, 6203 articles appeared in UK publications with almost 3000 in the month 12 November 2008 to 11 December 2008. Approximately 30 per cent appeared in the *Sun*. The online social work journal *Community Care* reported that Peter's social worker was named 55 times in 31 articles, editorials, opinion columns or readers' letters in 27 consecutive editions of the *Sun* from 11 November 2008. She was labelled lazy, useless, and one speculated on her mental health.[1] The GOSH paediatrician was described as 'a lazy cow' (*News of the World* 16/11/08, p.7). I was not out of the newspapers for more than two consecutive weeks in the first nine months and was variously described by a range of tabloids as smug, bungling, incompetent and arrogant. Before Peter's death a Google search of my name showed a handful of entries, but by April 2010 the search produced 24,700 results rising to 65,300 by July 2014.

Within hours of the convictions being made public, journalists gathered outside my home and stayed for considerable lengths of time every day and evening for four months. They returned at different stages in the story, sometimes for several days at a time, for example when Peter's mother was released from prison in November 2013. The volume of media coverage and the response from members of the public on social media, and in demonstrating on the streets of Haringey and marching in central London was extreme.

Less than three weeks after the public knew about Peter's death, on 1 December 2008, following the result of an emergency inspection by the regulator Ofsted, Councillor George Meehan, the leader of Haringey Council, and Councillor Liz Santry, the lead councillor for children, resigned. Minutes later I was removed from my statutory position of Director of Education and Children's Social Care Services at a press conference by Ed Balls, the Labour Secretary of State for Children, Schools and Families. The press conference was broadcast live on all major television stations and on websites. I watched the press conference and had had no warning that I was to be sacked live 'on air'. A week later, on 8 December 2008, a panel of Haringey councillors dismissed me from my job, making headline news on national television. Four Haringey social workers were later suspended and then dismissed on 30 April 2009 with high-profile publicity. After several hearings, including in the High Court, the GOSH paediatrician voluntarily erased her name from the register of medical practitioners in November 2010.

In March 2009 I began a Judicial Review of the decision to dismiss me. A Judicial Review challenges how a decision was made rather than whether the decision was right or wrong: the court does not substitute what it thinks is the correct decision. Almost three years later, on 27 May 2011, in London's Royal Courts of Justice in front of the Master of the Rolls, the country's third most senior judge, I won my case against the Secretary of State Ed Balls and Haringey Council, having initially lost in the High Court.[2] The case against Ofsted was not pursued on appeal as Ofsted was not directly involved in my dismissal. The Court of Appeal found that the Secretary of State and Haringey Council had acted unfairly and in breach of natural justice. Following my win on appeal, in August 2011, the Supreme Court turned down an application for permission to appeal against the Court of Appeal judgment brought by Ed Balls and Haringey Council. In the published appeal court judgment, Lord Justice Kay commented that I was 'entitled to be treated lawfully and fairly and not simply summarily scapegoated'.[3]

Responses to cases of familial child homicide were first described as 'moral panics' by Professor of Social Work Nigel Parton in his book *The Politics of Child Abuse* (1985) in relation to the murder of Maria Colwell in 1973. Thirty years later, reflecting on the response to the death of Peter Connelly, Parton (2014, p.69) describes the 'depth of anger' as 'much stronger and more prolonged than anything seen before'. Similarly, Professor of Social Work Ian Butler, and academic and Minister for Health and Social Services for the Welsh government Mark Drakeford, in a review of child deaths described the intensity, volatility and hostility of the public's attitudes to the social workers in the media coverage that followed news of Peter's death as reaching 'entirely new levels of irrationality' (Butler and Drakeford 2011, p.199). The difference, I suggest, was at least due to the volume of views and feelings communicated through social media such as Facebook and on online newspaper sites. For example, Professor of Criminology Wendy Fitzgibbon (2012, p.10) compared the 'computer-assisted voyeurism' that surrounded the death of Baby P with the much more 'respectful' coverage of the death of Maria Colwell. Finally, Professor of Social Work Ray Jones (2014, p.90) described how the *Sun*'s campaign 'whipped up and unleashed harassment and hatred', mainly against social workers.

In contrast, the editor of the *Sun* Rebekah Brooks, put forward the *Sun*'s campaign for 'Justice for Baby P' for the British Press Awards in January 2009, but failed to win. In the same month Brooks told students at the London School of Communications that she wanted to 'expose the lack of accountability and responsibility for Baby P's brutal death'.[4] But five years later in February 2014 her stance had changed. From the witness box of her own trial for phone hacking (for which she was acquitted), she admitted under questioning from her own lawyer that she had 'personally made a lot of mistakes in her 10–12 years as deputy editor and as editor' and in that context the 'balance went right out of the window' in attacks on 'social work leader Sharon Shoesmith' and that posting a photographer outside my home was 'cruel, harsh and over the top'.[5]

Nevertheless the names 'Haringey', 'Baby P' and 'Sharon Shoesmith' have virtually become household names. References to Baby P have become embedded in popular culture, for example in the story line of the BBC television soap opera *The Syndicate*. Aspects of the story of Baby P have been told in two BBC *Panorama* programmes in 2008 and 2009; in two documentaries, *Great Ormond Street Hospital – Too Important to Fail* in April 2012 by BBC London and *The Untold Story of Baby P* by director Henry Singer broadcast on BBC1 in October 2014; and in the book *The Story of Baby P – Setting the Record Straight* (Jones 2014).

The impact of Peter Connelly's death on children's social care

Peter Connelly's death had a serious and far-reaching impact on social care services nationwide. His death became yet another watershed in the history of child abuse and in the history of social work. The 'Baby P effect' came to describe the spontaneous reaction of social workers nationwide that brought thousands of additional children into care and identified many more as 'at risk' than had been the case before Peter's death (CAFCASS reports 2008/09, 2009/10, 2011/12). Social workers feared missing a similar case with all the attendant effects on them from media attention. In the first ten days after Peter's death made the national and international news, there was an unprecedented 26 per cent increase in applications for care orders which the head of CAFCASS described in a BBC interview as causing 'unnecessary and risk-averse interventions which could harm children and families'.[6] It is highly likely that not all these children needed to come into care, but the probability was that many would remain there throughout their childhoods. Further, the infrastructure for financing social care in local authorities, the timeliness of court processes, and the availability of foster and adoptive parents could not support the increase, and services in many local authorities came under severe pressure. The reverberations for vulnerable children and for the social work profession were not only instant but were to become far-reaching and enduring.

By the end of March 2011 government statistics[7] show that the number of children in the care of local authorities had grown rapidly to 65,500 children, 6000 more than in 2008. In Haringey the number in care increased by almost 45 per cent in the same time period. Simultaneously the number of children deemed 'in need' overall in Haringey rose to become the highest rate in England at almost four times the English average (1272.4 children per 10,000 compared with the England average of 346.2 children per 10,000). A year later, at the end of March 2012, the number of applications for care proceedings in England had increased by 79 per cent compared with October 2008, reaching an historic peak in the number of referrals to more than 10,000 applications in a single year (CAFCASS 2010/11, 2011/12). In contrast, during the 15 months between Peter's death and the public being aware of it, these government figures show that there had been no significant change in the number of children brought into care either nationally or in Haringey.

The context of this book

The impact of the responses to the familial homicide of Peter Connelly had far-reaching consequences for children, for social workers, and for the individuals 'named and shamed' in the media. On a personal level the responses to the death of Baby P had a serious effect on my mental health which I had to work hard over several years to recover from. On a professional level, the responses brought my career in education and children's social care of over 35 years to an abrupt end. I was deeply stigmatised. Four social workers also lost their jobs, and although none were removed from the register of social workers (see page 132), they each suffered years of unemployment and have had to work hard over several years to recover their mental health. A paediatrician also lost her profession and her livelihood. Nevertheless, this book is not about 'my story', or the story of the other professionals who lost their jobs. Neither is it an attempt to seek retribution or to pursue restoration. The research and this book are about *understanding* the responses to the familial homicide of Peter Connelly.

The approach of this study

The approach of this study is that the response of any person to an event is influenced by that person's unique biography or psyche, influenced over time by many influences in the 'outside world'. That is, reactions and responses to events are a unique combination of the 'psyche' and the 'social' or the 'inner' and the 'outer' experiences of each individual. This interaction of an inner world, which includes both conscious and unconscious thought, with the outer world influenced by social, cultural, historical and political factors I position as a 'psychosocial perspective'. From this perspective the responses to the familial homicide of Baby P were therefore a combination of the psyche and the social, or the 'inner' and the 'outer', not functioning as separate entities but as one dynamic psychosocial process.

The approach assumes that we inhabit a world which is structured by perceptions and concepts usually expressed in language. With many different perceptions, what individuals, including myself, thought they knew about Peter's death was partial, incomplete, fallible and diverse.

I have based my work on a theoretical stance of 'critical realism'. Critical realism assumes that what causes a particular phenomenon, in this case the responses to the homicide of Peter Connelly, is multi-layered and complex. At the same time, critical realism accepts that 'a real world' exists beyond our thoughts, knowledge and ideas about it and that our representations of the world are our own interpretations. Critical realism seeks to explore and to understand the mechanisms and processes which lead to particular interpretations. Peter Connelly's death was a real event but the portrayal of his death was a series of interpretations and re-interpretations from interactions between multiple individuals. Critical realism has been used in a range of research topics, for example to illuminate the complexity of healthcare, in particular issues in midwifery (Walsh and Evans 2014).

My approach therefore is that no simple 'cause and effect' explanation of the responses to the familial homicide of Peter Connelly existed, no simple 'answer' would be found, and no 'correct' interpretation could be made. Instead my aim was to *understand the nature* of the psychosocial dynamics of the responses to the death of Baby P. Given the seriousness of the impact on children and on the social work profession I argue that understanding these responses is important. It is not simply about *my* understanding of the responses, but an attempt to improve my understanding and that of others, of how, and to some extent why, events took place as they did. I anticipated multiple interpretations and a network of understanding.

Documents used in the research for this book

The documents used in my research were all 'naturally occurring' as the responses to Baby P's death unfolded. That is, I have not 'created' any documents or evidence from interviews or observations, and no contact has occurred with any actor referred to in the book. Instead I have worked with a range of documentary evidence written, or contributed to, by specific individuals, including email correspondence. Documents have advantages over other forms of data such as interview or observational data, since they represent a moment in time or a particular social context such that the data are relatively fixed (Prior 2003). Altheide (1996, p.2) argues that documentary evidence can provide 'an array of objects, symbols and meanings that make up social reality shared by members of society'.

The book refers to five categories of documents which provide a breadth of evidence across the many actors who responded to the familial homicide of Peter Connelly. More importantly they enable the analyses of the interactions between the content of different categories of documents which allows me to grasp the dynamic interaction between key players.

The five categories of documents are: media coverage; views and opinions of members of the public who posted on social media and wrote to newspapers; utterances by politicians and views of civil servants and Ofsted inspectors expressed in email correspondence; documents related to the Haringey Joint Area Review (JAR) including 17 drafts of the JAR; and finally the two Serious Case Reviews (SCRs) into the death of Peter Connelly. The documents used are listed in Appendix 3.

Considering the ethics

I have considered issues of ethics in relation to the subject of this book both generally in terms of responsible conduct in social research (Iphofen 2009; Mauthner 2002) and specifically in how the book is written. I have also been influenced by the views of Emeritus Professor Frank Furedi (2003, p.646) who suggests that there should be no 'no-go' areas for research and he condemns any suggestion that special dispensation should be granted by 'authorities' for research into sensitive topics. He argues that 'no matter how sensitive the issue is, there must be no curbs on the freedom to conduct intellectual exploration'.

I have taken account of ethics in three ways. First, the theoretical stance of critical realism assumes that different individuals construe different realities or truths in relation to any phenomenon. A key word in my research question is 'understanding'. That is, understanding the responses of multiple actors in a particular context, rather than discovering or proving what they did was 'right' or 'wrong', 'ethical' or 'unethical'.

Second, I have considered my personal relationship with the research in some depth. Whilst this book is not about me or the others who lost their jobs, we all have strong personal and professional connections with its contents. Arguably I am the most prominent character in the story, which made my subjectivity and reflexivity in the processes of researching the book crucial. Carolyn Ellis, Professor at the University of South Florida and regarded as a prominent researcher into reflexive approaches to research, suggests that the researcher's introspection, having lived through an experience with questions and queries, is a useful source of data (Ellis 2004).

However, whilst I had lived through an extraordinary experience and had some aspects of knowledge outside what was generally understood, I had no contemporaneous knowledge or understanding of the detail of how the narrative emerged at the time or prior to undertaking my research. I had never met the majority of the actors in the story, and in particular I had never met Peter Connelly or members of his family. At the same time my experiences and those of my colleagues gave me a strong personal motivation to seek a deeper understanding of the events that followed the death of Peter Connelly: to research events and to write this book. Throughout the research I was keenly aware of my own subjectivity, which made me pay constant attention to my emotional and intellectual responses. I questioned my use of the research materials, constantly challenged my own interpretations, reflected on how my findings are presented, and invited others at different stages to provide critiques.

Third, once all legal proceedings were complete I invited the head of Ofsted and the Ofsted Board to discuss my findings. They declined. I also sought a meeting with Secretary of State Ed Balls, but received no reply. Further, at the time of the publication of the second SCR I informed Tim Loughton MP who was Children's Minister (and who took the decision to publish the full SCR), the Chair of Haringey's LSCB, and the Head of Ofsted of my concerns about the mismatch between the SCRs which I discuss in Chapter 6, but again received no reply.

The book does not aim to be controversial or polemical. However, the very public nature of the events I have researched, the role played by many senior people, including prominent politicians, and the seriousness of the consequences of the responses to the death of Baby P may make this book contentious. The book may have the potential to create further professional and personal vulnerabilities given that I have received many threats online and two death threats delivered to my home.

Despite this, I believe that it is important that this book is written. In improving understanding and raising awareness of the nature of the responses to the familial homicide of Baby P it is my hope that the 'Baby P effect' might become re-characterised as a new and greater opportunity to learn, to reflect and to respond differently in the future to cases of familial child homicide.

Structure of the book

Chapter 1 explores the nature and prevalence of familial child homicide, and the history and perceptions of the London Borough of Haringey Council, which I argue both shaped the responses to the familial homicide of Peter Connelly.

In Chapter 2 I discuss the historical context of familial child abuse and homicide looking first at the emergence of childhood, the rise of modern day social work and the construction of the family. Second, I explore the impact of the early and continuing sequestration of information about child death; and third, I examine a number of inquiries into familial child abuse and homicide and I consider their legacies. I explore in particular how social, cultural and political factors shaped blame and denial and created a 'fear of failure' for child protection professionals, especially social workers.

In Chapter 3 I explore a number of theoretical ideas about blame, fear and denial and their effects. These theoretical ideas form a psychosocial perspective for the analysis of the responses to the familial homicide of Baby P.

In Chapter 4 I establish the socio-political and cultural context which contributed to how the responses to the homicide of Peter Connelly were shaped. In particular I explore the relevance of the political situation in the autumn of 2008 between the Labour government, especially its Prime Minister Gordon Brown, and the Conservative Opposition leader David Cameron, to the unfolding story of Baby P.

In Chapters 5 and 6, using the documents referred to above I undertake a psychosocial analysis of the responses to the familial homicide of Baby P. In Chapter 5 my focus is on the narrative that developed in the first six days after the public learned of the death of Baby P. In Chapter 6 I identify the blaming of child protection professionals, mainly social workers, for harm to children as a 'cultural trope'. The cultural trope is a psychosocial entity forged over time making the blaming of social workers compelling, potent and persuasive, and its effects far-reaching.

Finally, in Chapter 7 I summarise my findings, suggest some conclusions and discuss the implications for the social work profession of the government's proposals, especially the proposal for a criminal offence of 'wilful neglect' for social workers.

Chapter 1

The Background to the Familial Homicide of Peter Connelly

Introduction

The background to the familial homicide of Peter Connelly sets an important context for understanding the responses to his death. This chapter outlines the nature and prevalence of familial child homicide, and the history and perceptions of the London Borough of Haringey and its Council where Peter died, including the circumstances of the death of Victoria Climbié.

The nature and prevalence of familial child homicide

Familial child homicide is generally accepted as having always existed. However, data about familial child homicide in the UK are diverse and difficult to source. Despite the enormous focus on data analysis in public sector services, no single source of data on familial child homicide exists. Instead, information is drawn from the following six sources which each use different criteria, making comparison and monitoring virtually impossible:

1. The Office of National Statistics (ONS) Crime and Justice statistics which include convictions for the murder or

manslaughter of children under 16 years by 'a parent or known adult' in England and Wales.

2. Data on convictions under the Domestic Violence Crime and Victims Act (DVCVA 2004) which do not appear to be publicly available. I obtained data on these convictions through a request under the Freedom of Information Act (2000) to the government's Ministry of Justice. The DVCVA includes causing or allowing the deaths of children and vulnerable adults but not murder or manslaughter.

3. The World Health Organisation (WHO) Standardised Mortality Statistics which record deaths in four categories including homicide but are not as robust due to differences in the interpretation of different international laws.

4. Data from local authority child death reviews which are held by the government. These reviews record mortality statistics for England and include death by natural causes and homicide, and they use different age groups to other datasets.

5. Ofsted data which included deaths for England only for those aged 0–19 years where abuse and/or neglect have played a part and where charges had been brought.

6. ONS Child Mortality Statistics for England and Wales which include natural deaths and still-births.

The first dataset, that is, the Crime and Justice statistics from the ONS, is regarded as the most reliable since the statistics have been collected consistently over 40 years and can give a long-term view. These crime statistics for England and Wales show that familial child homicide, whilst appearing to be relatively rare, affecting approximately one in a quarter of a million children annually, translates into the death of approximately one child each week. However, the NSPCC and Ofsted (2008b) suggest that child death at a rate of one each week is likely to be a gross underestimate. For example, when neglect as a factor in a child's death is taken into account the rate increases to three or possibly four children each week.

At the same time, data from these Crime and Justice statistics are becoming increasingly unreliable in studying the incidence of familial child homicide as they do not include those parents or known adults convicted more recently under the DVCVA 2004. For example, the Crime and Justice statistics from the ONS do not include Peter Connelly's death because those responsible were convicted under the DVCVA with 'causing or allowing' his death and not with murder or manslaughter. Between 2006 and 2013, 27 convictions were made under the DVCVA, including the case of Peter Connelly, and may also include vulnerable adults. These figures underline the difficulty of accessing data and the overall unreliability of data.

Using the Crime and Justice figures from the ONS, the NSPCC suggests that two-thirds of those who are victims of familial child homicide are under five years old, and those under one year are eight times more likely to be killed than those in other age groups. Similarly, Ofsted (2008b) found that under-five-year-olds were the most vulnerable and that most of those who died were known to child protection agencies. It seems that Peter Connelly, as a 17-month-old child known to child protection agencies, was 'typical' of those children most at risk of familial child homicide. Notably the familial child homicide of those *not* known to social services rarely attracts criticism of social workers from the media or others; only those who *are* identified and known to child protection services appear to attract attention. This distinction is paradoxical in that it raises no questions about the processes of identification of children at risk in the community.

Familial child homicide (1997–2010)

In the 13 years that Labour served in office (1997–2010), the Crime and Justice figures from the ONS and the DVCVA statistics show that approximately 630 children were victims of familial child homicide. Between the deaths in Haringey of Victoria Climbié in 2000 and Peter Connelly in 2007, 416 children are recorded as having been killed by a known adult. Peter Connelly was one of 57 children who died as a result of familial child homicide in 2007.

Several other cases of familial child abuse and homicide at the same time as Peter Connelly were reported in the media between September 2007 and December 2008. For example, Tiffany Wright, a three-year-old who died in Sheffield and had been known to health and social care services. Her mother was convicted of her manslaughter, and her step-father of cruelty and neglect. Two-year-old Romario Mullings-Sewell and his three-month-old brother Delayno, also known to health and social services, were killed by their mother who was subsequently detained under the Mental Health Act. Finally, three-month-old Joseph Kompus died in the London Borough of Waltham Forest, which is a neighbouring borough to Haringey. Joseph's mother was convicted of manslaughter and had not been known to social services but was known to health professionals. None of these cases brought attention on the scale of the Baby P case. Other cases of child abuse and familial child homicide over a forty-year period have brought a degree of negative media attention.

One of the reasons why the case of Peter Connelly became so prominent in the media, I argue, was to do with the history and perceptions of the London Borough of Haringey and it's Council.

The history and perceptions of the London Borough of Haringey and its Council

Haringey's population

The London Borough of Haringey occupies eleven and a half square miles (30sq km) and is densely populated. Based on updates from the 2001 Census, at the time of Peter Connelly's death 224,700 people were residents of Haringey. At the time of Peter's death in 2007, approximately half of the residents came from minority ethnic backgrounds, making it one of the most ethnically diverse places in the UK. Haringey was the fourth most deprived borough in London and the fourteenth most deprived of 325 English LSOAs (Lower-layered Super Output Areas, a standard unit for presenting local demographic statistical information). Within the borough there were stark inequalities. For example, a boy born in the east of Haringey, in Tottenham, had a life expectancy seven years less than a boy born to the west in Muswell Hill. In 2008, long-term unemployment in Haringey was twice the national rate and almost twice the London rate. In May 2006, Haringey Council's own statistics showed that unemployment in Haringey was the highest in Britain and overwhelmingly concentrated in Tottenham where Peter Connelly lived.

Haringey's children

In 2008, one-quarter of the population of Haringey, approximately 55,000, were children and young people under the age of 20. Three-quarters came from minority ethnic communities, giving Haringey a rapidly growing ethnic minority population. The population had a high turnover and included a significant number of refugee and asylum-seeking children. According to the Index of Multiple Deprivation, in the year 2007/08 close to three in five children (approximately 25,000 children) lived in poverty, putting Haringey eighth highest in London and eleventh highest in England for childhood poverty. Eligibility for free school meals reflected these figures at over twice the national average (32% in Haringey compared with 15% nationally) but with a vast range across the borough, from 7.8 per cent in the Alexandra ward in the west to 50.7 per cent in the White Hart Lane ward in Tottenham to the east.

At the time of Peter's death, Haringey Council, through its Children's Services, had responsibilities for the 55,000 children who spoke 160 languages between them. The responsibilities included the education of children in 17 children's centres, 63 primary, infant or junior schools, ten secondary schools, one city academy, four special schools, one pupil referral unit, and a sixth-form centre. In terms of children who needed the support of social care services, 450 children were in the care of Haringey Council, 230 were unaccompanied asylum-seeking children, with 48 of those in care, 403 young people were identified as 'young offenders' and approximately 230 were deemed to be 'at risk' and had a formal child protection plan. This number of children with social care needs was in line with a small group of similar London local authorities known as 'statistical neighbours' which the government used to compare the performance of local authorities. But this number of children was much higher than the averages for England. For example, government statistics for England at the end of March 2008 show that 29,200 children or 27 per 10,000 were deemed 'at risk' and had a child protection plan compared with 230 in Haringey or 48 per 10,000, close to double the England average. Peter was one of the 230 children identified as 'at risk' and as a result he had a child protection plan.

Haringey's child protection services

Across the UK, child protection services include local authority social care services as the lead agency working in partnership with health services, police, lawyers, the judiciary and the voluntary sector. The statutory child protection services in the London Borough of Haringey at the time of Peter Connelly's death included social workers from Haringey Council's Children's Services, police officers from the Child Abuse Investigation Team (CAIT) of London's Metropolitan Police, paediatricians and health professionals from Great Ormond Street Hospital (GOSH) working in St. Ann's clinic in Haringey, the North Middlesex University Hospital (NMUH), the Whittington Hospital, and other health professionals employed by the Primary Care Trust (PCT). Working together, they protected children from a wide range of dangers and crimes. These included neglect, physical and sexual abuse, grooming, abduction, trafficking (in and out of the country), the protection of refugee and unaccompanied asylum-seeking children, support and protection of children affected by parental drug or alcohol abuse and/or domestic violence, protection from child-rearing practices linked to faith or culture (ranging from extreme forms of discipline, to witchcraft, female genital mutilation and to faith or so-called 'honour killings'), internet abuse, prostitution, sexual exploitation, radicalisation, youth crime including knife and gun crime, and familial child homicide.

Haringey Council and its past

Haringey Council has a history of progressive and pioneering Labour politics which prioritised the oppressed and disadvantaged but often caused controversy in the media and among politicians on the left and on the right. Jeremy Corbyn MP, who was elected as the left-wing Opposition leader of the Labour Party in 2015, served as a Labour Councillor between 1974 and 1983 in Haringey. By the 1980s, along with a small number of other London councils, Haringey attracted the pejorative label of 'the loony left', given its commitment to a number of anti-discriminatory and equal opportunity policies, many now part of UK law.

Before Peter's death, Haringey was memorable for three defining events. First, its plans to apparently promote gay and lesbian relationships in its schools culminated in extensive media coverage between May 1986 and March 1988. Professor of Law and Politics Davina Cooper (1994) argued that Haringey Council's policy intentions were both poorly communicated and distorted by a range of activists, and by Conservative politicians who convinced the public that Haringey intended to promote homosexuality and oppose heterosexuality. The controversy became high profile, with negative discourses around the Labour party's stance on the family, children and education perpetuated both by the media and by the Conservative government. The focus on 'loony-left' policies became so dominant that John Gyford, Steve Leach and Chris Game in their study of local politics in Britain (Gyford, Leach and Game 1989) argued that it allowed the Conservatives to win a third term in office at the general election of 1987.

In the second more serious and notorious event, police officer Keith Blakelock was murdered in 1985 during riots in the Tottenham area of Haringey. The murder took place in the context of unrest in several English cities and a breakdown of relations between the police and black communities. Three people were convicted of PC Blakelock's murder in 1987 but their convictions were quashed by 1991, and in 2014 a further murder trial of one man took place which also resulted in no conviction. Records of parliamentary debates at the time PC Blakelock was murdered (Hansard 5 December 1986) give some indication of the lack of trust in the police in several London boroughs, and the degree of poor relations between the local police and Labour councils, and specifically Haringey Labour councillors. Bernie Grant had become the MP for Tottenham in 1987 and was the first black MP in the country. After the riots in Tottenham, the same parliamentary debate reported that Grant had commented that the youths (in Tottenham) had given the police 'a bloody good hiding'. This remark led to him being denounced by the Labour whip for failure to condemn violence and he became a notorious hate figure in the tabloids and among right-wing politicians.

Both Bernie Grant and Haringey Council became the butt of tabloid criticism. Examples cited by Cooper (1994) include: 'Barmy Bernie is going coffee potty' (*Sun* 5/11/85, p.4), a story that alleged that the council had ordered its workers to show solidarity with Nicaragua by drinking the Marxist country's 'grotty' coffee, when no such order had been given; 'the racist bin liner is blacked' story (*Mail on Sunday* 02/03/85, p.6) which claimed that black bin liners had been banned by Haringey Council because they were racially offensive; and 'Baa Baa Green Sheep' (*Daily Mail* 09/10/94, p.5), which claimed that Haringey Council had banned the nursery rhyme and replaced it with 'Baa Baa Green Sheep', when such a proposal had never occurred. Reporters hung around playgroups in the borough but failed to find evidence, and 'day after day, Haringey has been crawled over by journalists from the Murdoch empire, searching for dirt and salacious gossip' (Jeremy Corbyn, Labour MP, Hansard 5 December 1986).

The third notorious event was the murder of Victoria Climbié in Haringey in February 2000. Victoria was a seven-year-old girl who was a migrant from the Ivory Coast entrusted by her family to the care of her great-aunt, Marie-Thérèse Kouao in 1998. It is probable that with a child presented as her daughter, Kouao had a greater chance of being prioritised for housing and for welfare benefits. Kouao and her boyfriend, Carl Manning, were both convicted of Victoria Climbié's murder in 2001. Victoria had been known to London's Metropolitan

Police Service, The North Middlesex University Hospital (NHUH), the four London Councils of Enfield, Ealing, Brent and Haringey, and to the NSPCC, but she had lived in Haringey during the last six months of her life.

The public inquiry discussed the part that race may have played in the failure of services to protect Victoria given that she was black, those convicted of her murder were black, and the social worker, her manager and the police officer were all black. Issues were raised as to whether the social worker and the police officer, being black, were afraid of being accused of racism by their own communities in taking action against Kouao, or that they may have made faulty assumptions based upon their own cultural perceptions about the African family that prevented them from acting (Laming Report 2003, paras 16.1–16.13). These complex matters were interpreted in different ways, including an accusation from the Director of the Race Equality Unit at the Laming Inquiry that Haringey Council found it acceptable for ethnic minorities to receive poor services under the guise of 'superficial cultural sensitivity' (*Guardian* 25 March 2002).

Alongside these concerns about race, what was emerging in the Inquiry was a case of familial child homicide linked to, or as a result of, a belief in 'spirit possession' or 'kindoki'. Kindoki is a belief practised in some African countries, and to different degrees in some African churches in Haringey. But the Inquiry report made only passing reference to these matters (Laming Report 2003, para. 3.79). Possibly the presence of kindoki was judged too unpalatable or too unbelievable for the public. It was not until another murder in 2012, this time of a 15-year-old boy, which involved witchcraft, that politicians and press acknowledged the existence of kindoki and made links with Victoria's death (*Guardian* 5 March 2012; BBC News 4 March 2012).

In the year Victoria died, ONS crime and justice statistics show that 82 other children across England and Wales were also victims of familial child homicide. Why a decision was made to hold a public inquiry into Victoria's death rather than any of the other homicides raises questions such as, why this case and not another?

Concerns about the protection of children nationwide were already emerging in the period 1998–2001 in an investigation by eight inspectorates (including the inspectorate previously headed up by Laming) and reported by the government (DH 2002a). These concerns were also reflected in a raft of other reports, for example in outcomes of focused research on child abuse (DH 1995, 1996, 2001), on guidance on modernising social services (DH 1998) and on interagency issues in child abuse investigations (DH 2002b). These reports, especially the report from the eight inspectorates (DH 2002a), had already identified many of the issues reported as recommendations in the Laming Report, a point acknowledged in later DCSF guidance (HM Government 2006, para. 1.6).

The Laming Inquiry made no criticism of government policy and instead located the need for improvement in the work of individual practitioners from all services and in local government processes of accountability and governance (Laming Report 2003). The government's official response (DfES 2003) was jointly to the Laming Report and the findings of the eight inspectorates. Major legislation followed swiftly. The Children Act 2004, and its strategy Every Child Matters (DfES 2004) were both positioned as a response to Victoria Climbié's death. I suggest that both were a result of the earlier government report (DH 2002a) which outlined nationwide concerns about child protection. But in being linked to the Laming Report and the high-profile death of Victoria Climbié, the legislation was much less likely to meet with resistance. Many of the recommendations made in the Laming Report were never implemented in the Labour government's policies or guidance.

I argue that the Laming Inquiry provided the 'New Labour' government with a convenient opportunity to manage a number of issues. The Laming Inquiry and its findings deflected attention away from the nationwide problems with the protection of children identified by the eight inspectorates (DH 2002a). Instead it located them in a few London Councils and in particular Haringey Council. 'Troublesome' Haringey Council represented much of the 'loony-left' politics that 'New Labour' wanted to sweep away. The perception of Haringey Council's 'over-promotion' of equal opportunities, the anger surrounding the death of PC Blakelock, and its controversial black MP Bernie Grant, I suggest, provided a subtext to the Laming Inquiry. Bernie Grant MP died in April 2000 and the obituary in the *Guardian* (10 April 2000) which described him as 'a red rag to the bulls of right-wing politics' gave an indication of the degree of controversy.

Victoria's death came to represent Haringey Council's inability, with all its commitment to race issues, to protect a young black African immigrant girl. Ian Willmore, a former Labour deputy leader of Haringey Council, writing in the *Guardian* at the time (26 January 2003) summed up the effect: 'in Haringey 'equal opportunities' came in the end to this – the death of a black child and the ruin of black staff'.

Evidence from the Laming Inquiry taken up by the media was that Haringey senior managers had managed to escape responsibility and that only junior staff members were punished,[8] that documents were withheld,[9] others tampered with,[10] and that inaccurate prior assessments had been made by the Social Services Inspectorate.[11] Despite the involvement of four London boroughs, London's Metropolitan Police and several hospitals, Haringey became the borough, and of all the professions involved social workers became the profession most associated with Victoria's death. The Laming Inquiry silenced 'troublesome Haringey' and stigmatised its social care services. I return to the case of Victoria Climbié in the next chapter.

Haringey Council's improvement and decline

By the time Peter Connelly's death became known on 11 November 2008, I had been Director of Haringey Children's Services for three years. I had come to Haringey Council in 2001 as an employee of the private sector company Capita on a two-year contract to improve Haringey Council's education department, following a highly critical inspection in 1999, only several months before Victoria Climbié died. Without the private sector as employer, Haringey Council could not attract staff to run its services. I had worked in local government as a teacher, adviser and education manager for almost thirty years and just before coming to Haringey Council I had been an HMI (Her Majesty's Inspector) of schools and local authorities with the regulator Ofsted. In Haringey I led on the work to improve educational standards and at the completion of the contract between Haringey Council and Capita, following a competitive process, I was appointed by Haringey Council as its Director of Education in 2003.

As a consequence of the Children Act 2004, which ostensibly followed the inquiry into Victoria Climbié's death, new departments of Children's Services were established in English councils combining previously separate education and children's social care departments. From 2005 I became the Director of Haringey Council's new joint department with 1300 staff and a revenue budget of approximately £250 million.

By 2008, when Peter's death became known, Haringey Council was a much improved local authority with its Children's Services consistently graded 'good' by external inspectorates and the overall Council also deemed 'good' in its Comprehensive Performance Assessment (CPA) (Audit Commission 2009). The CPA was a process of assessing how well Council services served local people and was a key element of the government's programme to modernise public services. It categorised Councils as either excellent, good, fair, weak or poor.

During my time as Director, between 2003 and 2008 standards of educational achievement for 16-year-olds in Haringey schools improved at twice the national rate year on year. As a Children's Service this progress continued. In the three consecutive years between 2005 and 2008 in Joint Area Reviews (JARs) and two Annual Performance Assessments (APAs) Ofsted judged educational attainment to be 'good', and it reported rapid improvement in children's social care from 'adequate' to 'good' (Ofsted 2003, 2005, 2006, 2007a). JARs were three-yearly reviews of the performance of social care, education, health and police in delivering services to children and carried out over five months. APAs were an annual audit of performance data usually with a single day visit by inspectors. Both JARs and APAs resulted in a grade of 1 to 4 representing 'outstanding', 'good', 'adequate' and 'inadequate' respectively.

Inspections of specific social care services, for example Haringey Council's Fostering Service (Ofsted 2008c) and its Private Fostering Arrangements (Ofsted 2008d), were also judged 'good' early in 2008 along with thematic inspections of services for 'home educated pupils' in September 2008, and pupils excluded from schools in October 2008. Lastly, the educational attainment of children in care of the local authority had increased steadily over three years, and by 2008 these young people were achieving GCSEs at twice the national average for children in care. Haringey's Children's Services was now consistently 'good' and Haringey Council overall through its Comprehensive Performance Assessment was 'improving well' (Audit Commission 2008). In 2007 the council was nominated by the Improvement and Development Educational Agency (IDeA) as one of four 'most improved' councils.

But following the media coverage of the familial homicide of Peter Connelly an emergency inspection or Joint Area Review (JAR) took place between 17 and 21 November 2008 on the order of the Secretary of State Ed Balls. It judged Haringey Children's Services as 'inadequate' (Ofsted 2008a), making Haringey Council's CPA 2008/09 also inadequate. Only four councils in the country were deemed inadequate and none showed the sudden decline that characterised Haringey Council.

Conclusion

Given the benefit of hindsight, despite the improvements since the death of Victoria Climbié, Haringey Council remained deeply vulnerable. Sara Ahmed (2004), Professor of Race and Cultural Studies uses the term 'sticky' to describe how a person or entity, because of past events, can attract negative connotations which simply attach to it and begin to pass as a form of 'common knowledge'. Labour-led Haringey was 'sticky'. Haringey's vulnerability in 2008 was not only from the tabloids, but also from politicians on the right, *and* those on the left at that time in government. I argue that the psychodynamics of the effects of that vulnerability are part of the story of the response to Peter Connelly's death. Haringey Council could have defended itself against the many untruths reported in the media, but it appeared unable or unwilling to do so. The death of Baby P as a fourth defining event can in part be located in perceptions of Haringey Council's past, which in turn had the potential to determine its future.

In the next chapter I look more broadly at the historical context of familial child homicide and the high-profile public inquiries, including the last inquiry which concerned the death of Victoria Climbié.

Chapter 2

The Denial of Crimes Against Children

Introduction

In contemporary culture, familial child homicide, especially where it involves the mother, breaks *the* most fundamental taboo of all. As the progenitor, the notion of motherhood signifies natural love for, and the instinctive protection of, her child. Criminologist and sociologist Professor Barry Goldson argues that childhood is 'a barometer of the "state of the nation"' (Goldson 2001, p.34) suggesting that how we care for children is the very embodiment of who we are as individuals and as a society. Lee Edelman, Professor of English, goes a step further. He suggests that children are 'eternal life' when he states that children represent 'the telos of the social order and come to be seen as the one for whom that order is held in perpetual trust' (Edelman 2004, p.11).

This chapter explores the historical context of familial child abuse and homicide and in doing so draws upon the dynamic interaction of the social, cultural and political in shaping responses to familial child abuse and homicide. First, I explore the emergence of childhood in 'the sentiment of the nation', the symbiotic rise of modern-day social work and the construction of the family as a unit of social control. Second, I discuss the impact of the early and continuing sequestration or concealment of knowledge about child death, including familial child homicide, on the family, on social workers and on the public generally. Third, through the lens of a number of high-profile familial child abuse and homicide inquiries I draw out and discuss the emerging issues, especially the interactions of the media and politicians, and notions of 'prediction and prevention' that focus the responsibility for harm to children on child protection professionals. My analyses indicate a complex interaction of the denial of familial child abuse and homicide, and the blaming of professionals, usually social workers, which has become habitual and which puts children at greater risk.

Childhood, the family and social care services

Children occupy a special place in the sentiment of the UK nation. This valuing of childhood is central to how people respond to crimes against children. The history of childhood suggests that the notion of childhood has been constructed and reconstructed according to the social, moral, economic and political circumstances prevailing at the time, and that it is subject to contexts of class, race and gender (Ariès 1962; Jackson 2000; James and Prout 2005; Jenks 2005; James, Jenks and Prout 1998; Postman 1994; Stainton-Rogers 2001). For example, the industrialisation of the eighteenth century made children 'objects of utility' (Zelizer 1985, p.5), or symbols of potential economic growth and hence of great value to their families and to the country's future.

At the same time child deaths from ill-health, poverty and neglect were commonplace and in the eighteenth and nineteenth centuries were usually treated as 'minor events' often met with 'indifference and resignation' (Zelizer 1985, p.25). Historical views differ about the nature and prevalence of the ill-treatment of children and hence the causes of death. For example, DeMause (1974) takes the view that the further one goes back in history the more likely it was for children to be abandoned, beaten, terrorised and sexually abused. However, Corby, Shemmings and Wilkins (2012) argue that what appeared as harsh treatment of children was not so much about abuse or ill-treatment but a reflection of the tough social and economic conditions of the time that affected the health and welfare of poorer children.

Harry Ferguson, Professor of Social Work, in his analysis of child welfare in this period charts the development of care and concern for children (Ferguson 2004, p.38). He suggests that by the turn of the twentieth century, these 'hazardous social conditions began to be re-framed in terms of a new conception of parental responsibility and welfare'. Improvements in medical care led to better standards of health and social care and to progress in the social conditions for children which were gradually enhanced by access to education. Consequently, by the late 1940s child death had reduced dramatically, especially for infants under one year old (Cunningham 1991).

Early welfare services both contributed to these improvements and developed as a result. In the early to mid-nineteenth century welfare services were usually philanthropic Christian charitable groups. They sought to 'rescue' children not so much from abusive families, but rather to protect society from growing numbers of 'delinquent' children (Cree 1995). Clapton, Cree and Smith (2013, p.203) reviewed the strategies that such groups used to raise awareness of the plight of children and also to help develop their services. For example, they agreed that the NSPCC engaged with the media and used 'shock tactics' to draw attention to the plight of poor children. Such tactics built public support and much-needed funds for its work. In effect, the media was fed by the NSPCC's 'wrenching propaganda which dramatized the defencelessness of the young' to get support (Behlmer 1982 cited by Clapton *et al.* 2013, p.206).

This growing support and awareness of the need to protect children led eventually to the 'Children's Charter' or the Prevention of Cruelty to, and Protection of, Children Act 1889. The Children's Charter was the first major legislation to protect children by outlawing child cruelty. Whether the children were victims of poverty or cruelty was ill-defined. But the Children's Charter gave welfare workers powers to forcibly remove children, usually to charitable organisations such as the NSPCC (Harris 2008; Powell 2001).

In relatively short time-scales referrals doubled and quadrupled and the NSPCC established itself as a national children's charity.

Developments in health, welfare and education in the period after the Second World War and into the mid-1950s shaped children as 'objects of sentiment' to be nurtured, cared for and educated. In contrast to being an 'object of utility', this 'economically useless' child emerged as the 'emotionally priceless' child creating 'a new and enduring sentimentalization of childhood' (Zelizer 1985, p.209). Families had become more visible and accessible through the census process and particularly the compulsory registration of births, marriages and deaths. Ideas of what constituted acceptable standards of family life, especially child-rearing, were gradually constructed, communicated, reinforced and valued, producing notions of the 'normal family' (Parton 2006, p.12). Good standards of mothering, especially in child-rearing, were important and became a symbol of respectability and good moral standards. For example, 'well-adjusted' children emerged from decent families with good relationships, especially between mother and child (Parton 2006, p.14).

The newly formed welfare state of the mid-twentieth century gave rise to a sense of optimism that class differences would diminish and poverty would be eliminated. The expectation that children could and should be protected through intervention was well established (Ferguson 2004). But poverty, overcrowding, hunger and disease were the realities for many families.

Social workers had little control over these wider social issues. Their emphasis was on working with families to keep them together. To do so, social work was influenced by psychodynamic theories in the work of Donald Winnicott (1964), particularly his notion of 'the good enough mother', and also in the work of psychoanalyst John Bowlby (1969) on 'attachment theory', which emphasised the importance of the mother and child relationship for the future well-being of the child. Social workers worked with families, mainly mothers, to develop acceptable child-rearing practices. In doing so, problems of child welfare became located not so much in the negative effects of social policies, but 'within' the individual client, usually the mother, casting the problem as the mother's inadequacy and ultimately a consequence of her own actions. Increasingly the needs of these families became redefined in terms of moral failure (Parton 2006).

Given these tensions, social work developed as a politicised profession. Issues of class politics were, and are, at the centre of the work of social workers and the development of the profession. In the 1970s, in a period of both Conservative and Labour governments, a more radical social work voice emerged. It highlighted the effects of poverty and inequality, and especially questioned the expectation that social workers should ignore the effect of social policies in the lives of their clients. The movement rejected approaches to social work which drew upon psychoanalysis and psychodynamics, arguing that they pathologised individuals and their families (Featherstone 1997).

At the same time, new social work departments were established by a Labour government following the Seebohm Report (Seebohm 1968). The report emphasised notions of 'universality' which initially brought growth and a sense of optimism. But the incoming Conservative government of 1970 with its 'New Right' thinking was highly critical of these new approaches and especially of increasing costs (Dickens 2011). The need for 'eligibility' criteria to access services with a consequent need for rules and their adherence began to emerge. Modes of intervention changed and welfare services that had started out to protect children and support families gradually became more intrusive through expectations that they should police and 'normalise' child-rearing practices, usually with marginalised groups such as lone mothers and ethnic minorities (Parton 1991). Social workers had an increasingly difficult role of surveillance and intervention on behalf of the state with families that, in line with government policy, they were working to keep together (Ashenden 2004). Simultaneously, social workers were expected to manage families away from the public gaze, thereby enhancing social order.

In effect, family disorder, breakdown and disadvantage became elements of a class politics that encouraged unpalatable elements of family life to be kept invisible. For many mothers the new role of the social worker made them less willing to seek help, and more keen to avoid attention, reflected in the decline in families seeking voluntary care for their children in difficult times (Payne 2005). The radical social work movement challenged right-wing thinking and gave voice to the lack of attention given to the social context of the need of some families and the tendency to blame families and not the state for their inadequacies (Bailey and Brake 1980). But the high aspirations of Seebohm were never realised for reasons that still resonate today: underfunding, lack of clear roles for social workers, loss of social workers' skills, autonomy and status, cumbersome management, inflexibility, increase in bureaucracy and increasing demand for services (Dickens 2011). By the beginning of the 1970s the high point for social care was already in decline, especially its professional image (Parton 2006; Payne 2005).

In the latter part of the twentieth century the more radical voice of social work became marginalised and virtually silenced. This was most likely the result of reactions to public inquiries from politicians and the media rather than the findings of inquiries per se. I suggest that the political opportunism that emerges from my analysis of the inquiries that follows may have had some relationship with the need to silence the more radical voice of social workers. Eileen Munro, Professor of Social Policy (1996), supports that suggestion. She found that almost half the inquiries she researched did not fault social workers, but that several high-profile cases publicly vilified social workers for both identifying and failing to identify child abuse and homicide. Social workers were positioned increasingly as responsible and accountable when cases of child abuse and familial child homicide came to public attention. Implicit in this blaming of social workers was the lack of knowledge and awareness of the incidence of child abuse and homicide.

Sequestration of information about child death

From the turn of the twentieth century the NSPCC reported on, and exaggerated, the incidence of child abuse to promote the need for its services (Cree 1995). Between 1915 and 1936 the NSPCC reported on the rate of child death from hunger and poverty, including familial child homicide, as an indication of its success in reaching children even though some died (Ferguson 2004). In those 21 years, 10,774 children known to the NSPCC died (presumably others not known to NSPCC would also have died). The number decreased from 951 in 1915 to 277 in 1936, which represented a small minority (0.25%) of all children involved in NSPCC casework. But from 1936 the NSPCC ceased to make figures about child death available to the public (Ferguson 2004, pp.83–84).

This withdrawal or sequestration of information, Giddens (1991, pp.155–156) suggests, is the 'structured concealment of potentially troublesome information which threatens the trustworthiness of expert systems'. The sequestration of this information about child death may have been to promote trust and confidence in the emerging social care services (Ferguson 2004). But there may have been other reasons. First, the sequestration may have reflected a concern about the growing numbers of social workers and welfare services, especially their increased costs, and the continuing poverty that led to a persistence of child death. Second, it may have been to disguise the success in reducing the number of deaths which could have resulted in the withdrawal of financial support and public sympathy for the work of the NSPCC during a period of financial crisis. Third, it could have been to promote trust in government social policy in a period of growth in welfare services. Overall, exposing unpalatable information, (usually) about 'poor' children dying from neglect or homicide, was hardly beneficial to governments or social workers. In effect this forged a psychosocial context for child abuse and homicide and the sequestration of information.

The effects of sequestration

The high expectations of family life that developed in the mid-twentieth century, especially the sentimentalisation of motherhood and childhood, and the sequestration of information about child death, I suggest, assisted the concealment of abuse within the family. Mothers were not only held to be morally responsible for how their children behaved, but motherhood was idealised (Dally 1982; Chodorow and Contratto 2012, first published 1989). Feminist researchers argued that it is usually the mother who is the protector of the child, but it was the child who was removed when abuse was suspected, often instead of, or more often as well as, the perpetrator (Gordon 1988; McIntosh 1988; Nava 1988).

For the mother, revealing familial child abuse risked losing her child(ren), her home and her livelihood, as well as suffering shame and a deep sense of failure as a wife and mother, which might lead to ostracism in the community and in her wider family. Such circumstances may well have resulted in an incentive for her to keep things quiet and try to manage the problems herself. In attempting to control what was beyond her control, the mother was culpable when things went wrong (Parker 1997). In consequence, consciously or unconsciously, mothers may have protected the perpetrator. In turn, perpetrators, usually fathers or close male relatives (Frosh 2002b), consciously or unconsciously did not expect to be challenged. When child abuse, especially child sex abuse, became explicit it was often blamed on the child's lack of morality or promiscuous behaviour (Jackson 2000). Such 'within child' explanations may well have avoided even greater consequences such as homelessness and destitution for the family, a position that often made 'the unsafe home the only refuge for women and children' (Atmore 2003, p.28).

Early in the twentieth century, Freud (1975, first published 1915) revealed evidence of the sexual abuse of girls by their fathers drawn from the disclosures of women undergoing psychoanalysis. Freud's findings emphasised the psychosocial nature of child sex abuse. But the social response was so hostile that Freud re-characterised the abuse as the daughter's sexual phantasy about her father or her 'hysteria', which influenced generations of psychiatrists (Rosen and Etlin 1996) who were mainly men. 'Secretly and privately it was accepted that [Freud] was right' (Crawford and Conn 1997, p.278) but the legacy was a denial or a re-interpretation of childhood sexual abuse. In the next chapter I discuss the work of Kitzinger (2004) and

Walker (1997) which illustrates the effects of this re-interpretation in which women abused in childhood blamed themselves for the abuse.

Psychosocially, the lack of awareness of the maltreatment of children, coupled with the idealisation of motherhood and childhood and notions of 'natural love', disguised the mother's capacity for harming her child, placing them both in danger. Crawford and Conn (1997, p.280) reviewed the literature on female perpetrators and argued that the UK had not begun to recognise female sex abuse, which research evidence shows is more common than has been assumed. They suggested that child sex abuse by the female may be an expression of the oppression of female sexuality. The feminine stereotype characterised by 'asexuality, passivity, and maternalism are socially required and individually incorporated' but they disguise aggressive drives in women that can be repressed but occasionally break through.

Female cruelty is often believed to be the result of male violence, suggesting that women lack agency (Crawford and Conn 1997). But there are other explanations. As a result of impoverished childhood experiences which may have included violence, women can turn their cruelty inward onto themselves or onto their children, whom they regard as extensions of themselves. Overall it is easier to deny rather than to acknowledge that motherhood can accommodate sadism, brutality and perversion (Motz 2008).

The denial of child abuse and expectations about motherhood concealed abuse, whether the perpetrator was male or female. Testimonies from women around violence, rape and abuse when they were children (McIntosh 1988) and from men, for example of abuse from priests during childhood (Ryan Report 2009), show the kinds of secrets that may well have their origin in these kinds of beliefs. The evidence of harm to children, especially within the family, has been difficult for society to acknowledge.

Social work was, and has remained, a predominately female profession with its roots in philanthropy and in feminism, given the role of social workers in supporting the rights and needs of women, often lone mothers (Milner 2001). As such it has attracted both positive and negative comments about the empathy that social workers might, or might not, develop with mothers, thereby affecting their professional judgments.

The lack of knowledge and awareness of familial child abuse and homicide not only places the family, and especially the child, in danger, but it also has an impact on the relationship between the social worker and the mother. A mutual dependency can develop, for example, in relation to a state of denial of the risk to the child. Could the mother's denial be accepted by the social worker who unconsciously cannot bear to know? Can a social worker 'not consciously knowing' reinforce the mother's sense of 'not knowing'? Given the belief in 'natural love' of the mother I suggest that each can become locked in an unconscious state in which familial child homicide is an outcome neither can countenance. It describes a case of 'knowing and not knowing' (Steiner 1993) which I return to in the next chapter.

Featherstone (1997) reviewed a range of mainly feminist literature which explored the issues raised by 'women working with women'. She examined the complexity of the relationship between a female social worker and a mother, especially the implications of experiences they might share, and also of their possible mutual disapproval, relations which were central to processes of decision-making but yet had received little attention. Further, Reder and Duncan (2004), in an analysis of child deaths in which the parent(s) demonstrated a state of denial about the neglect of the child, suggested that where the parent(s) made a relationship with the child protection worker, a 'double bind' was unwittingly (unconsciously) created in which the child protection worker entered into denial with the parent. If this complexity of denial worked for mothers and social workers, I suggest that it also worked for paediatricians, police, politicians and for the general public. Denial 'protected' everyone, including social workers themselves. Consequently, children and their families, including perpetrators, and social workers were all at greater risk from a lack of knowledge and awareness of child abuse.

Growing awareness of 'child abuse'

An awareness of harm to children grew in the latter part of the twentieth century. Paediatricians in the USA (Kempe *et al.* 1985, first published 1962) and orthopaedic surgeons in the UK (Griffiths and Moynihan 1963) began to identify injuries to children which they labelled 'battered baby syndrome'. The term described harm to young children which was due to physical and emotional abuse by a parent(s) which could cause significant disability or death and had previously been misdiagnosed as a clinical condition often referred to as 'cot death'. Both Parton (2006) and Powell and Scanlon (2015) give comprehensive accounts of the 'rediscovery' of child abuse and the roles played by the medical profession and the NSPCC in establishing its significance.

High-profile cases of child abuse brought controversy from both within and outside the medical profession. For example, the case of mother Sally Clark who was convicted of the infanticide of her two sons and was eventually acquitted brought claims and counter-claims of the existence of familial child abuse. This controversy within the medical profession is best illustrated by the case of UK paediatrician Dr David Southall. In a research project at two London NHS hospitals beginning in the 1980s, Southall identified parents who fabricated illnesses in their children as a disguise for the harm they had inflicted on them themselves, known as 'Munchausen Syndrome by proxy'. Thirty-three prosecutions took place and twenty-three parents were diagnosed with fabricating illnesses in their children.

However, the cases created such controversy that Southall was removed from the medical register of doctors after being found guilty of professional misconduct by the General Medical Council (GMC) in December 2007. Despite having the support of the Royal College of Paediatrics and Child Health, Southall became associated with miscarriages of justice in cases of assumed 'cot deaths', and in a BBC documentary in 2009 Southall was dubbed as either 'one of Britain's most hated and dangerous doctors – or one of its most dedicated protectors of vulnerable children'. By 2010 he was reinstated after an appeal, and in 2012 the GMC dropped all cases against him.

The controversy of 'cot deaths' and the diagnosis of 'Munchausen Syndrome by proxy' added to the complexities of diagnosing child abuse and child sex abuse. Parton (1985) suggested that doctors became reluctant to make firm diagnoses of child abuse for four reasons, which I argue are still relevant today. First, they were not aware of baby battering (or child abuse); second, they were unwilling to believe that parents could do such a thing; third, they saw themselves as treating disease or medical need and so were unwilling to break patient confidentiality; and fourth, they were reluctant to become involved in criminal procedures. Other doctors saw their role as the guardian of the child, with a moral obligation to expose the problem in order to tackle it. The case against Southall, which was taking place during the life and subsequent death of Peter Connelly, led to enormous concern and caution among paediatricians about the risks in diagnosing child abuse. I argue that it may have had a bearing on the reluctance of paediatricians to make a definitive diagnosis of child abuse in Peter's case.

Lead agencies that had access to families and children, such as doctors, social workers and police officers, developed conflicting perspectives about child abuse both within and between their professions, which I return to in the next chapter. Finally, child abuse had a low profile for governments; for example, the NSPCC acted to tackle 'baby battering' by establishing a Battered Child Research Unit in the early 1970s, but there was limited interest or funding available (Parton 1985; Powell and Scanlon 2015). This is in sharp contrast to the Independent Inquiry into Child Sex Abuse led by Justice Lowell Goddard set up in 2015 to look into allegations of historic child abuse.

Contemporary knowledge of familial child homicide

Today, in an age replete with statistics, no single comprehensive source of data on familial child homicide exists. Different types of information are contained in the six incompatible sources discussed in Chapter 1. The absence of accurate information about such a serious issue, in which on average one child a week is the victim of familial homicide, suggests a legacy of this sequestration. Earlier I argued that this lack of knowledge of the incidence of familial child homicide increased the risk to children. This lack of knowledge of how many children are victims of familial child homicide was demonstrated in December 2008 when Christine Gilbert, the head of the regulator Ofsted, advised the Parliamentary Select Committee on 10 December 2008 that 282 children had died at the hands of parents or known adults in England in a 17-month period ending in August 2008. This was a rate of four children each week. No one on the committee questioned the figure, such was its own lack of knowledge. Shortly afterwards Ofsted withdrew the figure as it included accidental deaths and the deaths of terminally ill children (Gilbert 2008). Ofsted corrected its advice to concur with the crime statistics cited in Chapter 1 that one child each week is a victim of familial homicide, and accepted the NSPCC position that the figure rises to three or four each week when neglect is a factor in a child's death. In effect, not only the public but also public bodies that regulate and judge social care services were unaware of the incidence of familial child homicide. Familial child homicide had remained largely invisible.

The sequestration of information, or the 'disappearance of death' (Ferguson 2004, p.87), reaching back to the earlier part of the twentieth century, draws into question not only what the public and the regulator understand, but also what social workers themselves understand. Anecdotal evidence from discussions between 2011 and 2014 with members of the British Association of Social Workers (BASW) suggests that many social workers are also unaware of the rate of child death. The 'Baby P effect' discussed in Chapter 1 is, in essence, a demonstration of social workers acting on either new, or renewed, awareness of the possibility of familial child homicide and their fear of 'missing it'. As a result, the threshold at which children were removed from their families was spontaneously lowered across the country, rapidly increasing the numbers of children being brought into local authority care.

Six high-profile inquiries into familial child abuse and homicide

High-profile government inquiries into familial child abuse and homicide illustrate the influence of the contemporary attitudes and beliefs discussed above. Six cases that made headlines over a 30-year period from 1973 to 2003 illustrate the degree of denial that existed and how they shaped different aspects of a developing cultural narrative that blamed social workers for harm to children. These are the familial homicides of Maria Colwell in 1973 (DHSS 1974), Jasmine Beckford in 1984 (London Borough of Brent 1985), child sexual abuse in Cleveland in 1987 (Butler-Sloss 1988), alleged satanic abuse on the Isle of Orkney (The Orkney Report 1992), the murder of James Bulger in 1993 which was subject to a murder trial rather than an inquiry, and the familial homicide of Victoria Climbié in 2000 (Laming Report 2003).

These inquiries were legal or quasi-legal processes and, in common with the murder trial, they searched for some kind of objective truth or rationale to explain some deeply unpalatable crimes against children. In all cases there was a stated desire to find a way to cease incidents of harm to children. The inquiries illustrated the impact of the interaction between the media, politicians, political opportunism, notions of risk, issues of class, race and gender, and the overwhelming sense of shock and horror at the degree of harm to children. Three main outcomes emerged from these inquiries. First, professionals, especially social workers, were increasingly held responsible for the harm to children. Second, 'an emotional public sphere', a term first used by Richards (2007) in relation to terrorism, was created which added to the blaming of social workers and denied the complexity of recognising and tackling familial child abuse and homicide. Third, new social policies for children were enacted as a result of each single case of high-profile abuse or homicide, and, given the emotional outrage, they were easier to implement creating an 'emotional policy sphere'. These outcomes, led by the blaming of so-called 'incompetent' social workers, I argue, became the defence against knowing about the extent of familial child abuse and homicide.

Maria Colwell

Maria was seven years old when she was killed by her step-father in 1973, whilst known to social workers. Comprehensive accounts of the case are given by Parton (1985) and Butler and Drakeford (2011). The handling of the case by politicians and the media brought child abuse and child homicide suddenly to the attention of the UK public. The response to the case was therefore fuelled by class politics. The background of the case was one of declining family life, growing 'permissiveness' and increasing fears of violence (Parton 1985).

There was also political turbulence. The Conservatives had to concede defeat in 1974 following attempts to form a coalition with the Liberals and in a second election in the same year Labour won with a slim majority. Conservative Minister for Social Services, Keith Joseph, set up the Inquiry (DHSS 1974) and was vocal about his rejection of Labour's post-war consensus on welfare. He had views on the 'intergenerational transmission of deprivation', or pathology passed through the generations, which referred to some mothers as being unfit to be parents given their low intelligence, suggesting that 'our human stock is threatened' (Jones 2012, p.45).

Media coverage of the Inquiry was characterised by extreme hostility towards social workers, with daily headlines, for example in *The Times*: 'Social Worker Made Error of Judgment' (3 November 1973) and 'Social Workers Wrong, QC Tells Inquiry into Death of Maria Colwell' (8 November 1973) (both cited by Parton 1985, p.92).

Against this media coverage, leading social work academic and member of the Colwell Inquiry panel, Olive Stevenson, in a minority report attempted to establish a wider context for the case:

> it was 'the system', using the word in the widest sense, which failed [Maria]. Because that system is the product of society, it is upon society as a whole that the ultimate blame must rest. Indeed, the highly emotional and angry reaction of the public in this case indicates society's troubled conscience. It is not enough for the state

as representing society to assume responsibility for those such as Maria. It must also provide the means to do so, both financially and by ensuring that the system works as efficiently as possible at every level so that individual mistakes which must be accepted as inevitable do not result in disaster. *(DHSS 1974, para. 242)*

This view of the responsibilities of the state or 'society's troubled conscience' perhaps reflected other central and local government reports at the time suggesting that Maria's death was 'simply the tip of a much bigger iceberg' (Parton 1985, p.101) of potential child abuse. But these reports were never brought to public attention.

The effects of the Inquiry were, first, that the public was deprived of the knowledge and information of the extent of child abuse, thereby strengthening the view that Maria's death was an isolated case of poor social work practice. Second, as an example of the 'emotional policy sphere', the Children Act 1948 was updated to the Children Act 1975 and, despite the criticisms of social workers, the new Act gave them greater powers to remove children from their homes (Parton 1985). The effect was that the number of social workers increased, costs rose and social workers were criticised for providing little 'investment return'. The view was reinforced, especially for politicians, that social workers would maintain social order among 'difficult families' (Parton 1985). Lastly, social workers were publicly blamed for Maria's death. For politicians, publicly blaming social workers when things went wrong may have been more preferable than attacking the morals of 'the poor' or risking criticism of the social policies of the government.

To break the perceived cycle of deprivation, many took the view that poor children should simply be taken from their families and adopted at an earlier age as opposed to more costly longer-term intervention with 'inadequate birth families' (Morris 1984; Maluccio, Fein and Olmstead 1986). Such arguments have endured and re-emerged in the wake of Peter Connelly's death, for example in a report commissioned by Barnardo's children's charity (Hannon, Wood and Bazalgette 2010) and in government initiatives to increase the rate of adoption set out in the Children and Families Act 2014.

Such a stance exposes the dichotomy between 'failure to parent' being the result of inherent inadequacies of the parents and mainly the mother, and the effects of social policies that produce poverty, ill-health and dependency, or a combination of the three.

Jasmine Beckford

Jasmine Beckford was killed by her step-father in 1984 in the London Borough of Brent. Jasmine had been known to social workers, and the Inquiry, led by a barrister, made significant criticism of them (London Borough of Brent 1985). But the Inquiry also looked more broadly at the context of Jasmine's death and raised issues for the first time about multi-agency work with health, education and the courts. Three interrelated themes emerged from the Inquiry (Parton 1986) which have had long-term effects on both social work practice, and perceptions of it.

First, a legal and judicial framework was the basis of attempts to find a 'rational' account that defined what went wrong. Social work was cast as defined by law, and social workers as law enforcement officers who had simply failed to enforce the law. Consequently, social workers were accused of failing to save Jasmine, given that the law demanded that she should be protected, implying that protecting Jasmine was a simple case of complying with the law, for example in making use of 'Emergency Protection Orders' which would have saved her life.

Second, the Inquiry claimed that social workers were distracted from their enforcement role by the 'rule of optimism' which led them to interpret the actions of the parents favourably and therefore fail to challenge them. At the core of the 'rule of optimism' are the notions of 'cultural relativism' and 'natural love'. 'Cultural relativism' is a respect for other cultures in which a person (social worker) from one culture has no right to judge another culture using his/her own cultural standards. 'Natural love' is a 'generally accepted belief', of which social workers are a part, that parents have an instinctive love and sense of protection towards their children which is embedded in their human nature. It was a case of when in doubt about a child's best interests, favour the links with the natural parents (Dingwall, Eekelaar and Murray 2014, first published 1983).

The Inquiry team, influenced by their expert witness Cyril Greenland, a British-born professor of social work from Canada, (mis)interpreted 'the rule of optimism' as the way in which social workers retained their enthusiasm for the job and a sense of being able to make a difference, suggesting that they were thoroughly subjective and blind to the risk of child abuse (Parton 1986). 'The rule of optimism' arises from a much more nuanced process for social workers of striking the right balance between intervening on behalf of the state with families who, in line with their professional training and the 'law of the land', they are working to keep together (Parton 1986). With limited social or moral legitimacy for intervention, or no legal or technical tools to support intervention, 'the rule of optimism' was about a balance of risks between the family and the state which favoured the parents. Crucially, the Beckford inquiry ignored these broader issues and reduced the problem to individual professional attitudes, or 'within social worker' issues, thereby removing any societal responsibility.

The third theme that emerged from these 'within social worker' considerations concerned the skills required by social workers to overcome these 'failings'. The Beckford Inquiry accepted the fundamental position that Kempe et al. (1962) had argued in relation to 'baby battering', that familial child abuse was 'a disease' carried by the parent whose victim was the child (Parton 1986). Similarly, the Inquiry was influenced by evidence of Professor Greenland (1987, published after the Inquiry). Greenland provided the Inquiry with eight characteristics of abusing families developed from his research into 168 cases of familial child homicide, arguing that almost all applied to Jasmine Beckford. But identifying common elements in cases of *actual* child homicide, given the benefit of hindsight, is a simpler matter than attempting to use these as criteria to *predict* child abuse. Most child homicides are likely to demonstrate Greenland's eight criteria, but not all those families who demonstrate the criteria will abuse or kill their children (Parton 1986). A list of factors common to cases of familial homicide published by Ofsted (2008b) over thirty years later was virtually the same, for example drug and alcohol misuse, incidents of domestic violence and mental illness among families where child death or injury had occurred.

Crucially, the Beckford Inquiry, in its endeavour to prevent further deaths, accepted that familial child abuse was a disease inherent in the parent which could be 'diagnosed', giving rise to fledgling ideas of managing risk. The Inquiry concluded that it was the social workers' lack of knowledge of the facts of cases of abuse, or their failure to understand their significance, that led them to fail to identify the risk that Jasmine was in. Using the evidence of Professor Greenland, the Inquiry developed the notion that child abuse could be 'predicted and prevented'. It recommended that social workers should be trained to identify 'high-risk' families and to remove those children to care. The dual concepts of 'prediction and prevention' became dominant in a new discourse of the 'science of child abuse' (Parton 1986, p.522) which I return to in the next chapter.

But the Inquiry went further by placing the responsibility for ensuring the training of social workers on local councils. In doing so, the responsibility to predict and prevent child abuse and homicide not only rested with social workers but also now with those who led local councils. The Inquiry had high expectations of the impact of its findings, and it made sweeping assumptions of the new 'science of prediction' when it suggested that:

> [s]ociety should sanction, in 'high-risk' cases, the removal of such children for an appreciable time. Such a policy, we calculate, might save many of the lives of the forty to fifty children who die at the hands of their parents every year, and at the same time would concentrate scarce and costly resources of Social Services Departments. *(London Borough of Brent 1985, p.182)*

Parton (1986, p.524) doubted whether the Inquiry panel was convinced about the ability to predict and prevent since it recommended the need for research by 'medical sociologists' to assist the techniques of prediction. Further, academics (Corby, Doig and Roberts 1998;

Parton 1991) and the government (DH 2001) questioned the ability to predict and therefore prevent. In a later Inquiry by the same barrister into the familial homicide of Kimberley Carlile, the ability to predict and prevent was questioned and appeared to reflect the Inquiry team's awareness of the doubts about prediction and prevention, and concern about attacks on social workers. The Inquiry report stated that, 'human judgment is fallible, society must tolerate the occasional failure. Staff who follow-up…child abuse are not creating those risks. They are inheriting the risks, and are accepting them on our behalf' (London Borough of Greenwich 1987, p.288).

But despite these misgivings, the message by the late 1980s was threefold: social workers should be able to predict and thereby prevent familial child abuse and homicide; they should shift their focus from the parent to the child; and they should intervene in a more authoritative way using the statutory powers they already have. These 'findings' marked the beginning of a sense that familial child abuse and homicide was an aberration that could be prevented by more intense surveillance. Failure to predict and prevent was a 'within social work' problem.

Media reporting in the case of Jasmine Beckford was extensive in its blaming of social workers, who were also roundly condemned by politicians. Any expression of the fallibility of social workers' judgments articulated by the Inquiry and quoted above was not repeated in future inquiries.

The notion of 'prediction and prevention' became embedded in the work of social workers and had a profound effect on social work and on children and their families. What had begun as a process of awareness of features of familial child homicide that could support preventative work over time became a *moral* expectation of social workers to prevent the risk of harm to children. Such expectations created high levels of anxiety among social workers and a 'fear of failure' that they would miss a case of familial child homicide. Over almost thirty years there has been no discernible reduction in familial child homicide. For example, crime statistics show that the annual 40–50 cases of familial child homicides the Beckford Inquiry referred to in 1985 has remained constant. Figures for March 2013 show that 50 children died at the hands of a known adult in the previous 12 months despite extensive 'improvements' and 'investments' in children's social care.

Compared with the number of children protected, incidents of familial child homicide are rare and therefore unlikely to be met by the vast majority of social workers. But the 'fear of failure' created by the intense vilification of social workers disproportionately affects the work of social workers in their day-to-day practice. The 'fear of failure' suggests that social workers have absorbed the high-profile criticisms of their profession. In turn such feelings have produced a pattern of uncertainty and insecurity in the profession evidenced by volatile practice in the face of public opprobrium, for example the sharp increase in children brought into care after the homicide of Peter Connelly.

Events in Cleveland, North-East England

Events in Cleveland concerned familial child sex abuse rather than familial child homicide, and the cases were on a much greater scale than anything that had gone before. Doctors and social workers in Cleveland had acted on the recommendations of the Beckford Inquiry by: making greater use of their legal powers; having regard for the newly developed notions of prediction and prevention; and maintaining a focus on children as opposed to parents. Doctors had diagnosed 121 children as having been sexually abused. Contrary to media accounts, only 26 children were seen to have been wrongly diagnosed. Although these facts were not available at the beginning of the crisis, once they were known many, including politicians, persisted in denying that it was possible that some 100 children had been abused.

Feminist writers and academics, especially Beatrix Campbell, had begun to raise issues about, and to politicise, child sex abuse in the 1980s, building upon radical feminist consciousness which had brought incest, rape and male violence to the fore (Atmore 1998; Campbell 1988; Gordon 1988; Nava 1988). In Cleveland, child sex abuse was 'suddenly' happening to ordinary children in ordinary families, it was 'not out there somewhere, but in our midst, in our hearts, in our histories, in our fantasies and our fears' (Campbell 1988, p.41). The emergence of the evidence that perpetrators were men and, worse, fathers and not strangers, and the realisation that this was not only a crime against women and children, but that the act of buggery was not confined to homosexuals, was politically too sensitive for the stability of society and was avoided in national debates (Freeman 1997). To some degree it is entirely understandable that the en masse buggery of children was too much for the public, press and some professional groups to comprehend (Nava 1988).

The interaction of the media, the politicians and police was formidable in its criticism of the paediatricians and social workers involved in the case. The method of diagnosis of anal intercourse which was so heavily criticised in the press was never discredited but it became *the* issue of public debate in Cleveland and in parliament rather than the incidence of sexual abuse itself (Campbell 1988; Freeman 1997). Many politicians and journalists simply disbelieved the incidence of sexual abuse, even given the evidence. In the midst of the confusion the police had withdrawn from acting on medical diagnoses even though it was their professional responsibility to do so. Instead they chose to support the local press in the 'Give us back our children' campaign, leaving social services in a dilemma as to how to intervene in families without police cooperation (Campbell 1988).

Political comment was extensive. The local Labour MP, Stuart Bell, in a speech in the House of Commons under parliamentary privilege accused one of the doctors, Dr Marietta Higgs who had made the diagnoses of sexual abuse, of having 'conspired and colluded' and he supported the police in wanting to sympathise with 'besieged families' (quoted by Nava 1988, p.115). He and several Conservative MPs, without any evidence, appeared to support the populist view and called for the resignation of Dr Higgs and the senior social worker Sue Richardson. In a parliamentary written answer the Secretary of State Kenneth Clarke wrote naively in terms of ensuring that such abuse should 'never happen again' (Hansard

Written Answer 9 November 1988). Despite the evidence of abuse, Conservative MP Tim Devlin was clear in his view that social workers and doctors had gone too far. He told the House of Commons that, '[t]he powers given to an outside agency operating on behalf of the State must be drafted carefully in order that gratuitous and free-ranging interference by an over-powerful agency cannot take place' (Hansard 6 July 1988).

At the same time the tabloid media led a gendered attack on Dr Higgs, which was:

> fuelled not so much by dislike but by fear: fear of the woman doctor, the professional woman, the woman with knowledge and public power. She was vilified for being a well-regarded career woman constructed as a problem, that she was anti-men and probably a feminist. *(Nava 1988, p.119)*

Further, the newspapers made an 'astonishing attempt...to displace guilt for the sexual abuse of children from the perpetrators on to Dr Higgs' (Nava 1988, p.119). Campbell (1988, p.67) summed it up: 'it was as if the disbelievers raised the politics on behalf of the patriarchs, and that the believers raised the problem on behalf of the women and children'.

In contrast, the *Observer* (28/06/87) claimed that Dr Higgs had 'lifted the lid on the horrifying scale of sexual abuse from which we have averted our eyes for too long'. Further, Atmore (2003, p.28) argued that casting the social workers, psychologists and doctors as folk devils served a "good' housekeeping narrative in which the 'ordinary' and 'normal' are kept intact from contamination by sexual violence'.

The Cleveland Inquiry, chaired by Lady Justice Butler-Sloss (Butler-Sloss 1988), supported the evidence of child abuse for some of the children and considered the impact on the children but made no comment on the behaviour of the men, or the views of the mothers, thereby failing to develop any knowledge of their perspectives. She made a strong admonishment of the behaviour of MPs and the press and suggested that social workers needed the support of the public to continue in the job the public needs them to do.

Once again the 'emotional public sphere' led to changes in legislation for children's social care. Government guidance, which was in the process of being updated when events in Cleveland occurred, was subject to subtle changes in emphasis (DHSS 1988a). In the draft that followed the deaths of Maria Colwell and Jasmine Beckford, agencies were to work together to safeguard children *from* parents, but given events in Cleveland, in the final document they were to work together *with* the parents (Parton 1991, pp.107–108). The subsequent Children Act 1989 balanced parents' and children's interests, rather than prioritising children's interests over parents' as the Beckford Inquiry had emphasised. A right-wing agenda had developed after the Cleveland Inquiry that suggested that parents needed protection from overzealous social workers and doctors.

The Children Act 1989, which remains the statutory basis of children's social care, brought the protection of children to prominence with new sets of procedures, committees and especially partnerships. Reflecting the Beckford Inquiry, the Act focused on the assessment of 'risk' which centred on whether children were at risk of 'significant harm'. The concepts of 'prevention' and 'prediction' of child abuse became established in the practice of children's social care. The notion of 'significant harm' was used to justify intervention with the family, but it relied on professional judgments and the availability of resources, meaning that thresholds varied across the country. Under the new Act no individual or single agency was to make a decision about sexual abuse in isolation, and lawyers and courts became involved with an emphasis on forensic evidence. Collectively they formed the child protection agencies, or multi-agency working, with social workers as the lead agency. Multi-agency working brought new complexities to the work of child protection which I return to in the next chapter.

The Children Act 1989 also tackled the thorny issues of responsibility and accountability. The Beckford Inquiry had explicitly recommended that local government elected councillors should be responsible for ensuring that social workers were trained in identifying high-risk cases. This new Act gave councillors a statutory responsibility to safeguard children rather than 'a duty to protect', which was a significant shift in the scale of responsibility.

The aftermath of the death of James Bulger

New complexities emerged with the murder of two-year-old James Bulger by two ten-year-old boys in Merseyside in 1993. The crime became understood in terms of pre-existing discourses of the 'trouble with youth', 'nasty videos', and a country in despair building upon a period of moral panic about lone motherhood (Roseneil and Mann 1996). Both the Conservative government and the Labour Opposition were in agreement with media and public condemnation but from different perspectives. The Conservative Prime Minister John Major called for a 'crusade against crime', and advised that society should 'understand a little less and condemn a little more' (*Sunday Times* 21/02/93). In contrast, Tony Blair, the Labour Opposition Home Secretary in a government that had opposed Conservative social policies, spoke of being 'tough on crime and tough on the causes of crime', which condemned the act but indicated a commitment to tackling social issues (*Guardian* 22/02/93).

The media and politicians had a high-profile presence in the case. It was the first occasion in which the *Sun* had run a campaign, under editor Kelvin MacKenzie, to increase the sentences given to the boys, and 20,000 people returned signed statements. Conservative Home Secretary Michael Howard interfered in the court sentencing by lengthening the ten-year sentence to 15 years. The BBC programme *Panorama* (BBC 9 October 1995) accused Howard of being influenced by the *Sun*'s campaign. Howard was later criticised in a House of Lords ruling in 1997 that his actions were unlawful and the sentence was returned to ten years, such was the level of political interference. The handling of the case was commented on in the European Court, which suggested that the government was giving more attention to satisfying public opinion than decisions that were right for the two perpetrators of the crime (Haydon and Scraton 2000).

Freeman (1997) suggests that what the public was unaware of, or was helped by the media and politicians to ignore, was that both boys came from disadvantaged families in which violence was present. Details of the serious degree of sexual assault of James Bulger emerged after the trial and Freeman (1997) suggests that its nature strongly suggested that at least one of the boys may have been himself subjected to sexual abuse. The presence of suspected sexual abuse of one or both boys would immediately have triggered psychiatric treatment for the boys, casting them also as victims. But the public response was such that they expected them to be treated as criminally responsible perpetrators and not as victims of abuse, and they were therefore charged and later convicted of murder. Freeman (1997) argues that to have brought sex abuse to light and therefore treated the boys as victims, or to have suggested that they were not criminally responsible and needed therapy, was simply not possible given the public views.

Sexual abuse within the family, similar to responses to events in Cleveland, or possibly because of them, was too unpalatable a subject to countenance. It may also have added to the discourse against lone motherhood and the break-up of the nuclear family which dominated the media after the death of James Bulger and which the Conservative government might have wanted to avoid. Freeman's (1997) suggestion that at least one of the boys had been the subject of sexual abuse was perhaps supported by the prosecution and imprisonment of Jon Venables for internet child sex offences in 2010, some nine years after he was released having served his sentence for the murder of James Bulger. Notwithstanding the horrendous nature of the crime, the case might indicate that it was more preferable to conduct a public trial and convict two ten-year-olds with murder than to confront the possible existence of their own sex abuse and their need for help. In common with the responses to the crimes in Cleveland, this was a case of choosing blame over painful acknowledgement of the realities of child sex abuse.

Satanic abuse

Satanic or ritual abuse includes torture and sexual abuse of children and adults, forced abortion and human sacrifice, cannibalism and bestiality, as part of magical or religious rites. Incidents of satanic abuse had been reported around the world and particularly in Australia in the 1980s and 1990s (La Fontaine 1998). From the late 1980s to the early 2000s allegations of satanic abuse were made in the UK in Nottingham, Rochdale and the Scottish isles of Orkney and Lewis. In the 1990s the NSPCC had supported the claims and reported that seven of their 66 teams in England, Wales and Northern Ireland were working with children 'ritually' abused.

Events in Orkney in 1991 where social workers and police removed nine children they thought were at risk of satanic abuse received extensive criticism in the media and by the public. The Inquiry led by Lord Clyde found no evidence of satanic abuse on Orkney, but rather cases of abuse that were sexually and not satanically motivated. Lord Clyde found that mistakes had been made by social workers and police but 'made in good faith' in line with what they thought had occurred. Lord Clyde called for reform and not recrimination. But despite his calls social workers were again vilified in the media.

Over 20 years later in 2013 a woman who as a child at the time had been taken into care disclosed the extent of sexual abuse by her father against her and her seven sisters. She had not disclosed who had been their abuser during questioning about satanic abuse, and their case was assumed by social workers and others to be part of organised satanic abuse. In an interview with the BBC she argued that events on the island may never have taken place if she had had the courage to speak up about abuse in her family by her father.[12]

Victoria Climbié

Victoria Climbié was one of 82 children who were victims of familial child homicide in the year 2000 according to crime statistics. 'New Labour' had been in government for almost three years. Lord Laming was appointed by the Labour government to chair the inquiry into Victoria's death. He had been the Conservative government's Chief

Inspector for Social Services between 1991 and 1998 when he was made a cross-party life peer. His chairmanship was questioned in the media and by Liberal Democrat MP Paul Burstow, not only because of his connections to politicians, but also because as Director of Social Services in Hertfordshire he had been strongly criticised for the handling of a child abuse case which led the local government ombudsman to make a finding of 'maladministration with injustice' in 1995.[13]

In Chapter 1 I discussed aspects of the Inquiry by Lord Laming into Victoria's death. I argued that in the context of Haringey Council, characterised as 'loony-left', the findings of the Laming Inquiry were used to give Haringey Council and its 'Old Labour' politicians a 'bloody nose' especially in a case that concerned a young black African girl in a London borough so vehemently committed to equality issues. The quasi-judicial nature of the Inquiry predisposed its business as the identification of the guilty parties and so the focus was almost exclusively on the conduct of individual professionals. The report endorsed the view that social workers could *not* predict child death but, despite that, it judged that social workers, police and health professionals had failed to prevent Victoria's death. Any exploration of systemic issues which may have helped to find explanations was neglected.

The context of the Laming Inquiry included extensive media and political criticism of Haringey, vilification of social workers and a culture of blame and recrimination. Haringey's barrister suggested that:

> [t]he atmosphere of blame...meant that this inquiry has lost the opportunity to allow those actually involved in doing the job at all levels to offer their reflections in an atmosphere of open-minded inquiry on what might have made a difference or how practice might be improved. *(Guardian 27/09/01, p.12)*

Others took up the issues of blame from different perspectives. Sociologist Michael Rustin (2004, p.11) suggested that since the Laming Inquiry focused on establishing individual guilt, not legal guilt but professional guilt, the report was unable to explain how those involved in the case interpreted, understood or evaluated what happened to Victoria. Such testimony, he argued, was vital to a full understanding. In the next chapter I discuss in greater depth the work of psychoanalytic psychotherapists Margaret Rustin (2005) and Andrew Cooper (2005). They described the defences of social workers, police and health professionals who had an unconscious need *not* to see what was unbearable. They use the term 'turning a blind eye' to suggest a 'psychic retreat' or a state of 'true denial', as opposed to the claim of the Laming Report which used the same term to imply intent. That is, the intent of the child protection workers to ignore what should have been obvious, which was translated by the Inquiry into failure, and consequently to blame.

Rustin (2005) concluded that the suggestion that professionals were incompetent masked the real reason that they kept a distance. She argued that the Laming Report recommendations, mainly about management and organisational matters, were not what the problems were about at all. She argued that professionals, who are exposed to inadequate resources, fear of blame and difficult families, experience unavoidable anxiety in how they think about cases. In particular they need processes which enable them to be aware of their potential distress and to be able to assess its impact on them and on the case if things are to be different. The Inquiry engaged in a technical, logical and legal process which neglected the emotional and moral aspects of the case (Cooper 2005) and it held the child protection professionals, especially social workers, to blame.

As in the aftermath of other high-profile child deaths or child abuse inquiries, once again the emotional policy sphere led to new government legislation. In Chapter 1 I argued that the government already knew the issues with safeguarding children from its own commissioned report (DH 2002a) but the Laming Report (2003) focused blame on social workers and others, and had the effect of deflecting responsibility from government. The Laming Inquiry is the last formal inquiry into a child death to have taken place and in completing it Lord Laming commented in a press interview that

Victoria's death would mark 'a turning point in ensuring proper protection of children in this country' (*Guardian* 09/09/2003). He also assured the government's Select Committee for Health (27/03/03) which was concerned that predecessor reports 'have ended up on shelves gathering dust' that this report would be different. But the turning point Lord Laming envisaged did not materialise.

Conclusion

The idealisation of motherhood and childhood in the 'sentiment of the nation', and the sequestration of knowledge and awareness of familial child abuse and homicide, both set a context for society's denial of crimes against children. I argue that the denial of familial child abuse and homicide kept crimes against children 'safe within the family' and in some institutions, for example the church.

Social work, with its origins in highlighting the plight of poor children, is intrinsically political. At its core are tensions as to whether the problems of families are the result of levels of poverty which are tolerated by politicians, or whether such problems are 'within' the clients and their 'innate inadequacy', especially 'within mothers'. On the political right and left, politicians expect social workers to keep such families from public view.

Efforts to keep unpalatable information from public awareness may be the origin of the sequestration of information about familial child abuse and homicide. Such sequestration and public blaming of social workers when things went wrong may have been more preferable for politicians than attacking the morals of 'the poor' or risking criticism of their government's social policies. But ongoing sequestration which results in a lack of knowledge of harm against children puts families, especially the children, and social workers, given their vilification, at greater risk.

Awareness of harm to children that emerged in the latter part of the twentieth century with cases of 'baby battering' and of familial child sex abuse and homicide were subjected to high levels of controversy, conflict and confusion. Characteristics of the six high-profile cases discussed included controversial media coverage, political opportunism (usually party political), a search for 'rational answers' using quasi-legal processes (Beckford Inquiry) or managerial models (Laming Inquiry), which led to a highly charged emotional public sphere and an emotional policy sphere in which children's social policy was incrementally adapted. The cases illustrated multiple interpretations as to whether aspects of cases were real, imagined, mistaken, constructed or concealed. But in all cases communicated mainly by the media and politicians, child protection professionals, usually social workers, were roundly condemned.

References to wider societal issues being at the core of cases of child abuse were made in the earlier Inquiries, but the sense that crimes against children were failures of social workers to apply their knowledge, skill and powers gradually dominated. Notions of predicting and preventing harm to children, introduced by the Beckford Inquiry, were predicated upon child abuse being a disease inherent (usually) in the mother, and upon emerging ideas about managing risk. But failure to predict and prevent became a 'within social worker' problem and established views that social workers were to blame for harm to children and should be held accountable. Successive Children Acts since 1975 focused not on improving circumstances for children and families but on improving skills of surveillance.

For social workers, the fear of either wrongly identifying or failing to prevent a case of child abuse has embedded a 'fear of failure' in the social work profession and a level of unavoidable anxiety which disrupts their work. Compared with the number of children protected, incidents of familial child homicide are rare but they disproportionately affect the work of social workers in their day-to-day practice. The social work profession lives with a high degree of uncertainty and insecurity.

At the core of the blaming of social workers by the media, the politicians and the public, I argue, was an expression of denial as a defence against such unpalatable crimes against children by a known adult. Part of the legacy of the denial is a 'gendered denial' which draws upon notions of 'the inadequate mother', 'female sexual phantasy', 'female sexualised behaviour', the ability of social workers (usually female) to support mothers, and misogynist media attacks.

By the time that Peter Connelly died I argue that a dominant and widespread cultural narrative was established that where deaths of children occurred, social workers were to blame. In the next chapter I develop a psychosocial approach to understanding the processes of blame, fear and denial that followed the familial homicide of Peter Connelly.

Chapter 3

Exploring Processes of Blame, Fear and Denial from a Psychosocial Perspective

Introduction

In the UK, for over forty years, cases of familial child homicide which have come to public attention have brought a sense of disbelief and shock. Responses to familial child homicide have been 'saturated with affect' (Ahmed 2004, p.95) but for different reasons and with different consequences. How individuals respond to such events is shaped by a wide range of 'inner' and 'outer' influences, or by the continuous interaction of the psyche and the social. Where the psyche and the social each begin and end, or if they ever do, is never clear. It may be that the values, norms and expectations of society are etched into the psyche, or that the experiences of the social world are shaped by the dynamics of the psyche.

In this chapter I develop a psychosocial perspective on the dynamics of blame, fear and denial that might enable a better understanding of the responses to the familial homicide of Peter Connelly. My psychosocial perspective draws first upon the work of psychoanalyst Melanie Klein (1882–1960) and other 'post-Kleinian' thinkers in the field of object-relations, in particular the psychoanalytic concepts of 'projection', 'introjection', 'splitting' and 'projective identification', ideas which will be explained in more detail below. Second, I consider how these personal worlds might shape and be shaped by the wider social world. To do so I turn my attention to the 'circulation of affect' in the work of Ahmed (2004), which I will explain offers some understanding of processes of 'public emotion'. Finally, to consider how the interactions of the print and broadcast shape 'public emotion' I consider three aspects: the work of Aeron Davis (2003, 2007, 2009), Professor of Political Communication, on 'mediated reflexivity', which describes the interdependence of politicians and journalists; the work of scholar of journalism and media Justin Schlosberg (2013) on the role of the media as the last line of public interest defence; and the work of Robert Entman (2004), Professor of Media and Public Affairs, on the 'cascade network of activation' which describes the interaction of politicians, the media and the public.

I conclude the chapter by exploring how some of these psychosocial processes have been applied in two research studies: the first by scholar and academic Jessica Evans (2003), which is concerned with events that followed the murder of Sarah Payne; and the second by Professor of Journalism, Media and Cultural Studies Jenny Kitzinger, which looks at perceptions of childhood sexual abuse.

The place of psychoanalytic concepts in the psychosocial

Psychoanalysis is distinguished from all other approaches to human psychology by the concept of the unconscious. The existence of an unconscious was first noted by psychoanalyst Sigmund Freud (1856–1939) through his work in enabling the 'expression' of what was in his patients' minds, rather than an approach focused on the correction of 'pathologies' through methods, such as hypnosis, practised at the turn of the twentieth century (Hinshelwood 1994, p.10). Freud's work cast doubt upon, and eventually overturned, the view that human behaviour was entirely the result of 'rational' thought. Unconscious emotional forces, he argued, had the capacity to disrupt and disturb our ability to think 'rationally'. For a useful overview of Freud's work see *Key Concepts in Psychoanalysis* (Frosh 2002c).

Today the unconscious is fundamental to psychoanalysis and it implies that humans can never be whole, never fully aware of why they act as they do, and never fully knowledgeable of themselves or in full control (Frosh 2002c). The existence of both the unconscious and conscious is referred to as 'split subjects' or simply 'splitting'. The unconscious is not accessible to conscious thought yet it has a profound influence on the psyche, constantly active and making things happen in the individual's life. Freud describes the unconscious as being in a state of dynamic activity, building and releasing tension in a constant process of repressing disturbing ideas. Such ideas, unavailable to conscious control, produce behaviours, feelings and experiences that are often unexpected and surprising. Unlike conscious thought, the unconscious is not constrained by 'reality', and it has no language to describe or express its experiences. Instead it is expressed in dreams, parapraxis (slip of the tongue) and, for some, in the symptoms of neuroses, or more seriously of psychosis.

Melanie Klein developed aspects of Freud's theories into a distinctive set of theories of human subjectivity known as 'object relations'. Object relations focus primarily on the very early relations between mother and child which lay the foundations for adult life. The innate human striving to be relational, and especially the development of thinking, was the basis of Klein's understanding of human development. Klein believed that infants (and subsequently adults) related consciously and unconsciously to a union of the psyche or the inner world, influenced by the social or the outer world, albeit she saw the psyche as the prime mover.

In particular, Klein saw anxiety as the emotion driving much of human behaviour and efforts to defend against anxiety as the driving force that shapes that behaviour, especially when things go wrong. Klein differentiated between two major groups of anxiety and defence: the 'paranoid-schizoid position' and the 'depressive position', and suggested that throughout life individuals move continuously between the two.

The paranoid-schizoid position describes the anxieties of birth and early post-natal life in the interaction of the baby with the mother (all references to the mother imply the primary care-giver). In the chaos of life as an object without a subjective 'I', the newborn experiences only satisfaction or frustration. In its desire to gain some instinctual gratification from an 'object' (the mother) the newborn distinguishes between what feels good and what feels bad. It 'splits' experiences of the immediate 'part-objects' of its mother into the 'good' and the 'bad'. The 'good object', usually the mother, is warm, safe, nourishing, comforting, understanding and experienced as loving. The good object is associated with the life instinct which forms the basis of trust and enables the development of love. In contrast the 'bad object' is the misery of hunger, coldness and loneliness, which brings the infant persecutory experiences of the mother. The experience of the bad object brings a sense of threat and feelings of hate.

Introjection and projection are unconscious intrapersonal defence mechanisms which help protect the ego and are the basis of how individuals relate to external objects from infancy into adulthood. For example, from the earliest stages of the paranoid-schizoid position, the baby is motivated to maintain positive feelings of goodness, and to rid him/herself of harm: the baby splits off bad feelings and projects these into objects outside him/herself, usually the mother. In most cases the mother contains the uncontrollable emotions of the infant and consoles the infant, allowing good feelings to predominate. At the same time the loving impulses of the infant are projected onto the good object, the mother, enabling the infant to keep goodness safe from the badness. Good objects are introjected, and idealised, thereby building up a store of internal protective good objects. This splitting, Klein maintained, allowed the infant to keep the experience of the good mother from the bad mother. In doing so the infant can overcome anxiety and fear, repair splits and achieve a sense of ambivalence that the world is neither all good nor all bad. The ability to love is simultaneously the ability to hate. It is not possible to know one without the other. Described in this way, this process of splitting is the basis of individual well-being, albeit such well-being is dependent upon good experiences predominating over bad ones (Segal 1973, p.37).

The 'depressive position' describes an important developmental milestone for the infant in which there is a degree of synthesis between good and bad objects. The infant perceives the mother as a 'whole-object' who 'brings' both joy (food and warmth) *and* sorrow (hunger and discomfort). The anxiety that has been present since birth has been reduced unconsciously in these early months through splitting, introjection and projection. As splitting diminishes, the experiences of the baby are less extreme, as he/she learns to fit things together better. The infant begins to realise that the part-objects resulting from his/her splitting, in particular the good and bad mother, are in fact a whole object, the mother, about whom he/she has already a range of feelings. The loving mother he/she realises is the same as the hated mother. In the depressive position the baby will introject the mother as a whole object of both 'good' and 'bad'. With the loss of a sense of omnipotence in controlling the world, the infant gradually becomes an interpreting individual and realises he/she has both good and bad qualities. The realisation brings a fear of losing the internalised good object, usually the mother, and carries with it a threat to the infant's identity.

Given favourable early experiences the infant will have strong ideal objects to relate to whilst becoming less afraid of bad objects and with it the need to defend against them (Segal 1973, p.67). This development allows the infant to go beyond self as object, and to achieve self as subject, that is, the development of 'I' or 'me'. Such developments make the infant more able to interact with the wider world and to tolerate ambiguity and uncertainty. Achieving the depressive position is part of a maturing process in which the self is better organised and strengthened against internal fears and the impact of the projections of others. In short, the initial experiences in terms of good and bad, that is, the paranoid-schizoid position, if all goes well changes gradually and is helped by positive experiences to overcome projections of frightening emotions enabling the world to be seen in more realistic terms. For a useful overview of Klein's work see *Introduction to the Work of Melanie Klein* (Segal 1988).

'Othering'

From infancy into adulthood these processes of introjection and projection are unconscious intrapersonal defence mechanisms which help protect the self and are the basis of how individuals relate to external objects or the world around them. The 'splitting off' of bad experiences from good, which are projected elsewhere, is part of human development. Bad experiences can be denied and good experiences idealised and exaggerated as a protection against anxiety.

Fear or anxiety which cannot be defended against is projected onto the 'Other' so that the sense of fear or danger becomes not within the self but is perceived as inherent in the 'Other'. In effect, when insecurity appears and anxiety rises the 'Other' can become the container for unwanted feelings and thoughts, much of it unconscious but with a wide range of consequences. The notion of the Other or the process of Othering is the identification of someone or others who do not belong to a particular group with which the self identifies. For example, discrimination against certain ethnic groups perceived to be different from one's collective social norm. The 'Other' therefore is a person who is perceived to not fit one's social norm.

Further, 'projective identification' as an extension of projection is an unconscious phantasy which is both interpersonal and intrapersonal and shapes each person's relational world. Projective identification 'splits off' and projects unwanted parts of the self into the other, and induces in the other the embodiment of the projection. For example, feelings projected into another person, such as hatred and fear, evoke in that person the thoughts and feelings projected, evoking a sense of being hated or fearful. Wilfred Bion (1897–1979), an influential British psychoanalyst who developed Klein's work, argued that intolerable anxiety can lead to a person resorting to excessive use of projective identification (Bion 1962). The Other can become a feared object or object of hate which produces a cycle of persecutory anxiety and the need to defend against it.

The Other can come to identify with negative projections and to own feelings which are not his/her own. The Other can come to believe that he/she is worthy of blame and deserving of abuse or of hostilities, with a wide range of consequences. There is a cycle of projective identification here which goes some way to describing the relationship between the public and social workers or the social work profession in general. Familial abuse or homicide is unthinkable; the anxiety it creates is projected onto social workers who in turn often characterise themselves in a moral position as containers for the nation's anger and disbelief.

Bion (1961) referred to 'dead containers' to describe those who had suffered the hostility of others and became an inert repository for their hatred and who could become ill as they struggled to contain the violent emotions of others. The projection of unbearable subjective feelings contained or not by the Other can bring relief for the projector. But the process can be a 'double-edged sword'. For example, Paul Hoggett, Professor of Social Policy and psychoanalytical psychotherapist, describes the vulnerabilities projected by one person and contained by the Other which create for the projector a world 'safe in its fearfulness' (Hoggett 2000, p.68). Borrowing from Hoggett, familial child abuse and homicide are projected as the failure of social workers and not as the reality for some children. This inability of individuals to grasp the unthinkable is dealt with by turning to the Other, in the belief that the explanation or the blame must lie elsewhere; and most especially it is not about 'my inability to face reality'. Hoggett (2000, p.12) refers to the ability of humans to deny what is 'unthought and unthinkable', a term that I argue can be applied to the complex circumstances in which the blaming of social workers for instances of familial child homicide appears as a rational explanation. Hoggett appears to sum things up when he argues that humans 'prefer stupidity and mindlessness to painful awareness and to those dispositions within us that are anti-life, which seek to avoid human complexity and contradictoriness by choosing shallowness' (p.12).

Denial

Between the depressive and the paranoid-schizoid positions, Klein (1952) suggested a state of 'pathological organisation'. The term describes a range of extremely rigid defences which enable a degree of illusory safety or psychic equilibrium. In his book *Psychic Retreats*, psychoanalyst and 'post-Kleinian' scholar John Steiner referred to this place of safety as a 'psychic retreat' where respite from anxiety can be sought and where 'reality' is neither fully accepted nor completely refuted (Steiner 1993). The psychic retreat is a defensive process of denial in which an individual is simultaneously 'knowing and not knowing' the reality of what is actually and metaphorically before his or her eyes. Steiner (1993) suggests that a person 'turns a blind eye' to what is seen or has come to be known as a reluctance to know the unpalatable truth, thereby remaining in a psychic retreat, or denial, where relations with reality are eschewed. From such a position a person can use 'perverse arguments' to deny or avoid the facts (Steiner 1993, p.92).

These processes of 'knowing and not knowing' are applied by Stan Cohen (1942–2013), Professor of Sociology, to his work on the denial of human rights abuses. Cohen (2001) suggests a threefold model of the denial of unbearable knowledge of human rights abuses. The denial can be 'literal' in a person being unable to believe that an event actually occurred, 'interpretative' in how the facts are accepted but the meaning is distorted through 'rational' explanations, or 'implicatory' in allowing the facts to be accepted but the psychological, moral or political implications to be denied. Cohen describes the justifications, rationalisations and evasions that people share and which bridge the gap between what they know about human rights and what they do, often in the form of stories that suggest a degree of 'moral accountability' (p.8). Bruna Seu, psychoanalytic psychotherapist and academic, captures the psychosocial nature of this 'moral accountability' in her work on human rights. She describes 'sociological forms of apologies, normalisation and neutralisation', but also 'psychological techniques of rationalisation, defence mechanisms and disavowal' which suggests that people retreat to 'a twilight zone of simultaneously knowing and not knowing' (Seu 2013, pp.19–21).

The dynamics of denial

These analyses of the dynamics of denial suggest that an unpalatable event such as a case of familial child homicide brings unconscious denial and with it a search for some kind of rational answer, usually in the form of someone to blame. In the previous chapter I discussed the valuable insights that psychoanalysts Margaret Rustin (2005) and Andrew Cooper (2005) provided into the role and function of denial (and subsequent blame) operating in the child protection workers (social workers, police and health professionals) in the case of the familial homicide of Victoria Climbié.

Rustin (2005, p.11) suggested that it was crucial to understand the way in which the professionals who were involved in the case of Victoria Climbié 'faced or avoided the mental pain'. She argued that the unconscious defences of child protection workers were enacted when they became aware of the dreadful circumstances that Victoria was living in. Rustin described their reactions as defences against recognising the reality which 'involved severe distortions in the mind's capacity to function'. The result was an *unconscious* need *not* to see what was unbearable (my emphases). Rustin (2005) drew on Steiner's notion, suggesting that it was a simultaneous 'knowing and not knowing' that allowed child protection workers to 'turn a blind eye' indicating 'psychic disturbance' or a psychic retreat on their behalf. Rustin argues that the professionals retreated to the structures and practices of their organisations which allowed them to become convinced that they could avoid thinking about their encounters with Victoria and her aunt. I suggest that each might have consciously or unconsciously left it to other professionals to raise concerns. In applying Steiner's term 'psychic retreat' to describe the effect of 'turning a blind eye', Rustin (2005, p.12) provides a different perspective on the many actions of professionals judged as incompetent in the Laming Report. She suggests that perceiving the actions as incompetence masked the real reason that the professionals kept a distance, which was because of the 'intense feelings stirred up by exposure to human cruelty and madness'.

Cooper (2005, p.8) also engaged with the notion of 'turning a blind eye' and argued that child protection workers, and society at large, can enter into a state of 'true denial', meaning that we are 'unable to struggle consciously with the conflict, the dilemma, or with the anxiety arising from [some situations]'. It is a 'very ordinary defence', and we do it when we are 'deeply conflicted about what we are seeing or about what we have come to know'. Cooper suggests that it is well beyond the everyday psychological capabilities of most people 'to be capable of thinking about and linking up apparently inconsistent elements of experience'. It would be a case of being able 'to think the unthinkable'.

Cooper's (2005) position on familial child homicide reflects that of Money-Kyrle (2015, first published 1961) when he argues that some facts of life have a simultaneous acceptance and disavowal, for example the reality of death. Applied to harm to children, we know children are abused and that some are killed by their parents but we cannot face it. More explicitly, Cooper (2005, p.9) suggests that there is a deep ambivalence about facing up to these issues and that the 'pain of knowing [that abuse of children happens] is too great for us to be able to sustain our attention'. 'Knowing and not knowing' is in effect a defence against linking things that appear to be connected but which create 'painful anxiety' (Rustin 2005). For example, the black African social workers, police officers and doctors who saw Victoria may have been in unconscious denial of linking 'black child', 'black family', 'spirit possession', 'torture' and 'murder'. Psychoanalytically, 'knowing and not knowing' described by the metonymy of 'turning a blind eye' suggests the complexities of unconscious denial rather than conscious wilful neglect on behalf of child protection workers, or a form of racism suggested by the Laming Report (2003, paras 16.1–16.13, discussed in Chapter 1). The Laming Inquiry's explanation is in itself an example of the inability to face what Hoggett (2000, p.12) refers to as what is 'unthought and unthinkable', but instead seeks 'rational' answers, or 'shallowness' that avoids human complexity.

Cooper (2010) suggests that social work is an ideal object for the negative projections of others since social work intervenes (at times forcefully) between those perceived to be 'good' families and those regarded as vulnerable, damaged or damaging. The perceived incompetence of social workers then functions as a defence for society generally against having to tolerate knowledge of what is 'bad'. Cooper suggests that social work as a profession exists in a cycle of idealisation–denigration and social workers become the 'receptive mother who is in tune with society's projections of its own destructiveness and by internalizing these projections offers society containment of its unbearable feelings' (Cooper 2010, p.10).

Similar dynamics emerge in other 'caring' professions. For example, Menzies Lyth (1988, first published 1960) in her classic study of nursing found that in dealing with life and death, primary primitive anxieties were stirred up for nurses. But the organisational changes taken by hospitals to defend nurses against anxiety depersonalised their engagements with their patients and created secondary anxieties expressed in a different range of defences. Nurses demonstrated their collective power to 'split off' their anxieties and to project them into others, usually management. Further, in order to avoid the fear of having to take responsibility for errors, they avoided specific definitions of who was responsible for what. Nurses began to perceive patients as 'part-objects'; for example, their attention was focused on the medical needs increasingly indicated by machines, rather than on the well-being of the whole person.

Paediatricians also get drawn into processes of denial from inside and outside their profession. For example, Dr Southall identified parents he claimed fabricated illnesses in their children as a disguise for the harm they had inflicted themselves, known as 'Munchausen Syndrome by proxy'. Controversy about his claims led to Dr Southall initially being removed from the medical register and later reinstated when his claims were accepted as real. I discussed aspects of the case in Chapter 2.

Blaming and scapegoating

Psychoanalytically, blaming and scapegoating are the manifestation of processes of denial and Othering. Both are regarded as the product of the projection of unwanted feelings and emotions. Blaming and scapegoating suggest an unconscious urge which brings psychic relief (Welch 2006; Cooke 2007). The scapegoat is the person/group/society forced to take the blame for something which is not his/her/its fault. For example, Welch (2006, p.36) argues that the use of scapegoating in the aftermath of the terrorist attacks on New York's World Trade Centre in September 2001, known as '9/11', provided a 'cathartic ventilation of frustration by displacing aggression onto a suitable target', mainly Arabs and Muslims. But the scapegoating failed to identify the real causes of and solutions to the political violence. The scapegoat was in effect the observable 'social outcome' of the psychoanalytical processes.

Sociologists suggest that scapegoats are created to bear the blame for threats to society's way of life and moral values (Girard 1986; Jeffrey 1992). Anthropologist Mary Douglas (1984/66, 1986, 1992) in developing her cultural theories argued that blaming and scapegoating functioned to maintain social cohesion and social order by removing threats to social boundaries and basic moral values. Scapegoating in effect draws a virtual line between the righteous 'us' and the transgressive 'them', which provokes a reaction to matters that are experienced as out of place or that disturb the way in which the world is ordered. Blaming another for perceived ills removes the presence of the 'pollution', either literally or symbolically. The 'transgressions' of the scapegoat become a moral failure.

From a psychosocial perspective, blaming and scapegoating allow individuals to split away from distressing events and to construct some kind of explanation. In the context of familial child homicide, blaming and scapegoating enable individuals to split away from the anguish and horror of such a deeply held social taboo into some kind of explanation that can be tolerated. The belief that social workers and others are to blame for familial abuse and homicide can become a habitual response embedded in individuals, groups and whole societies. At the same time the blaming and scapegoating of professionals shapes their work as individuals, but also as professions and as multi-disciplinary teams. Dykman and Cutler (2003) argue that organisations as well as individuals can become the victims of scapegoating. The social work profession, and to some degree paediatricians, have developed a 'fear of failure' and as professions they experience vulnerabilities with far-reaching implications which I return to in subsequent chapters. Further, scapegoating can reflect a culture of authoritarianism and social solidarity in which control and harsh penalties respond to, and satisfy, public outrage creating a mentality of 'we' versus 'them' (Welch 2006, p.43). Harm to children can create a particular form of public outrage which makes it, and the professions who work to prevent harm to children, particularly susceptible to blame and scapegoating.

The effects of social media

Earlier I suggested that social media played a part in shaping the responses to the death of Peter Connelly. At the time, communication by social media included email, text, internet sites such as Facebook, online blogs, video-sharing sites such as YouTube, but not Twitter. Different views exist as to the role and function of social media. Psychoanalysts John Bird (2003) and Michael Civin (2000) suggest that unconscious expression of defences of Othering and denial can be exacerbated by social media. For example, visual and bodily cues and emotional relatedness, essential to learning and communication, are absent in online communications, making them much more fragile. The absence of such cues can lead to primitive aspects of psychic life described by Klein (Bird 2003, p.123), such as 'splitting', or 'a kind of detached hostility'.

At the same time, multiple communications among a virtual crowd can develop a complex fusion of passions all happening simultaneously, which hampers the capacity of individual members to reason things out. The crowd's emotions are dynamic, moving, and developing in response to views and new perspectives that fit with the crowd's emotional narrative. The suggestibility and ease of influence between members of a group online becomes rapid, often encouraging the group to find fascination in certain images (Hoggett 2009).

Further, Bird (2003) suggests that a pattern of attachment can occur between people in virtual groups which is much stronger than attachment occurring between 'present' groups. But such attachment is in his opinion 'primitive, shallow, persecutory, schizoid and absurdly grandiose and supportive of one another, making cyberspace a 'bad object'' (p.124). Similarly, Civin (2000) suggests that anxieties cannot be managed or contained in social media and that users can become insulated from personal contact. Writing twenty years ago, Holland (1996) produced research evidence on 'internet regression' which suggested that users can demonstrate a level of intimacy or openness, and extraordinary generosity, but at the same time a loss of boundaries, a lack of inhibition, increased vulnerability and a level of foul-mouthedness that is unrestrained. It was evidence of these negative effects that led to new notions of 'cyber-bullying' and online harassment, and to the new Defamation Act 2014 which brought the potential for criminal convictions.

Sociologist Zygmunt Bauman (1993) argues that the ability to be moral lies in proximity to others, which raises a problem not only of sociality in social media communication but also morality. Bauman sees virtual relating as a gradual disintegration of citizenship and the weakening of the ethical self. Bird (2003, p.125), on the basis of Bauman's position, asks whether it is the embodied presence of others that makes us human and, if so, 'has the prosthetic of the virtual world made us less human?' If so, the increasing use of social media in responses to cases of familial child homicide makes such responses even more concerning. More recently, Professor of Psychology Geoff Beattie, in an interview with the BBC (6 August 2015), described the effects of the excessive use of the smartphone. Beattie argued that it denied its users the face-to-face interactions which are the foundation of the social world where humans learn about reciprocity and how to interpret emotion and develop empathy.

In contrast, the work of Neubaum *et al.* (2014) provides a contradictory perspective. Their research looked at the psychosocial functions of social media following the loss of life at 'The Love Parade', an electronic dance musical festival and parade in Germany in 2010. The event and its participants received widespread condemnation in the international media. Neubaum *et al.* (2014, p.30) identified a process of social sharing of emotion online among those who had been present. In particular, they identified a specific need for people to express their internal states to others following an emotional event. They found that people used social media to express their empathy and sympathy with the people concerned, as well as to emotionally support each other, suggesting that social sharing of emotions accounts for a considerable share of active social media communication in disaster contexts. In effect, 'social media seem to serve as instruments for individual emotion regulation'; further, individuals seemed to have a need to 'comprehend the consequences of a disaster on an individual level' and social media fulfilled this need by offering more 'authentic and personal information than traditional media' (Neubaum *et al.* 2014, pp.32–39). In particular, engagement with YouTube, Facebook and weblogs was associated with beneficial effects such as feeling better, the sense of not being alone, and the efficacy to cope with the extreme situation.

'The circulation of affect'

The discussion thus far has been concerned with developing a psychosocial perspective on denial, Othering, fear, blame and scapegoating which might aid understanding of responses to crimes against children. Sara Ahmed (2004, p.117) challenges the assumption that emotions are 'a private matter, that they simply belong to individuals, or even that they come from within the individual and *then* move outward toward others' (emphasis in the original). She is critical of the 'inside out' model or the 'me', which assumes an objectivity of the individual; and she is critical of the 'outside in' model or the 'we', which assumes the social.

Ahmed argues that emotions are not 'in' the individual or the individual's psyche or 'in' the social. Emotions are not something that 'I' or 'we' (the crowd) have. She asks what emotion does rather than what it is. Rather than seeing emotions as a psychological state, it is a case of looking at the ways in which emotion facilitates the relationship between the psyche and the social. Ahmed argues that it is emotions that create or structure the psyche and the social as objects, making the psyche and the social *effects* of emotions rather than the *cause* of emotions. In the social world, patterns of meaning and feelings get attached to objects that give rise to emotion. Ahmed describes 'the circulation of affect' arguing that 'it is the objects of emotion that circulate rather than the emotion' (p.11). The death of a child, especially where it involves the mother, is an object of emotion.

Ahmed explores how the use of metonymy as a 'figure of speech', and the power of performativity, are used by the media and politicians to shape both the public nature of emotions, and the emotive nature of the public (Ahmed 2004). Metonymy describes the substitution of the name of a thing or a concept by the name of something with which it is closely associated, and performativity describes the capacity of speech and communication not simply to communicate but to create new realities simply by being uttered.

Ahmed uses examples from newspaper articles, websites, government reports and political speeches to demonstrate how the use of metonymy and performativity create emotions such as hate, fear, shame and disgust which then establish a social and emotional value, and a meaning that defines both the inside and the outside of the person, group or nation. For example, Ahmed describes 'the slide of metonymy' which can create causal relations; for example, the use of the words 'terrorist' and 'Muslim' together mobilises fear and anxiety. Similarly the words 'nigger' or 'paki' generate negative affect. Such words are performative and have transformative power; for example, the black man or the Muslim becomes an object of hate and fear. Ahmed argues that it is the 'futurity of fear' or the anticipation of fear which is not yet present, and although it may not occur, the sense of fear is not overcome and people remain fearful. Fear then becomes a symptom which maintains the distance between the fearful and those feared. The fear does not come from, or reside in, the black or the Muslim man but through the circulation of fear; each comes to feel the fear as his own and 'becomes' fearsome. The black man and the Muslim man come to fear the impact of the white man's fear.

Further, the word 'disgust' works performatively to generate that which it appears to name; for example, the homeless person, a pregnant schoolgirl or the 'fat cats' (rich bankers). Disgust then takes on a cultural meaning and a moral value that shapes who or what is disgusting and it generates affect. It distances 'us' from disgust by casting out 'disgust', and pulling 'us' away from disgust.

Similarly, hate does not reside in the individual but the circulation of 'hate' can, for example, connect the asylum seeker with the terrorist and others perceived to invade the body of the nation. The hatred 'slides' across to Arabs, Muslims and South Asians and accumulates affective value over time. The hate generates the Other as an object of hate to be defended against. The proximity of the object of hate becomes threatening, moving communities to align themselves against the object.

It is through what emotions do rather than what they are that 'we' and 'others' emerge. As 'we' and 'others' emerge, an 'us' versus 'them' creates space between the two. Together 'we' hate and it is 'us' who are wronged. Thus boundaries between I / we / other are formed, and social norms and expectations emerge. The effect of Othering in phrases such as '*bogus* asylum seekers' communicates to 'the British' people those who are 'not us' and who 'threaten or endanger us'. The narrative communicates a 'you' who is understandably enraged about those who 'take' what is 'yours' (Ahmed 2004).

Ahmed (2004) refers to this process of the circulation of affect as an 'affective economy'. The circulation of affect shapes individuals and communities, it legitimises political decisions, and 'sticks to some objects' in the process. Some objects through the power of affect are shaped by histories in which fixity emerges, making them 'sticky'. Consequently, emotions influence how lives are lived and experienced.

I suggest that this process of the circulation of affect has parallels in how perceptions of social workers have evolved. The social worker anticipates the fear of being blamed in a case of child abuse or homicide. Fear becomes a symptom of her work and the work becomes fearsome, making anxiety and defensiveness implicit to the social work profession. The volatility is borne out in the increasing numbers of children taken from their families after high-profile events, for example as demonstrated by the 'Baby P effect' following the death of Peter Connelly. Simultaneously, mothers can be reluctant to seek help for fear that their child will be taken from them. I explore some of these processes in subsequent chapters.

The interaction of the media, politicians and the public

The media and politicians played a prominent role in shaping the responses to the death of Peter Connelly and understanding these processes is central to developing a psychosocial approach to an analysis of events. In this section I look specifically at three areas concerned with the media, politicians and the public. These are the impact of relationships between the media and politicians; the media's role in holding power to account; and engagement with the 242 public.

The impact of relationships between the media and politicians

Traditionally, power and politics have been located in a belief that the 'ruling classes' or 'elite groups' sustained themselves through the control of ideas communicated to the masses via the media. However, this simplistic stimulus–response model assumes that the media is an independent entity affected by the thinking and behaviour of politicians. Rather than this primitive model, Aaron Davis,

Professor of Political Communication, asserts that power lies in the interdependence of the media and politicians (Davis 2007). In effect, those in power are the main sources, main targets and some of the most influenced recipients of news, making the news media the conduit for negotiations between those in power and in opposition with the public 'no more than ill-informed spectators' (Davis 2003, p.673).

Davis (2009) researched relationships between politicians and journalists during the latter part of Labour's third term in office, which was the same period in which Peter Connelly died, and as such gives a useful contemporaneous perspective. Davis found close relationships between senior MPs and national political journalists from the broadcast and print media. Their relationships were symbiotic and mutually beneficial. Each needed the other's cooperation to do their jobs, but they were also aware of the potential for conflict. MPs in the main mistrusted journalists, with half of those interviewed acknowledging that the media had a role in influencing the rise and fall of ministers. Journalists were keen not to appear too close to politicians, which might compromise their reputations. In essence their relationship was one of 'antagonism and useful exchange', but with potentially damaging effects of 'conflict and mistrust' which led to news coverage which could be too compliant or too aggressive (Davis 2009, p.210). Professional hierarchies dominated their relationships in that back-benchers were often excluded, and the most favoured connections were with government ministers rather than Opposition shadow ministers. Consequently, Opposition shadow ministers focused more often on exploiting populist news stories to get attention.

A high degree of antagonism, conflict and mistrust between journalists and Labour MPs developed during Labour's last term in office. For example Labour MPs spoke of a decline in the ethics and quality of journalism and described the media as acting 'unashamedly as an opposition' (Davis 2009, p.210). Their views reflected those of Prime Minister Tony Blair (who stepped down during Labour's last term in office) who referred to the potential for the media to wield serious damage, commenting that the media is 'a feral beast tearing people and reputations to bits' (Blair 2007), suggesting that politicians were at the mercy of journalists.

The complex interdependence of politicians and journalists represented an intricate web of attitudes and relationships that defined the political arena itself. Journalists were not simply reporting on political positions or giving their interpretations, but they had become part of the interpretation itself in a process of 'intense reflexivity'. Journalists had become the tools of party politics or party conflict (Davis 2009).

In effect, journalists had become political key players but with their own agendas and resources. The 'whole way of life nature' of their shared culture and their thinking, behaviour and practices suggested a process of 'mediated power' (Davis 2007). As a result, Davis describes media/political relationships as the social and symbolic construction of the political arena, or a form of institutionalised and intense 'mediated reflexivity' (Davis 2009, p.205), in which 'journalists themselves have become political sources, intermediaries and political actors' (Davis 2009, p.215).

Mediated reflexivity describes a two-way relationship between the media and politics, in which, unlike the elite–media–mass paradigm, neither is cause nor effect, but each is both cause and effect. Both shape their own norms, beliefs and constructed narratives for their own means through this process of mediated reflexivity. Kuhn (2007) described how this power and control could shift swiftly between the politicians and journalists, with prime ministers and editors of tabloid newspapers each able to hold a precarious balance of power which, through processes of 'smear', 'flak' and 'spin', shifted in ways that could threaten democracy.

The media's role in holding power to account

Given these relationships, the degree to which the media can fulfil a role in holding politicians to account is questionable. Accountability legitimises power and authority and is the means by which the public can monitor power. Public bodies have processes of accountability through which their decisions and actions are open to scrutiny, ensuring that their powers are held within the democratic consent of the voting public (Bovens, Schillemans and Hart 2008). Justin Schlosberg (2013, p.195) argues that the media is, in effect, the last line of public interest defence: 'where formal mechanisms of accountability fail, journalists step into the front line of public defence'.

Schlosberg tested his assumption in relation to three high-profile stories taking place between 2006 and 2010 and therefore during a similar timeframe to the work of Davis (2009) above, and the death of Peter Connelly. The first was the long-running 'Al Yamamah' story, which focused on the alleged corruption in the British arms trade through British Aerospace Systems (BAE). The second concerned British scientist David Kelly who was found dead in July 2003 two days after it was revealed in the press that he had questioned the government's position that Iraq had weapons of 'mass destruction'. The third was the leak in November 2010 of US diplomatic communications by Wikileaks (an international online, journalistic organisation which publishes secret information, news leaks and classified media from anonymous sources).

In each of the high-profile stories a lack of critical attention from the media failed to fulfil its presumed role as the last line of public interest defence. As a result media attention declined in all three cases and ultimately ended giving the impression that justice had been done or that it was unnecessary, despite events and evidence that indicated otherwise. Schlosberg studied the reasons why the media had in effect failed to consider other explanations or 'frames' which resulted in its failure to fulfil its accountability role in these three cases (Schlosberg 2013).

First, there were four constraints: 'abstraction', which shifted stories into historical contexts and neglected important elements in the present; the limits of schedules for news broadcasts that forced the story into late-night programmes; the limited 'shelf life' of the story, which created a 'desperation for closure'; and the nature of relationships between journalists and politicians. The result was that key aspects of stories were unresolved (Schlosberg 2013, pp.197–201).

But these four constraints, Schlosberg argued, overlapped with four other reasons for failure. The first of these was a process of 'indexing', which is a theory of news content and media–state relations developed by Bennett (1990, 2011). Indexing predicts that how the media reports on public policy issues will generally support the political view when politicians are in agreement. In effect, where there is consensus, especially across political parties, the media will probe less, thereby neglecting to give critical attention to the issue, compared with events where there is political debate or dissent. Those who supported the media and the political view had an unopposed voice in the media, making indexing more likely to diminish the diversity of views and opinions thereby reducing the media's role in holding politicians, including government, to account (Bennett 2011).

A second reason for failure of media scrutiny concerned a degree of caution about possible libel action which had produced a more 'directed' and less 'risky' journalism. A third was the way in which journalists restricted themselves through an 'a priori filter' or 'cultural blind spots' of preconceived ideas about outcomes. And lastly, official sources used a range of strategies to withhold information which went unchallenged in the media (Schlosberg 2013, p.205).

Schlosberg considered whether the containment or account-ability failures he observed amounted to an ideological force or worldview. He rejected liberal pluralist accounts that suggested that market forces or organisational limitations were to blame for the constraints. Instead, Schlosberg took a nuanced position in observing a 'significant tendency towards ultimate containment in news controversies that threaten the discourses that legitimise state–corporate power'. The containment he observed was not entirely representative of how the media works in all cases, but it was not random, suggesting systematic characteristics. There are parallels in how cases of familial child abuse and homicide are reported.

For example, the media and politicians are themselves part of culturalisation processes in which people learn the requirements and expectations of their surrounding culture and acquire the values and behaviours congruent with that culture. Schlosberg suggests that these culturalisation processes need to be 'thought-out' if the ideological function of news is to be understood. The ideological function in the three cases, that is, the socio-political stance, had the effect of muting the public responses which could have challenged the stories. For example, greater public engagement may have enabled the media to achieve better levels of accountability and therefore greater pressure on policy-makers to pursue the detail of these three cases.

Engagement with the public

'Populism' in political ideology emphasises the importance of the views of 'ordinary people'. Populist leaders see themselves as 'the voice of the people' and they engage with popular opinions and grievances. 'Media populism' seeks to connect with populist views and sentiments often related to areas regarded as controversial, for example immigration. Given the close relationships between politicians and the media, 'mediated populism' or a kind of complicity between the news media and political populism can emerge (Mazzoleni 2008). Finally the media and/or politicians often engage in 'punitive populism', for example in 'turning a blind eye' to difficult or sensitive matters but allowing the public to raise the issues and demand solutions that politicians can deliver, a process discussed later in relation to the Portsmouth protesters (Evans 2003).

In relation to US foreign policy, following the terrorist attacks known as '9/11', Entman (2004) developed a 'cascade network activation' model which describes the interaction of politicians, media and the public. He focused on what was essentially the interaction of politicians with the American people (and arguably people worldwide) communicated via the media in the context of extreme shock, anger and distress at the huge loss of life in 9/11. For example, the words used by President Bush included figures of speech such as metaphors and metonymy, and performative utterances that conveyed 'a clear, concise emotionally compelling 'frame' of unity, of a struggle for 'good versus evil,' and 'a war on terror' which received overwhelming approval and evoked patriotic zeal well supported in the media' (Entman 2004, p.1).

Bush used words that aroused intense thoughts and feelings or 'schemas', such as clusters of ideas and feelings, that were both psychological and physiological, in the minds of a large section of the public (Entman 2004). These thoughts and feelings formed a 'network of knowledge' with emotional, visual and aural images; for example in relation to 9/11, images of people jumping from the World Trade Centre, the building tumbling to the ground, the horror for the relatives, the bravery of the fire department, or the face of Osama bin Laden. Once the 'network of knowledge' was established, further information was processed in relation to the powerful thoughts and feelings it contained. The 'network of knowledge' is an example of Ahmed's (2004) circulation of affect which attached fear and hate to the object of bin Laden.

The 'cascade activation model' conceptualises how the network of knowledge flows. Information moves downwards from the politicians to the media, who may frame it differently and communicate it to the public who in turn respond (Entman 2004, p.10). The response of the public is relayed back to politicians via the media. But the public responses that the media engage with might be selective or misrepresentative of public sentiment. As the information travels down the chain the more it becomes distorted from the 'real' situation that began at the top with the politicians and the 'reality' that is communicated to the public. Each actor adds to the mix of thoughts, ideas and feelings and the result is that what is communicated between the groups is 'packaged into selected framed communications' (Entman 2004, p.12).

The cascade network activation model acknowledges the power of hierarchy but not hegemony per se. A successful frame will need unity among politicians in the same political party and in some cases between political parties. But as with 'indexing' discussed above, the media is more likely to support the political framing if there is consensus within the party, and much more so if there is cross-party consensus. Where similar thoughts and impressions are expressed by politicians, other elites and news outlets, the more the words and visual images communicated to the public will reflect the same framing. It is the presence of dissidence among politicians that makes the framing factional and threatens the success of the frame in communicating the preferred narrative of the political elite.

'Cultural congruence' and 'cultural incongruence' may interact with the preferred frames and preferred narrative. Cultural congruence is concerned with the degree to which preferred frames are fully congruent with schemas habitually used by most members of society. Journalists repeatedly construct and reconstruct schemas that associate aspects of a story which concur with the public's thinking. For example, media frames that immediately followed the terrorist attacks of 9/11 needed no cognitive effort to connect with the frame offered by the politicians. The American people were united in intense anger against bin Laden as the perpetrator, with little attention directed at the security services whose 'intelligence' might have been expected to have anticipated such an attack.

Similarly, culturally incongruent interpretations create disso-nance with the dominant schemas and create psychic disturbance. For example, those portraying bin Laden as a 'freedom fighter' who was striking against 'decadent America' were simply rejected as part of the problem. The cascade network activation model suggests that when matters are unmistakeably culturally congruent or culturally incongruent, counter-claims are usually silenced and political control is at its highest. In relation to 9/11, the media was unable to raise dissent either upwards to officials or downwards to the public because of the public's reluctance to tolerate any opposition to the US role (Entman 2004). What might appear as hegemony is only in these clearly defined cases.

When the response to an event is ambiguous the media and politicians will contest the frame. If a president loses control of the frame or cannot find a compelling frame, political and other elite opponents, journalists and the public can together achieve as much influence as the president. But if the public supports the president then all opposition from politicians and from journalists dissipates. In contrast to a hegemonic or deferential stance, presidential power therefore can be limited by how much combined support there is from journalists and the public. Journalists become political players themselves, supporting some positions and solutions and demeaning others. They can shape frames to draw in public opinion and become powerful actors and 'presidents are well advised to stay on the good side of these schemas' (Entman 2004, p.157).

Two research studies

To conclude this chapter I look at two research studies concerned with responses to child abuse reported in the media. Both studies draw upon the interaction of the psyche and the social and have some insights that I apply to the case of Peter Connelly in Chapter 5.

In the first, Jessica Evans, with specific interests in the psychoanalytic aspects of the public sphere, reported on events in Portsmouth in south-west England in 2000 when a group of some 100 women attacked homes they perceived to be those of 'paedophiles' (Evans 2003). The attacks followed the murder of eight-year-old Sarah Payne by a 'paedophile' in 2000 and they were fuelled by information published in the *News of the World* about possible 'paedophiles' living on the women's estate. Evans found that many of the women were working class lone parents often accompanied by their children on the protest marches and many, including their leader, self-identified as victims of childhood sexual abuse. Some were also clients of child protection services because of concerns about their own children.

Evans drew on psychoanalytic concepts of unconscious projection, and on the work of Walker (1997) who found that women abused as children often introjected explanations which are made in the media. In particular, Walker found that the women had come to believe that the abuse was their own fault since they were positioned as having been able to stop it, but failed to do so. In the context of the Portsmouth protesters, Evans argued that the extreme degrees of hatred, aggression and moral condemnation that the women displayed externally may not have explained the meaning of their actions internally. She suggested that the women's defensive behaviour may have been an expression of their feelings about their own abuse; that it was their own fault. Consequently, on an unconscious level they identified with the 'paedophiles' or parts of the 'paedophile' they perceived to be part of their own psyche. The presence of the 'paedophile' may have evoked unconscious feelings of conflict and deeply held anxiety, including guilt. Attempting to drive the 'paedophiles' out was an act of defence against the unpalatable reality of their own abuse. It allowed them to 'split off' the pain and distress of past experiences and project the 'bad' into the 'Other', in this case the 'paedophile'. Incited by their leader to protest, the women not only had an unconscious identification with the 'paedophile' but they also projected it into their children, injecting them with knowledge of the sexual aggression of men; a pattern observed in abusive families. They were 'disowning the aggressive and destructive anxieties about their own incapacities and bad inner objects from their pasts by projecting them onto the figure of the paedophile' (Evans 2003, p.177).

At the same time the government failed to manage events in Portsmouth. The response of the women enabled a process of 'punitive populism', discussed earlier, in which the Labour government instead of intervening endorsed and encouraged the 'purging mentality of the newspaper' (Evans 2003, p.171). The effect was that the media and politicians had a role in determining consequences, including sentencing and penal policy. The Labour government responded to the 'demands of the public', and at the same time the women achieved a degree of perceived moral integrity by claiming to be acting in the 'moral good' by publicly attacking and rejecting paedophilia.

In the second study, Jenny Kitzinger explored the effects of media communications on women who had been sexually abused in childhood. She found that the media shaped public knowledge and opinion, defined the social reality of child sexual abuse and set the agenda (Kitzinger 2004). The media used iconic and evocative images, and created untrue associations with other high-profile cases that acted as 'landmarks' in the public perception influencing their understanding and interpretation of the current case.

Critically, the personal experiences of women who had been victims of childhood sexual abuse were influenced by the mass media. For example, some of the women dismissed their experiences of abuse as not really counting as abuse, and they became confused as to whether they had consented, making them feel blameworthy and inducing guilt, confirming Walker's (1997) findings. The women had introjected the media's projections and came to blame themselves for the abuse. In effect the dominant culture represented in the media encouraged the denial of child sexual abuse among the public, and distorted how those abused in childhood came to understand their own experiences. Kitzinger (2004, p.215) concluded that the interaction of the media with these women's experiences had an impact on identity, how we talk with each other, how we interpret other people's stories, how we come to understand the world around us and 'even the landscape inside our own heads'. Similarly, Evans (2003) demonstrated that how the protestors had processed their experiences was in part dependent upon how sex abuse was defined in the social world, mainly through the media. The denial of crimes of child sex abuse was reinforced by the interaction of the media and politicians. Echoing Evans's findings, Kitzinger concluded that denial is a powerful defence driving responses of the media and the public.

Conclusion

The discussion in this chapter has drawn out a number of concepts and constructs that will form the psychosocial approach. In particular, it will include the psychoanalytic concepts of projection, denial and Othering, and their manifestation 'outside the clinic' in the form of blaming and scapegoating. I am especially interested in how 'the circulation of affect' might form views, perceptions and opinions in relation to the death of Peter Connelly. To do so, analysing the use of figures of speech such as metaphor and metonymy, and the use of performativity, will be important.

The work of Davis, Schlosberg and Entman brings together three strands of media and political interactions which are relevant here. These strands are the 'mediated reflexivity' between the media and politicians, the failure of the media to hold politicians to account, and the process of creating frames for public consumption. Their analyses also include one significant element in common, that is in relation to the public. Davis (2003, p.673) claimed that the public are ill-informed spectators. Schlosberg (2004) found that the media failed to carry out its role as the last line of public interest defence, giving the impression that justice had been done; and Entman (2004) argued that rather than promoting accountability to 'reflective or rational citizens' the government's responsiveness to public opinion is to curtail the ability of the media to publicise more balanced views. The cascade activation model suggests a degree of dependence for political leaders not only on journalists but also on public opinion, and especially a combination of the two.

The subject of my book is very different from the news items discussed by Schlosberg (2013) which were arguably embedded in the intricacies of politics and media. As such they were at some distance from the everyday experience of large parts of the population (whether they should or shouldn't be is not important here) and therefore from any palpable response from the public. Entman's (2004) focus on US foreign policy was also, although the events of 9/11 were an exception. As acts of terrorism they produced a strong sense of 'cultural congruence'. Richards (2007, p.137) describes terrorism in the UK as producing an 'emotional public sphere' in which interactions between the public and the media take place in a 'multi-dimensional space full of complex patterns of structures of feelings'.

In common with terrorism, crimes against children produce 'cultural congruence' in the degree of shared repugnance and fear they provoke in the public. Both Evans (2003) and Kitzinger (2004) demonstrate the far-reaching effects of views and attitudes towards child abuse, including for those abused in blaming themselves. How such powerful responses function psychosocially, I argue, had implications for developing everyone's knowledge, awareness and understanding, which might help in tackling crimes against children.

In the next chapter, I take a close look at the socio-political and cultural context which shaped the responses to the familial homicide of Peter Connelly. Then in Chapter 5 I apply this psychosocial thinking to the narrative that developed in the first six days, that social workers were to blame for Peter's death.

Chapter 4

The Socio-Political and Cultural Context of the Death of Peter Connelly

Introduction

The Labour government served 13 years in three terms (1997–2001, 2001–2005 and 2005–2010) under Prime Minister Tony Blair, except for the last three years which were served under Gordon Brown. In taking up power from the Conservatives after 18 years Labour faced a sense of a need for moral renewal in the aftermath of the murder of James Bulger. For example, a moral discourse had taken hold that focused on single mothers who were increasingly cast as an economically dependent underclass associated with many social problems (Roseneil and Mann 1996). To counter this moral discourse, Labour swiftly developed policies and discourses aimed at investing in the child and the family.

Victoria Climbié was murdered in the context of this policy background of 'investment' in children and families in 2000 in Haringey. It was the last year of the first of Labour's three terms in office, and the Laming Inquiry into the death of Victoria Climbié reported in the middle of Labour's second term. Towards the end of the second term, Labour implemented the Children Act 2004 with its strategy Every Child Matters (ECM) (DfES 2004), in an apparent response to the Laming Report (2003) and its blaming of social workers and their managers. ECM represented a high-profile and far-reaching strategy of investment in children and young people. Three years later, in 2007, in the middle of Labour's third term in office and shortly after Gordon Brown became Prime Minister, Peter Connelly became a victim of familial child homicide in Haringey.

This chapter is concerned with the significance of the socio-political and cultural context in shaping responses to the death of Peter Connelly. I consider three interrelated aspects. First, I look at Labour policies on families and on children's social care, including the changes introduced by the Children Act 2004 and ECM. Second, I consider the impact of ECM on how the blaming of social workers was shaped by the 'science of child abuse', beliefs about 'prediction and prevention', Serious Case Reviews, and systems of governance, partnerships and 'public accountability'. Third, I discuss the significance of relationships between the Labour government, the Conservative Opposition, the media, in particular the News International Group (now known as News Corp UK & Ireland Limited), and London's Metropolitan Police Service (MPS) in autumn 2008 in shaping responses to the death of Peter Connelly.

The impact of Labour policies on families and children's social care
New Labour policies for children and families
Across a wide range of Labour policies concerned with the family, parental responsibility was emphasised and made explicit (Driver and Martell 2002; Giddens 1998, 2002; Lewis and Surender 2004; Lund 2002; Newman 2001; Powell 2002). 'New Labour' challenged both the 'economic individualism' of Thatcherism and the free market, which it claimed failed to support families, and the 'social individualism' of 'Old Labour' which it argued was destructive of family life because of its overly liberal views (Driver and Martell 2002). Old Labour

was regarded as having been much too tolerant and supportive of a wide range of social problems, where New Labour now planned to intervene. It was a case of Old Labour paying too much attention to 'rights', and not enough to 'responsibilities', which later gave rise to the New Labour mantra of 'rights and responsibilities'. The alternative to both 'economic individualism' and 'social individualism' was New Labour's distinctive centrepiece, the 'Third Way' (Giddens 1998).

At the core of the Third Way was the idea of 'communitarianism', which perceived the community, and especially the family, as key to achieving moral renewal through social inclusion and equal opportunity. In the 25 years before Labour came to power, government statistics show that marriage had declined by 36 per cent and the proportion of children born outside marriage had increased fourfold. Despite that, Labour promoted marriage as the best way to achieve stability for children, and to promote strong moral foundations for society (Blair 1996; Home Office 1999). Strong families and strong communities were seen as the infrastructure that could tackle a wide range of social problems such as drug addiction, alcohol and substance misuse, truancy, teenage pregnancy, youth crime and lone motherhood. The 'social investment state' came to describe this New Labour policy for children and families with its investment in their 'human capital', as opposed to the traditional welfare state provision of economic and social services that had gone before (Giddens 1998, p.117, italics in original).

The social investment state progressed under three main themes. First, it focused on paid work by promoting a new moral discourse that it was only through social and economic recognition that a family, especially the mother, and more specifically a lone mother, could find a route out of poverty for herself and her child to become 'worthy citizens'. Bridging the gap between financial deprivation and the ability to fulfil parenting requirements had a significant gender dimension as it most often targeted mothers (Featherstone 2006a). Recognising and countering women's poverty was critical to tackling children's poverty and to the general well-being of women themselves (Woman's Budget Group 2005). But women's work was often low paid, making women disadvantaged in the labour market, a factor that New Labour had not targeted in its welfare-to-work programme.

Second, the idea of the social investment state was future-oriented. It saw children as the workers of the future, not the children of today with needs in the present (Featherstone 2006a). Children were 'becomings' rather than 'beings' (Fawcett, Featherstone and Goddard 2004, p.17).

Third, the needs of certain groups were reframed in terms of personal responsibility rather than any structural economic, social or equality factors which might contribute to their circumstances (Lister 2006; Featherstone 2006a). The emphasis on paid work devalued full-time parenting and created conflict about what was regarded as 'good' for children and their families (Levitas 2005, first published 1998; Lister, 2006; Williams 2004). Full-time mothering, for example, 'is now only available to those who do not need state support' (Featherstone 2006a, p.305).

The moral renewal of the family was aligned with economic development as the route to social integration. But for many families, dependency on welfare services was enduring as they were unable to benefit from the economic developments, or take advantage of the 'opportunities' available. They were increasingly perceived as victims of their own misfortune, or worse, their own lack of effort. Poorer families dependent on benefits and welfare had increasingly become, in the years preceding the New Labour government, subjects of a 'moral underclass discourse' or 'MUD', which described an underclass of the poor regarded as having little responsibility or observance of moral values (Levitas 2005/1998). But poverty was defined as children living in households which have incomes less than 60 per cent of the median national income and it was difficult to separate out the relationship between 'dependency needs', material needs and the effects of poverty. Writing towards the beginning of Labour's time in office, Hoggett (2000, p.166) argued that many families had emotional dependency rather than material needs, and that the welfare state focused on the latter. He made the observation that 'the care and compassionate face of the welfare state seemed to have become lost to a harder edge of human worth'.

The impact of the 'market' ethos involved Labour in 'culture politics' which sent messages to society about who and what was considered 'good' or 'bad' and where boundaries were drawn (Webster 2001b). The demonisation of dependency on the state had the effect of forming a 'moral boundary' around the dependent 'underclass'. In doing so it functioned to create a symbolic order or divisions in society (Douglas 1984, first published 1966). The subsequent moral discourse (see page 83) was far-reaching in its capacity to construct 'particular sorts of preferred subjects in society and demonising others' (Driver and Martell 2002, p.51). The process is characteristic of the blaming and scapegoating discussed in the previous chapter. Such moral boundaries are 'pollution taboos' (see page 83) evident in social order in that 'polluting matter' is matter out of its proper place; it fails to belong (Douglas 1984/1966, p.124). The difference between those who could be socially integrated and 'what remained', that is, the moral underclass or 'polluting matter', did not belong in acceptable society.

The effects of these Labour policies had resonances with the views of Conservative Minister Sir Keith Joseph in the early 1970s and later during the Thatcher years, when Conservatives were influenced by the views of Murray and Hernstein (1994). In their infamous book, The Bell Curve, crime was blamed on factors within the (disadvantaged) person, that is, biological, psychological or intellectual deficiencies. Any link with the social and economic policies of governments was ignored, with 'lower classes' referred to as the 'new rabble'.

It is well established that 'poor' children, usually those deemed as the 'underclass', experience higher levels of mortality, illness, neglect and physical abuse, poor housing and homelessness, teenage pregnancy, suicide, mental illness, involvement in crime, and poor educational outcomes (HM Treasury 2008). They also often repeat childhood patterns in adulthood as parents themselves (Bynner 1999; HM Government 2011).

Further, strong relationships exist between poverty, low income and child maltreatment (Baldwin and Spencer 2004) and between low emotional well-being and child maltreatment (Radford *et al.* 2008). The clients of social workers are predominantly poorer children who are disproportionately represented in child protection caseloads, in part because access to 'middle class' families is subject to a complexity of (mis)perceptions of what constitutes child need. For example, it is not child poverty per se that influences decision-making about the need to protect specific children, but factors of poor housing, stress and violence in the home, mental health, child neglect and substance abuse by the parents (Stokes and Schmidt 2011). More middle class children are less affected by these economic issues and therefore less likely to come to the attention of social workers. This misperception that crimes against children only occurred in 'poor' families was at the core of responses to events in Cleveland which affected what appeared as 'ordinary families' and therefore fuelled the denial.

Disadvantaged or poorer people are more likely to vote Labour, the assumption being that poorer people perceive a Labour government to show greater concern about the less well-off. These poorer people are traditionally Labour's people (Johnston and Pattie 2011). Well into the twenty-first century and after three terms in office, New Labour failed to change the lives of its neediest citizens, maintaining a 'moral underclass' that had limited access to the economic renewal of the family. It was this 'moral underclass' that formed the clients of social workers and this 'moral underclass' that social workers were expected to keep from public view. Reactions to familial child abuse and homicide were not just about the denial of unpalatable knowledge of child suffering but also about the repugnance of a 'polluting matter', a moral underclass that was perceived to commit crimes against their children. Familial abuse and homicide placed such a moral underclass well outside all that was civilised.

In the previous chapter I argued that the criticism of social workers had become embedded as cultural responses to crimes against children. It was as if social workers, in working to support this moral underclass, had become outside all that was civilised themselves. They had become an underclass, a polluting matter that had failed to keep such repugnance from public view. A moral tension had developed between social workers and society. Social workers were gradually positioned outside of 'proper' professions, occupying the lowest position in the symbolic order of welfare professions, compared with doctors and nurses who possessed the skills to keep us healthy and the police who protect us.

Labour and social care policies in Every Child Matters (ECM)

In responding to the Laming Report (2003), the Labour government introduced new structures, systems and processes under the Children Act 2004 and its new strategy Every Child Matters (ECM 2004). ECM was constructed against this background of family policy, child poverty and blaming of social workers. ECM was a national framework for every child 'to fulfil his/her potential' through achievement in five outcome areas: 'Be Healthy', 'Stay Safe', Enjoy and Achieve', 'Make a Positive Contribution' and 'Achieve Economic Well-Being'. ECM reflected New Labour's focus on 'rights with responsibilities', but its scope in tackling broader issues such as health inequalities or child poverty was regarded as implicit. The ethos was one of high aspiration without too much attention given to the constraints.

The new structures had far-reaching effects. First, Children's Services were created by combining local authority education departments and children's social care departments previously part of Social Services departments. The 'thinktank' DEMOS described the new Children's Services, which focused on children and families, as the most significant change seen in the history of local government, making them the largest departments with the highest proportion of the local authority budget (Lownsborough and O'Leary 2005).

Second, Children's Trusts were established which provided joint governance for the new model of partnership working between the local authority social workers, health authorities and the police, collectively known as the child protection agencies. Third, Local Safeguarding Children Boards (LSCBs) were overseen by the

Children's Trust and had responsibility for coordinating the work of the child protection agencies in all matters related to safeguarding children. Fourth, Serious Case Reviews were carried out under the auspices of the LSCB (HM Government 2006, para. 8.2) when a child who was known to the child protection agencies died or was injured, and abuse or neglect was suspected. By April 2008 SCRs were applied to all deaths of children, for example those children who died of natural causes.

SCRs enabled each of the child protection agencies to open themselves up to self-scrutiny and the scrutiny of each other, in order to learn the lessons of the death or injury of a child known to them. Executive summaries of SCRs were published by LSCBs on local authority websites, but full reports remained confidential to both protect the children and their families, and encourage openness among agencies (HM Government 2006, para. 8.33). In 2008 the vast majority of LSCBs were chaired by the Director of Children's Services in line with government guidance (HM Government 2006, para. 3.49).

Lastly, the Children Act 2004 placed overall responsibility for the protection of children in a single Director of Children's Services (DCS), who had the overall professional lead, and in a single elected member designated the lead member (LM) for children and families, who had the political lead (DfES 2005).

The delivery of social care

The quality of delivery of social care to children was defined by the achievement of national and local targets known as the Personal Social Services Performance Assessment Framework (PSSPAF) (CSCI 2007). These PSSPAF indicators increased rapidly to well over 100 different elements, for example improving take-up of breast-feeding, reducing teenage pregnancy, increasing the rate of adoption, reducing the numbers of young people not in education, employment or training, or reducing the number of children deemed to be 'at risk' of harm.

The ethos was such that if a desired outcome, perceived to safeguard children in the broadest sense, could be evidenced, then it could be measured and targeted for improvement. Such a concept had its origins in a 'scientific model of knowledge' which relies upon factual evidence (Newman 2001). Single indicators and groups of indicators were systematically monitored and compared with the performance of 'statistical neighbours' by different government teams. Each team sought their own action plan from the local authority to deliver improvement, which in turn formed an indicator for their team outcomes and for their personal performance.

At Haringey Council, for example, following the death of Victoria Climbié, the number of children taken into care had risen significantly above its 'statistical neighbours'. This rate had to be reduced before Haringey Council could get a 'green light' on this indicator from government advisers. Performance in children's social care became reduced to monthly 'traffic light indicators' (red, amber and green) with convincing explanations needed for the appearance of a 'red' or the failure to remove a 'red', for example in failing to reduce teenage pregnancy. Little allowance was made for local factors; for example, in Haringey there were many young Turkish couples who married in their teens but their teenage pregnancies were included in the statistics that Haringey Council needed to reduce.

In practice, under the PSSPAF regime, managers and elected council members developed their knowledge of performance indicators and challenged services and employees in a new 'PAF' language of numbers and targets. The world of performance indicators extended to partners in health, although not to the same degree of stringency. For example, the police had performance indicators but without comparable levels of detail, government monitoring or ranking in public league tables. The tightest control was reserved for local government (Newman 2001).

The range of data used to monitor outcomes for children very quickly became vast, and by 2003 required sophisticated e-enabled systems to collect, report and analyse the data. The Integrated Children's System (ICS) was the e-enabled answer, produced to a national format, with standard procedures, workflows and rigid timescales. For example, it measured whether timescales in making assessments of risk had been reached (for example seven days in the case of initial assessment), and automatically produced performance data in real and historic time. Embedded in the automatic electronic collection of data and the real-time production of statistics of ICS was the transparency of each case. In a process reminiscent of Foucault's panopticon (Foucault 1995), each case showed the recording of when and by whom every piece of information and data was entered. Only trained and registered users could access ICS, and every occasion it was accessed was recorded. Crucially, ICS was tamper-proof.

Systems of governance, partnership and accountability

Delivering ECM was subject to Labour's strategy on governance and accountability. Janet Newman, Professor of Social Policy and Criminology argues that Labour sought to shift away from old forms of governance characterised by hierarchies (Newman 2001). But in many aspects Labour increased the 'top-down' approach, which conflicted with its aim to devolve responsibility (Newman 2001; Powell 2002; Powell, Bauld and Clarke 2005). Newman's work on social policy included four models of governance: the self-governance approach, the open systems approach, the rational goal approach and the hierarchical approach (Newman 2001). The vast majority of the changes brought about by ECM reflected Newman's 'hierarchical model of governance' with its formal patterns of accountability. The new Children's Services and the ECM initiative were established with little to no consultation, due in part I suggest to the perceived link between the Laming Inquiry and the emotional policy sphere it created. This 'top-down' approach is characteristic of control, surveillance and questioning of professional knowledge, which reveals a complex form of power and is at odds with devolved responsibility (Newman 2001).

A main characteristic of the new Children's Services was the interdependency of the partnership between three sovereign bodies: the local authority, the National Health Service and the police service. The promotion of partnerships, networks, and the all-important notion of 'joined-up government', to be achieved both centrally and locally, was to enable the partnership to intervene early to prevent problems developing. But partnership working brought together different management and governance models, professional expectations, public perceptions, budgets, priorities and power networks (Daly 2010; Ferguson 2004; Hills and Waldfogel 2004; Newman 2001; Parton 2006; Payne 2005; Powell 2000, 2002; Powell *et al.* 2005).

Each service had to rely on the other's performance and resources to deliver successful outcomes for children. This ECM model of 'matrix management' and partnership was in contrast to a hierarchical model. It was more characteristic of Newman's 'open-systems' model of governance in which accountability is seen to be 'low' (Newman 2001, p.42).

At the same time the local authority Children's Services existed as part of local government which was encouraged to develop towards Newman's 'self-governing' model. This meant decentralising services and delegating decision-making to communities and implementing models of accountability that depended upon community engagement with services. Newman (2001) argues that mixed models of governance and accountability led to clashes of power and logic. These mixed models of governance were all represented in the new Children's Services.

Inspection of Children's Services

The inspection of the performance of each local authority area Children's Services was conducted by the regulator Ofsted. Ofsted had inspected education services of local authorities, including schools, since 1992 and under the Children Act 2004 took over responsibility for the inspection of children's social care from the Commission for Social Care Inspection (CSCI). In doing so, the top-down model of Ofsted inspection brought an end to CSCI's advisory and development role. From April 2005 the new Ofsted inspection regime included Joint Area Reviews (JARs) and Annual Performance Assessments (APAs). The quality and effectiveness of the work of local authority social care and education services, health and police services were inspected via JARs. The work of the three agencies was reduced to a single grade of 1 to 4 representing 'outstanding', 'good', 'adequate' and 'inadequate', respectively.

Despite being a grade that reflected three sovereign bodies, the single grade was 'weighted' and 'added to' grades for other local authority services such as the quality of 'the environment' and a further single grade was produced for the whole council in its Comprehensive Performance Assessment (CPA) and published in a national league table. The grade had been distilled through so many layers that it was virtually meaningless. The CPA as a model for local authority evaluation was revised and replaced in 2009. Further, significantly, Laming in his second report (Laming 2009, para. 6.5) identified weaknesses, not in the system of measuring local authority effectiveness, but in the inspection processes due to a lack of expertise and limited experience in child protection, most notably in Ofsted.

From April 2007 Ofsted also took responsibility for the evaluation of SCRs. The evaluation focused on the quality of the SCR report rather than the work to safeguard children per se, and it failed to give enough focus on the SCR as a learning tool (Laming 2009). In its initial report into the quality of the first 50 SCRs, 40 per cent were found to be 'inadequate' (Ofsted 2008b), a pattern that persisted in 2009 with 34 per cent of 173 SCRs deemed inadequate (Ofsted 2009). Following criticisms in the Laming Report (2009) of the quality of Ofsted's evaluations of SCRs, from 2010 Ofsted ceased to undertake this task.

The impact of Labour's Every Child Matters (ECM) initiative

The science of child abuse and its effects

Child protection during Labour's time in office became a 'sophisticated' risk management process based on e-enabled systems of assessing and responding to the perceived risk of harm to children. In his treatise on the 'risk society', Ulrich Beck (1992) described a stage in late modernity which produced risk entirely as a result of human progress. Beck argued that risk is inherently unpredictable but the overwhelming desire of humankind to make progress creates a need to identify, predict and prevent risks. Systems of risk management followed in many aspects of the public and private sectors and were characteristic of a 'society increasingly preoccupied with the future (and also with safety)' (Giddens 1999, p.3).

In the context of social care the notion of risk was about preventing harm to children, and the focus was one of finding ways to reduce the potential for error in professional judgments rather than any attempt to look at social factors that may have reduced risk. More importantly, the use of ICS in children's social care exacerbated the notion that child abuse could be objectified, represented in an e-enabled system, and crucially could enable prediction and prevention. The belief in predicting and preventing had an enduring appeal since it was first put forward by the Beckford Inquiry (discussed in Chapter 2). It may be that the social work profession came to believe in 'a specialised professional expertise' that allowed them to predict abuse even though simultaneously they risked professional failure when children were harmed.

It followed in this ethos of managing risk that if the e-enabled system, with its enforced timescales and electronic workflows which prioritised completion of records in specific timescales, was properly implemented then risk of harm to children would be minimised. Managing the risk of harm to children thereby became a proxy science – a 'science of child abuse' – but it failed to secure reliable predictions of harm to children which might lead to prevention (Brandon *et al.* 2008; Brandon 2009a; Littlechild 2008; Fitzgibbon 2007).

Consequently, risk in the 'systems theory' which underpins ICS produced 'a self-referential logic or rationality' (Zinn 2008). That is, there was no 'objective' standpoint from which to identify risk as might be claimed by science. Nevertheless, the 'science of child abuse' focused on assumed knowledge of what constituted risk, and the ability thereby to reduce the potential for error in professional judgment (Littlechild 2008). ICS was embedded in the work of social workers, such that these risk assessment tools themselves developed agency, not only influencing the human agency of the social workers, but also in some cases becoming the dominant agency. Such a phenomenon is theorised by 'actor network theory' (Law 2009; Latour 2005) in which objects, in this case ICS, are treated as part of social networks on the same basis as human beings.

ICS became the cornerstone to reduce or remove risk of harm to children and thereby suggested a degree of perceived control over risk. The literature offers evidence to the contrary, summarised below in six examples.

First, the people, the events, the communications, and the multi-agency settings in which social workers work vary so much that rules and procedures in risk management systems such as ICS cannot always apply (Munro 2010). Second, 'child neglect', which is the most common reason that children are assessed as 'at risk', is more difficult to define and to quantify than the theory would suggest, and so outcomes in terms of harm are unpredictable (Macdonald and Macdonald 2010; Masson, Pearce and Bader 2008). Third, encouragement to place too much faith in results generated by 'scientific instruments' (such as ICS) erodes professional autonomy (Broadhurst et al. 2010a; Munro 2005) and devalues the use of intuition or 'gut feelings' (Gigerenzer 2007 cited by Munro 2011), or similarly 'the smell' of practice (Ferguson 2004). Fourth, social workers draw upon empathy, compassion, care and concern which are relational experiences that produce moral dilemmas, including a sense of moral responsibility, that are difficult to systematise (Broadhurst et al. 2010b; Cooper 2005; Horlick-Jones 2005; Ruch, Turney and Ward 2010). Fifth, informal levels of risk management that operated outside the formal e-enabled systems and included spontaneous, individualised, pragmatic and tailored responses to cases, social relations or team culture (Broadhurst et al. 2010b; Munro 2010) were found to be central to professional practice and were 'under-emphasised and under-theorised' (Broadhurst et al. 2010b, p.1052). Sixth, Rustin (2005) and Cooper (2005) described the unconscious emotions of social workers and others when faced with dreadful circumstances that they must face on behalf of society which mean they must 'think the unthinkable' (discussed in Chapters 2 and 3). In a report after Peter Connelly died, Lord Laming specifically criticised the government's reforms in relation to ICS:

> the direct engagement with children and their families which is at the core of social work is said to be at risk as the needs of a work management tool overtake those evidence-based assessments, sound analysis and professional judgment about risk of harm. *(Laming Report 2009, para. 3.17)*

Multi-agency working raised new problems and new risks. For example, social workers, doctors, heath visitors, police and courts in relation to their work with children have different histories, systems and cultures. They each believe in their own expertise, and manage cases through their different professional lenses, drawing upon different thresholds about child protection (Ferguson 2004, pp.114–118). Yet they must work together as a multi-disciplinary team to safeguard children in the context of public emotion which is potentially volatile and which each has already experienced. For example, doctors might treat presenting medical issues in a child but overlook or be reluctant to deal with the potential 'social' issues in making diagnoses of abuse, leaving those considerations to another profession. At the same time social workers become reluctant to act to remove a child without a medical diagnosis, and the police want clear evidence to bring charges. The 'fear of failure' I identified in the previous chapter leads to concerns about getting judgments about whether abuse has occurred, which encourages each agency to draw unhelpful professional boundaries. In effect, prediction and prevention, multi-agency working and notions of responsibility and accountability were key developments that both helped and hindered the work to protect children.

Risk management

The management of risk also functions in providing a 'framework for managing our fears' (Roth 2010, p.470). The desire to banish risk can become compelling, and a belief that risk can be controlled fortifies the human desire for certainty (Beck 1992; Douglas 1992; Giddens 1991). Certainty brings a sense of 'ontological security', meaning that a sense of certainty is essential to secure our very existence. Diligently following rules or systems reduces the discomfort of uncertainty and makes uncertainty seem less uncertain (Hunt 2011), as in the use of ICS. This notion of banishing, controlling or denying uncertainty convinces us that we can know something which is unknowable and that the achievement of certainty is possible (Beck 1992, p.21). Believing that risk can be controlled acts as a defence or denial of the realities of risk.

This ever-present search for security creates an overwhelming sense of 'needing to know' which is inescapable, uncontrollable and prone to unintended consequences (Beck 1992). Politicians, for example, are attracted by discourses (and practices) that appear to resolve uncertainty in the social world given its desire to deliver 'certainty' to its citizens and to maintain social order (Hollway and Jefferson 199?). This 'needing to know', 'believing we know' and 'banishing uncertainty' reflects Bauman's (1992) central thesis, that modernity's quest is to extinguish existential uncertainty, making the denial of ambivalence in itself a defence against uncertainty and disorder.

I argue that the positivist notion of 'predicting and preventing' harm to children came to function as a defence against uncertainty or as ontological security. MacDonald and MacDonald (2010) explore the difference between risk and uncertainty. Risk is about 'not knowing for certain that something will happen but knowing the odds' and uncertainty is about 'not even knowing the odds' (Knight 1921 cited by Macdonald and Macdonald 2010, p.1175). Uncertainty is critical in social work and gets lost in the discussion of risk in many child death inquiries. For example, neglect is the most frequent reason that children are referred to as 'at risk'. But neglect is difficult to define and to quantify and outcomes are uncertain (Macdonald and Macdonald 2010). For social workers several hundred children may be registered as 'at risk' with the majority registered as a result of neglect, but there is uncertainty about all of them as to whether any or all are at risk of serious injury or death and should be removed from their parents. Given that virtually all of the situations social workers deal with are uncertain – the people, the events, the accuracy of assessment, the communication of concerns – taking one action as opposed to another is inherently risky, especially in a multi-agency setting. Macdonald and Macdonald (2010, p.1179) argue that the difference between risk and uncertainty is important, especially given that little attention is given to the reality of uncertainty when issues of accountability and blame of organisations and of individuals dominate. When 'management of risk' fails, social workers themselves became a threat to ontological security (Warner 2013b).

Nevertheless, in Labour's time in office ICS became the tool, if properly used, that was to facilitate predicting and therefore it was a key element in preventing harm to children. How the 'belief' in the ability to 'predict and prevent' developed in the social work profession can be traced through Serious Case Reviews.

Serious Case Reviews (SCRs)

SCRs had been designed by government as processes through which child protection agencies could learn lessons from cases of familial abuse or homicide of children known to them. But judgments about whether deaths could have been predicted or prevented began to emerge in SCRs. This may have been an attempt to defend against actual or potential criticism in the media, but the judgment of whether a death could have been predicted and hence prevented was problematic. Brandon (2009b, p.1110) in a study of SCRs concluded that 'the worst outcomes were mostly too complex to be predictable or preventable.' But SCRs have continued to make this judgment and the media has continued to focus on it as evidence of the 'failure' of services.

In effect, SCRs have become distorted from their initial purpose into making judgments as to whether individuals were 'culpable' in their inability to predict and prevent harm to the child. In doing so,

SCRs became an example of Beck's (1992) 'organised irresponsibility', in which social care professionals, while preventing the risk of harm to most children, are unable to attribute 'errors', that is, abuse or homicide of children, to the system or risk framework that governs their work and which cannot guarantee the elimination of risk. For example, 'risk management by definition is a calculated attempt to reduce risk, but inherent [in such processes] is the acknowledgement that the ability to completely eliminate the possibility of things going wrong is impossible' (Giddens 1990, p.111). However, in the context of the death of a child it becomes difficult, or in effect entirely unacceptable, to articulate or defend the event in terms of a failure of risk.

I argue that the failure of risk in the context of child protection becomes a moral dilemma. As a consequence, when risk fails to be managed, the failure becomes not one of risk that could never have been fully controlled, but a failure on someone's behalf to manage the risk. A position of 'could not have known' is replaced with 'should have known' and in the context of individual responsibility becomes 'who is responsible' and 'who is to blame' and moves onward to expressions of 'what are the consequences'. Managing the risk of familial child abuse and homicide can reduce its incidence, but it is a chance event which is subjectified as something that can be controlled in all cases by human endeavour. Consequently, SCRs became a proxy for assigning blame to social workers. Borrowing Elliot's (2002, p.313) words, SCRs are a 'self-created dead-end'.

The impact of models of public accountability

Public accountability is an important part of the work of central and local government. It is the core of democracy and is concerned with the integrity of public governance and performance of public bodies. In short it seeks to achieve public confidence in government services (Bovens 2005).

Ofsted inspection was the cornerstone of the model of accountability for Children's Services. Ofsted's 'top-down' approach reduced the joint work of three large sovereign bodies (the local authority, health and police) to one of four grades as discussed earlier, which represented their degree of effectiveness. The grades enabled the production of national league tables which gave the media opportunities to 'name and shame', usually local authorities and their services, and not their partners in health and police. Hence the processes of accountability, and their potential to drive improvement, were compromised by struggles in both central and local government to avoid blame and potential reputation damage in the media if things went wrong.

The media's interest in negative stories – its 'negativity-bias' – made blame avoidance, rather than gaining credit, the prime motivator in public services in order to avoid the worst types of publicity (Hood 2002; Bovens 2005). The need to avoid blame becomes uppermost for the organisation and takes several forms: for example, delegating responsibility to individuals allowing the organisation to scapegoat an individual when things go wrong, but to claim the credit when things went well; or to use strategies of timing, stage-management or 'spin-doctoring' to deflect blame away from the organisation, a strategy characteristic of the Labour administration (Esser, Carsten and Fan 2000).

Risk in the form of blame avoidance can shape organisational culture (Hood 2002). The 'transparency' of systems and decision-making became an important watch-word in local government. For example, the e-enabled Integrated Children's System was characteristic of attempts to achieve transparency in the assessment of risks to children. At the same time, public managers learned to avoid risk by 'passing the buck', creating 'audit trails' and 'covering their backs' to shield themselves from potential criticism (Behn 2001, p.11). This discourse of blame avoidance became part of the lexicon of many public sector workers, especially in social work. Completed records in ICS, given its dominance in assessing risk, were perceived as insurance against blame and social workers invested in it. At the same time it set a context for the control, questioning and policing of professional judgment.

The Children Act (2004) and its guidance embedded accountability in the professional leadership of the Director of Children's Services (DCS) and the political leadership of the Lead Member (LM) as the individuals responsible. Such a model of public accountability is likely to have been influenced by the findings of the Laming Inquiry (Laming 2003) which stated: 'the single most important change in the future must be the drawing of a clear line of accountability, from top to bottom, without doubt or ambiguity about who is responsible at every level for the well-being of vulnerable children' (Laming 2003, para. 1.27).

However, what was less clear in the Laming Report was how these lines of accountability, embedded in the role of the DCS and LM, would work across the three major sovereign bodies, all answerable to the Children's Trust. The success of the new Children's Services was dependent upon the partnership between the three sovereign bodies. But the constitution and practices of each, and their different positions politically and consequently in the media, made their ability for 'joined-up working' at least challenging and often unachievable. The accountabilities of the DCS and the LM were contained in guidance related to the Children Act 2004, but gave DCSs and LMs responsibility without power. By 2008, Children's Trusts were reported to be 'confused and confusing' (Audit Commission 2008).

A year later, and after Peter Connelly died, Laming published his 'progress report'. He questioned his own model of 'linear or hierarchical accountability', when he stated:

> It is clear that within the existing landscape every organisation has only a partial view. There is none that has the breadth of vision across frontline agencies responsible for keeping children safe from harm, or the authority to achieve improvements across all the services with responsibility for safeguarding and promoting the welfare of children. *(Laming 2009, para. 73)*

The faulty reasoning about risk and its effects on social care renders the public accountabilities of the DCS and the LM a 'man-made hybrid' or a sophisticated process of blame avoidance by politicians.

Such blame avoidance is embedded in parliamentary inquiries, official investigations and public hearings. Such fora have the powers to pass judgment which creates public condemnation of a person or organisation. Coupled with the fluctuating nature of political agendas, blame may be attributed to some while avoided for others, in order to avoid negative publicity (Bovens 2005). Examples of 'lightning rods' who are individuals set up to 'take the heat' (Ellis 1994) have spanned governments of the left and right over many years. For example, the arms expert David Kelly who committed suicide two days after testifying to parliamentary committees about his press contacts regarding the (erroneous) claim of the Labour government that Iraq had weapons of mass destruction;[14] Derek Lewis, Chief Executive and Director General of the British Prison Service, sacked by Conservative Home Secretary Michael Howard following a politically sensitive prison escape in 1995;[15] Ken Boston, Chief Executive of the Qualifications and Curriculum Authority (QCA), forced to resign by Labour Secretary of State Ed Balls[16] following public concern about the reliability of the public examination system in 2009; Marietta Higgs, the paediatrician at the centre of the events in Cleveland in 1986 discussed earlier, who became the focus of severe criticism from politicians; and finally Wendy Savage, consultant obstetrician sacked from her job in 1985 for being a 'danger to her patients' but exonerated in a public inquiry.

In Chapter 3 I borrowed the notion of a 'twilight zone' (Seu 2013) to describe the reality of such a deeply held taboo as familial child homicide being split away from the anguish and horror it brings into some kind of 'acceptable' explanation through the use of blaming and scapegoating. The systems of governance, partnerships and accountability, developed in the context of eliminating risk, each function to provide a 'twilight zone', an 'acceptable' explanation when things go wrong. Public accountability in particular has become constructed as a process of defence, usually for politicians in establishing a route to blame and scapegoat others. As such, social workers are expected to tackle risk that cannot be defined or controlled, and in doing so, fear of failure becomes intrinsic to their day-to-day work and their profession, with far-reaching effects.

Whilst recognising the need for sanctions, the Centre for Public Scrutiny (2009) proposed building 'a culture of accountability' in the public sector with decision-makers using it as an opportunity for democratic debate and evidence-based policy-making. The report regards accountability as multi-faceted and complex, especially where there is partnership working across different services and concludes that 'individual accountability for individual organisations is no longer sustainable…[w]ork is going to have to be put into identifying and dealing with the governance implications' (p.17). Further, the report casts the media as 'well-placed to 'hold to account' decisions made by the powerful' but casts doubt on whether, given how it deals with emotive stories, it can 'move public discourse on'.

The political context preceding public knowledge of the familial homicide of Peter Connelly

At the time of Peter Connelly's death in August 2007, Gordon Brown had just become Prime Minister. By autumn 2008 when Peter Connelly's death became known publicly, the New Labour project was running into trouble. Brown had decided against risking electoral defeat in a general election in October 2007, and by May 2008 the Labour government had had its worst local government election results in 35 years.

Criticism came from within the Labour party and from the Conservative Opposition. Writing in the *New Statesman* in December 2007 under a heading of 'How Labour turned toxic', Labour MPs Jon Cruddas and Jon Trickett argued that the centralised or hierarchical model of politics of the Labour government had 'left the party floundering'. They pointed to the commercialisation of public services and in particular opined that the 'primacy of the economic over the social has created some winners, but many losers'. By April 2008, Roy Hattersley, previously a Labour cabinet minister, writing in the *Observer*, accused the government of not having a clear direction on social policy. Simultaneously, throughout 2008 the *Sun* and the

Conservatives developed a potent theme of 'broken Britain' which became a dominant part of their rhetoric.

Despite good economic growth, buoyant labour markets and targeted initiatives, Labour policies in three high-profile areas had run into difficulty, and I argue all had a bearing on the responses to the news of the death of Peter Connelly. The three areas of difficulty were: the lack of effectiveness of its social policies, problems in some NHS hospitals, and the early stages of the economic recession. A fourth area concerned relationships at the time between politicians and journalists, especially those in News International, and police officers not known until some years later.

In the first area of difficulty, Labour's social policies had failed to reach the most vulnerable families and their children. Hills, Sefton and Stewart (2009), in a major study of poverty and inequality, concluded that by 2008 success by Labour had been notable in reducing child poverty, albeit temporarily, in reducing the number of children living in workless households, and in improving educational achievement, particularly in poorer areas of London. But in the same study Hills and his colleagues found that, while Labour tried many things and many worked, there was a considerable loss of momentum in all policy areas after 2004 and up to 2007, and particularly up to the economic crisis of 2008. These findings are reflected in the figures on child poverty. In 1979 when the Conservatives took office, 1 in 10 children lived in poverty. By 1997 when Labour took office it had risen to 1 in 3 children (four million children). By 2008 there was only a marginal reduction. Of the four million children in poverty when Labour took office in 1997, the Daycare Trust reported that only 700,000 had been lifted out of poverty by 2005 and by 2008 the reduction reversed such that by the time Labour left office in 2010 it had reduced by only 500,000. By then, poverty was estimated to affect three and a half million children, 600,000 of whom lived in inner London (MacInnes, Parekh and Kenway 2010).

High rates of poverty impacted on social care, and specifically on children who had become looked after by local authorities. During Labour's 13 years in office overall there was a 24 per cent increase in the number of children who came into care (7500 additional children), but between 1997 and 2005 the number had substantially reduced by 18 per cent (5700 fewer children) reflecting the success in lifting increasing numbers of children out of poverty. But when the reduction in poverty stalled the numbers of children coming into care rose again. Between 2005 and 2008 government statistics show a 13 per cent rise. The increase in the number of children living in poverty and in the numbers of children in care suggests that the most vulnerable and dependent poor families, whom social workers work with, were not adequately reached by Labour policies. As a consequence, the children of poor families were increasingly taken from their families into the care of the local authority.

In the second area of difficulty for the Labour government, serious issues were emerging during 2007 and 2008 in some NHS hospitals, which were the subject of Labour's most high-profile flagship policy. The most serious issues concerned practices at the Mid-Staffordshire NHS Foundation Trust which led to a report that was so serious that it necessitated an apology on behalf of the government from the Secretary of State for Health, Alan Johnson, in March 2009:

> I apologise on behalf of the government and the NHS for the pain and anguish caused to so many patients and their families by the appalling standards of care at Stafford hospital, and for the failures highlighted in the report. *(Hansard 18/03/09, Column 909)*

A public inquiry took place which, given the change of government in 2010, was reported by the Conservative-led coalition's Secretary of State, Jeremy Hunt, in 2013. The Francis Report (Report of the Mid-Staffordshire NHS Foundation Trust Public Inquiry, Executive Summary) (2013) documented 'the appalling suffering of many patients...caused by a serious failure on the part of the provider Trust Board'.

Also in 2008 problems were emerging in Birmingham's Children's Hospital where senior doctors raised repeated concerns about the quality of care which they claimed were ignored by the management. The Chief Executive of Great Ormond Street Hospital, Jane Collins, was commissioned to investigate and write a report in 2008 at the same time as the SCR into Peter Connelly's death was underway. I argue that Opposition and media attention were later diverted from the role of Great Ormond Street Hospital in the case of Peter Connelly because of potential damage to the hospital's reputation, its work in supporting other hospitals, and Labour's record with the NHS.

The third area of difficulty was the economy. The economic crisis was becoming acute during the autumn of 2008 and by late October the British Chamber of Commerce Quarterly report showed that the economy had contracted for the first time in 16 years, indicating an impending recession. Gordon Brown intervened to secure several banks, followed by rescue packages designed to avoid their bankruptcy and restore confidence in the financial system.

Despite being under attack from the Conservatives for his economic credentials, the broadsheets reported that Brown fought back by demonstrating his ability to stabilise the banks. His profile internationally was growing and he became elevated to 'international statesman' for his handling of the financial crisis. Simultaneously, encouragement came from both the Populus Poll for *The Times* which showed that Labour had cut the Tory lead by nine points in a month and the Labour win in the Glenrothes by-election on 6 November 2008 which vindicated Brown's handling of the economic crisis (*Guardian* 08/11/08). Gordon Brown was preparing for the G20 summit of world leaders in Washington taking place a week later on 15 and 16 November 2008. Presumably he could build upon this growing positive profile by virtue of being on 'the world's stage'.

This potentially fragile political period is the context in which Jeanette Pugh, the DCSF Director of Safeguarding, exchanged some 40 emails with me in the 15 days before the verdicts in the Baby P case were announced on 11 November 2008.[17] Given this context the importance for Pugh in knowing the precise timing of the verdicts, and the content of what Haringey's child protection services planned to say to the press, now seems clear.

The fourth dimension of the context in autumn 2008 was revealed during the six years that followed through a combination of: the Leveson Inquiry (2012) into the culture, practice and ethics of the British media which concluded that the regulatory regime for the media had failed; the Parliamentary Select Committee in July 2009 which questioned the owners of News International; the trial of employees of News International known as the 'hacking trial' which concluded in July 2014; and finally an account of the trial and relationships between politicians, the police and the media (Davies 2014).

These four elements exposed, to different degrees, a complex set of relationships between politicians, the media and the police. In particular, relationships between: Gordon Brown (whilst he was Chancellor and later Prime Minister); David Cameron (whilst he was leader of the Opposition and later Prime Minister); the head of News International, Rupert Murdoch, and members of his family; his employee Rebekah Brooks, the editor of the *Sun*; his former employee Andy Coulson, formerly editor of the *News of the World* and, by 2007, head of communications for David Cameron; and finally members of London's Metropolitan Police. Following the 'hacking trial' Rebekah Brooks was acquitted and Andy Coulson received a custodial sentence. These relationships between the most senior politicians, the police and the world's second most powerful news corporation (Davies 2014) were revealed in the course of my research and became central to the responses to the familial homicide of Peter Connelly which I return to in subsequent chapters.

On Tuesday 11 November 2008 Prime Minister Gordon Brown was buoyant. Media coverage of his speech to the Lord Mayor's banquet the night before on his international economic role, for example in the *Guardian* (11/11/08), was supportive. That morning Brown and Cameron each gave press briefings an hour apart. Brown discussed his ambitions to tackle the global economy which he hoped to advance at the G20 summit of world leaders being held in Washington the following weekend. In the same press conference he was critical of Conservative proposals to offer national insurance breaks to private sector companies which David Cameron had launched an hour earlier. In public on this day the broadsheets show that Brown and Cameron were locked in high-profile conflict over tax policies.

At 11.30am the same day, 11 November 2008, the verdicts in the case of Peter Connelly were announced. It was in this political context, of which I was entirely unaware, that at 2 o'clock that afternoon I spoke to the press about the familial homicide in Haringey of Baby P.

Conclusion

Labour reforms for children and families maintained a 'moral underclass' whose children were predominately the clients of social workers. Governments on the right and left had positioned disadvantage 'within' clients, rather than in the effects of social and economic policy. Social workers, given their proximity to the 'moral underclass', occupied the lowest position in the symbolic order of welfare professions compared with doctors and police.

Every Child Matters established the 'science of child abuse' as a risk management process which built upon notions of prediction and prevention. The fundamental fault line was that not all risk could ever be eliminated, but that a failure to predict and prevent harm to children is a failure on behalf of the social worker and not of the risk management framework that governs her work. Given this background, Serious Case Reviews that explore the circumstances of harm to children in seeking to judge whether a death was predictable or preventable function as a proxy for blame.

Against this background, children's social care developed an authoritarian and disciplinary ethos with strict lines of accountability through Ofsted inspection and through the roles and responsibilities of DCSs and LMs for children's services. Efforts to establish multi-agency partnerships from three sovereign bodies created a pattern of accountability for DCSs and LMs of responsibility without power.

The complex interaction of social, cultural, historical and political dimensions discussed in this chapter has denied harm to children by known adults, and instead blamed social workers for failing to predict and prevent. In its 'suture' between the psyche and the social it is a psychosocial process of blaming social workers for harm to children. By autumn 2008, when the public learned about the familial homicide of Peter Connelly, this psychosocial process was well-established.

Peter Connelly had died in Labour-led Haringey Council, the same borough where Victoria Climbié died, and Labour's reforms were ostensibly based on the outcomes of the inquiry into her death. Peter's death had the potential to be interpreted as a symbol of the Labour government's lack of progress and lack of impact of all the expenditure and all the rhetoric of a decade in power. Haringey Council was already 'sticky' and alongside its social workers, and the Labour government, they were all vulnerable.

In the next chapter I examine how these fragilities and vulnerabilities became manifest in the immediate narrative of what happened to Baby P.

Chapter 5

The Narrative about Baby P Emerges

Introduction

In the six days that followed the convictions of those responsible for Peter Connelly's death, 11–16 November 2008, complex and dynamic interactions took place incrementally between many actors. These included the Prime Minister Gordon Brown; his Secretary of State for Children, Schools and Families Ed Balls; the leader of the Opposition David Cameron; Liberal Democrat MP Lynne Featherstone; the print and broadcast media; social and health care professionals; police officers; employees and elected councillors of Haringey Council; and members of the public who signed petitions, posted on social networking sites, wrote letters to newspapers and demonstrated on the streets.

Those interactions produced a dominant narrative that blamed social workers and me for the death of Baby P. To understand how the narrative emerged I have taken a psychosocial approach working with, and building upon, a number of concepts discussed, and arguments presented, in previous chapters. For example: the interaction of the denial or disavowal of harm to children especially by the mother; the range of social, cultural, historical and political influences; the dynamics of the interdependence of the media and party politics and the symbiotic influence on the public; the power of figures of speech; and the use of performativity in speech and in images. Since the temporal nature of the interactions is important to the analysis, the chapter is presented as a chronology of interactions over six days.

Tuesday 11 November 2008

The trial of those responsible for the death of 'Baby P' concluded on 11 November 2008 with the convictions of Peter's mother Tracey Connelly, her boyfriend Steven Barker, and his brother Jason Owen. The fear of blame, I argue, was already established among social workers and in particular among Haringey's child protection agencies (Great Ormond Street Hospital services [GOSH], the Metropolitan Police Service [MPS] and Haringey Council's social workers). The fear of blame was producing different responses well before the case of Peter Connelly came to public attention. All three child protection agencies had concerns about how the death of Peter Connelly would be treated by the media.

Increasingly, Local Safeguarding Children Boards (LSCBs) provided briefings for the media when a child known to their services was a subject of familial child homicide. But the Haringey LSCB was a partnership of members of unequal status and power, especially given the different perceptions of each partner. GOSH, according to its website, was a 'global centre of excellence in child healthcare' and was well-established in the sentiment of the nation, characterised by its work with very sick children and its ability to raise many millions in charitable donations annually. London's MPS with over fifty thousand employees was a powerful organisation with interdependent links with both the politicians and the media. Haringey Council with its 'stickiness', discussed in Chapter 1, and its social workers, by virtue of their perceived lower professional status, was much more vulnerable.

The plan of Haringey's LSCB to brief the media was, in effect, its engagement with the embedded culture of blaming social workers, albeit from different vantage points for each member. To give a press briefing was, with hindsight, paradoxical given that convictions had just been made in the court for those responsible for Peter's death. Those convictions and the publication of the SCR summary on the same day could have sufficed.

In effect the press briefing was the opportunity to tell the press that the child protection agencies were *not* responsible for Peter's death. It was an act of defence against our own anxiety and fears about blame in the media. But it is unlikely that GOSH, given its position, needed any form of defence. Perhaps its presence at the press briefing even functioned to deflect attention away from its wrongdoing onto social workers. The MPS's Child Abuse Investigation Team (CAIT) took no part in any defence. On the day the jury retired to consider its verdict (5 November 2008), it was clear that there was unlikely to be a murder conviction and police officers briefed the media separately. In that briefing, according to a journalist interviewed for the BBC documentary *The Untold Story of Baby P*, the police were critical of social workers.[18]

Jane Collins, Chief Executive of GOSH, and I briefed approximately 40 journalists, mainly men, mostly crime correspondents, the majority of whom had attended parts of the trial and the negative police briefing. We told the press how well our services knew Peter Connelly, by then known as 'Baby P', together visiting him sixty times, but presenting ourselves as a partnership we declined to give the breakdown of 38 visits from health, 17 from social workers and five from police. Collins informed the press that the GOSH paediatrician who had examined Peter two days before he died had been referred to the General Medical Council (GMC). I referred to the disciplinary proceedings taken against the social workers and informed them that there was no evidence of gross misconduct in terms of wilful neglect or intent that meant they should lose their jobs. This position was later upheld by the General Social Care Council which at the time scrutinised the conduct of social workers. 'Sticky Haringey' was immediately in evidence with hostile attitudes towards me as the Haringey Council representative and Director of Children's Services (DCS). Several journalists demanded sackings and named a social worker whom they wanted me to agree to sack. None of this behaviour was used towards Jane Collins (or the police).

My defence of the social workers was equated with complacency and I came under personal attack. If I would not sack the social workers then I was invited to 'throw myself on my sword' there and then and to say that my department was failing. Ofsted had told me consistently in six inspections that my department was 'good' and so I defended this record when journalists invited me to blame Peter's death on my 'poor department' and 'incompetent social workers'. Crucially it was not these questions but a question that came later in a BBC *Radio Five Live* interview on the same day which wanted me to attribute responsibility for the death to social workers and asked me to guarantee that no more children would die. I could give no such guarantee. My response was:

> The issue you raise is the hardest one of all and that is that no agency, no director of Children's Services, no paediatrician across the country can say that we can stop people who are intent on harming children and that's the saddest fact of all. No-one can give you that guarantee and I think that's something we must be honest about.[19]

These words conveyed a message that was 'unacceptable' in the media and was presented as such to the public. The question and the media's response exposed a combination of a lack of knowledge of the existence and rate of familial child homicide, a need for certainty, and an underlying denial of familial child homicide. In particular it drew upon the moral imperative that social workers should 'save' all children, as discussed in previous chapters. Alternatively, this may have been an opportunity for some elements of the media to exploit a human interest story and sell more newspapers. In either case the public was misinformed and misled from the outset.

Next day my words were extensively criticised and throughout the week used to label me as complacent and worse: 'callously disdainful as well as absurd' (*Sun* 17/11/08, p.8). Others were more ambivalent, describing my words as 'tactlessly accurate' (*Sunday Times* 16/11/08, p.18) and 'she may have made this claim in an effort to exonerate herself and her employees but her statement is true, nonetheless' (*Independent* 15/11/08, p.19). These criticisms underline the denial of the existence of harm to children but also acknowledged tangentially that social workers could not be responsible for familial child homicide. But the newspapers simultaneously avoided expressing any view that social workers were *not* to blame. This denial of the existence of harm to children was turned against me and at the same time the reality of familial child homicide formed a 'submerged narrative' which failed to come fully to the surface. Instead the dominant narrative in the media was in line with previous cases of child abuse and homicide: that social workers had failed to save Peter. Blaming social workers might have been a more palatable explanation than the unbearable emotion inherent in the killing of an infant, especially where it involved the mother.

Gender became another submerged aspect of the narrative. At the press briefing Collins and I presented ourselves as strong, decisive and resilient women. We each expressed sadness and regret at Peter's death but we did not make any form of apology that may have given the sense of accepting responsibility for his death. Perhaps our 'professional' attributes did not convey enough feminine or motherly concern for these (predominately male) journalists and I was cast as a 'cold bureaucrat' in ways that may not have occurred had I been male. Several months later a journalist from the *Guardian* suggested that if I had cried things may have turned out differently. But such emotion, as Ahmed (2004) suggests, could have had conflicting meaning, for example as 'a woman who can't cope', or 'a sign of culpability'. I return to matters of gender at different stages in the story.

At this early stage other professionals perceived the news differently. For instance, Stuart Young, Assistant Chief Executive, Haringey Council, who was known to me, conveyed the message, '[h]ope all is OK…think you did very well on the news tonight', and Sir Paul Ennals, Chief Executive of the National Children's Bureau

(NCB), who was not known to me, '[w]ell done, Sharon, on how you have been handling the media attention over this case. Seriously tricky stuff, but you have been getting the tone just right.'[20]

But media reports that evening were challenging. London's *Evening Standard* reported, '[t]hey left the boy to die like Climbié' (11/11/08, p.1), '[w]ritten warnings but no sackings' (11/11/08, p.6), 'social workers saw [Baby P] 60 times' (11/11/08, p.1). The sixty visits remained attributed to social workers and dominated the immediate narrative reproduced in most publications and persisted for many years. Other comments implied criticism of government policy, for example 'Climbié reforms fail to stop new tragedy' (11/11/08, p.5), but these issues were secondary to the dominant narrative about social workers being to blame. Evoking the death of Victoria Climbié was an example of 'abstraction' (Schlosberg 2013), which shifted the story to an historical context and gave the public 'the landmark' (Kitzinger 2004) which influenced their interpretation of the current event.

Within hours of the press briefing, the death of Baby P was communicated to the public through existing schemas about Haringey Council especially related to negative connotations about Victoria Climbié's death. This 'stickiness' of Haringey and the 'circulation of affect' by the media created Haringey Council and its social workers as objects of emotions of anger and hostility. They were portrayed as having failed to act or, worse, ignoring the 'torture' of Baby P. The GOSH paediatrician was singled out for criticism but the very first reports in London's *Evening Standard*, for example in its editorial with the title 'Unforgiveable', suggested, 'the spotlight will also [as well as those convicted] fall on the social workers in Haringey who ignored or missed signs of abuse and neglect...[d]octors who saw the child behaved correctly' (11/11/08, p.12, my emphasis).

These words reflected the positioning of the different professions, with social workers, given their role with the 'moral underclass', being culpable compared with doctors and nurses who performed life-saving tasks and police who protect us from crime, and are not even included by the media. With their greater power and influence, both GOSH and the MPS were each able to succeed in keeping attention away from their conduct in the case. No comment or criticism was made of the MPS or of GOSH as organisations.

The 'slide of metonymy' (see page 87) (Ahmed 2004) was in evidence, which began to strengthen the case against social workers. In the example above, social workers 'ignored', 'missed', neglected', but doctors 'behaved correctly'. The responses of the public were being shaped by misinformation and performative modes of communication which created new realities, in particular that social workers denied the help Peter needed. The responses of the public were in turn responded to by the media and politicians who had created them in the first place, characteristic of Entman's (2004) 'network of knowledge' or 'cascade activation'.

Party political opportunism interacting with the media stance, which was characteristic of previous high-profile cases discussed in Chapter 2, was immediate. Liberal Democrat MP Lynne Featherstone had been a Liberal Democrat Councillor in Haringey during the period in which Victoria Climbié died and she was active locally in challenging Labour-led Haringey Council, especially its leader. Without any detailed knowledge of the case, she 'seized the moment' and suggested on Sky News (11/11/08) that she would 'refuse to stand by and watch [Haringey Council] squirm out of responsibility again', and that Peter had fallen through 'safety net after safety net.' Featherstone had been informed of serious concerns about GOSH medical provision in Haringey before this case came to public attention. Despite that, her comments reinforced connections between Peter's death and that of Victoria Climbié and focused blame on Haringey Council, especially the Labour leader and myself as DCS.

In contrast, the Secretary of State Ed Balls's department, the Department for Children, Schools and Families (DCSF), published a press statement on 12 November 2008. It referred to the 'tragic case that will have shocked and appalled the country. It makes us all question how someone could do such a terrible thing to a child and set out to deceive the very people trying to help' (Hansard 12 November 2008, Column WS 49).

The press statement was relatively neutral, suggesting that those who perpetrated the crime were responsible. Social workers were not held responsible since they were deceived. But this apparent neutrality risked being incongruent with the media's blaming of the social workers. Permanent Secretary David Bell, and Director of Safeguarding Jeanette Pugh, both in Ed Balls's department, the DCSF, in a late-night email exchange on Tuesday 11 November 2008, appeared to reveal the government's 'comfort' with the media position. Their communication indicated a tolerance of attacks on social workers. Pugh informed Bell that:

> so far I think we've handled this as well as we could and Government is reasonably well positioned. ...SoS [Secretary of State Ed Balls] reported to be pleased. Haringey coming under heavy fire. GOSH less so thus far. The police seem to be briefing behind the scenes though publicly come across as measured and reflective.

The email went on to refer to 'the progress report' that Ed Balls had commissioned from Lord Laming which Balls was keen should not be seen as 'an inquiry or review', and Bell and Pugh exchanged concerns about potential criticism of government policy from prominent social work academic Professor Eileen Munro and the usual ranty stuff from the likes of the British Association of Social 'Workers...' Finally Pugh anticipated possible issues resulting from the *Panorama* programme scheduled for 17 November 2008 and a 'news spike' when sentencing of those convicted took place on 15 December 2008. The exchange suggested that an escalation of the story was not anticipated. This was reinforced by a phone call to me from Jeanette Pugh the next day suggesting that we meet the following week when media attention had calmed. The government in effect saw itself as potentially vulnerable to criticism in the press but 'well-positioned' to respond.

The case of the police is notable throughout, and I return to it at different stages. At this early stage Pugh's comment about the police 'briefing behind the scenes' seems to signify an acknowledgement and tolerance of the police conduct in three respects. First, Pugh was aware of the police shortcomings in the case, having received successive drafts of the SCR.[21] Second, she was aware that the forthcoming *Panorama* programme was likely to include accusations given that she had read Haringey Council's 'right of reply' to the BBC in which Haringey Council rebuffed allegations made by the police. Lastly, Pugh had briefed ministers about the findings of the SCR shortly after the convictions of those responsible and made no mention of the shortcomings in the police case reflected in the recommendations for the police in the Serious Case Review. The emphasis was on the recommendations for social care and health.[22]

In less than 24 hours the story had been shaped. Haringey social workers were positioned as responsible for the death of Baby P. Haringey Council's 'stickiness' may well have functioned as 'a priori filters' or 'cultural blind spots' (Schlosberg 2013, p.205). But the blaming of social workers was characteristic of the customary response, or the cultural response. It was the established way in which such events were communicated. The use of metonymy and performativity gave patterns of understanding, meaning and feeling to the event and began a process of shaping social workers as objects of hate and resentment.

Wednesday 12 November 2008

On Wednesday the 'circulation of affect' developed dramatically. Emotions were shaped by the interdependence of party politics with some sections of the media, especially the *Sun*. Reporting restrictions about the identity of Baby P, his mother and her boyfriend which had been established by the court to protect Peter's family meant that the only images available were those of Jason Owen, who was one of the three convicted, the social workers, the paediatrician and myself. From Wednesday 12 November these images filled the front pages of many newspapers. The power of visual images in the media became central to how the narratives in relation to Peter's death were constructed, represented and communicated to the public, usually with hidden codes of meaning (Lippmann 1992; Sturken and Cartwright 2001). In the print media, for instance the *Independent*

(13/11/08, p.13), and broadcast media, the image of me was with eyes half-closed looking like a very stern, unfeeling and uncaring bureaucrat. These images of me and the others added to the 'network of knowledge' and positioned us as 'the people responsible', 'those to blame', 'those who failed to prevent such a brutal death'.

Of particular note in the media were briefings from police which were both defensive of themselves and accusatory of social workers, which escalated the blaming of social workers. For example, reports in London's *Evening Standard* (11/11/08, p.1) were explicit: 'the police had suggested three times that the baby should be taken into care, and sought legal advice, but social workers sent him back to his mother', also repeated in *The Times* (12/11/08, p.7). In the *Daily Telegraph* (12/11/08, p.21) a police officer was quoted as saying that the death of Baby P was 'a tragedy that could have been avoided', implying that someone was to blame. At the same time computer-generated images of the body of a baby and a 'close-up' of a baby's head which purported to represent Baby P's injuries as they had been recorded at his post-mortem, plus images of his blood-stained clothes, appeared in the majority of UK newspapers and on their websites (*Guardian* 12/11/08, p.10; *London Lite* 13/11/08, p.1; *The Times* 12/11/08, p.7; *Daily Mail* 12/11/08, p.4). These images were provided by the police. Some weeks earlier the police had informed me that they would not use actual video material of Peter at nursery as these were too emotional for the public; instead they would use computer images. I had no sense of how these would look or how they would be used in the media. In effect these images were powerful signifiers not only of the injuries but suggested suffering, neglect and torture. It is questionable whether the police would issue or have ever issued such images of a child or an adult who was the subject of a road traffic incident, for example, or murdered by an unknown adult. Why release such images of a victim of familial child homicide and blood-stained infant clothing given that they were guaranteed to provoke shock and revulsion?

Most of the newspapers built upon the dominant narrative. For example: '[a]s in Climbié case, no senior staff likely to lose job'

(*The Times* 12/11/08, p.7); 'borough will always be linked to deaths' (*Daily Telegraph* 12/11/08, p.9). Social workers were to blame: '[they] saw *tortured* boy 60 times' (*Daily Express* 12/11/08, p.7, my italics); and, in relation to Haringey Council's image of some 25 years before, 'loony council that has endless smug initiatives' (*Daily Mail* 12/11/08, p.13). Other articles focused on the harm done to Peter expressed in gross terms, for example: '[t]reated like a dog, used as a punchbag' (*Daily Mail* 12/11/08, p.4).

But an article in the *Sun* with the headline 'BLOOD ON THEIR HANDS' (12/11/08, p.1, capitals in original), was exceptional in its direct accusation. The article included profiles of those convicted and images of the paediatrician, the social workers and me, which resembled police 'mugshots' making a connotative suggestion of criminality which added to the public anger. In the article, the *Sun* focused its attacks on me: 'she refused to resign as it emerged that she led the 'independent' review of the case;' 'Sharon Shoesmith concluded that NONE of her social workers should be sacked.' These headlines provoked anger against me personally given the new suggestion of an 'abuse of power' on my part in leading an SCR and making a decision not to sack social workers. In its editorial the *Sun* (12/11/08, p.8) drew upon the 'stickiness' of Haringey. It suggested that Laming's nationwide review 'should start by dissolving Haringey Council, sacking its useless welfare squad – barring the lot from ever holding public office again'.

The exchange at Prime Minister's Question Time

An exchange between Prime Minister Gordon Brown and the leader of the Opposition David Cameron at PMQs (Hansard 12 November 2008), combined with the images released by the police and the headline in the *Sun*, reinforced 'the direction of travel' of the story dramatically. Just when the Prime Minister had much to sound confident about in his handling of the economic crisis (see Chapter 4), Cameron deflected attention away from his achievements and into a far-reaching party political clash about Baby P.

Brown appeared unprepared for this attack, which further reinforces the view that senior civil servants did not anticipate such party politics. Cameron's utterances at PMQs, especially viewed visually on the BBC website,[24] were dynamically performative in that they were spoken with authority from the seat of government, the House of Commons, and were not just descriptive but in this context changed the 'reality' of what had occurred. From the House of Commons Cameron reinforced and built upon the developing narrative: 'this is the same children's services department as Victoria Climbié' and 'nobody [is] taking responsibility and nobody has resigned'. Referring to the SCR he suggested that 'Haringey's inquiry is completely unacceptable, being led by Mrs Shoesmith who is the council's own director', 'she cannot possibly investigate the failure of her own department'. In his response Gordon Brown added to the complexity with what appeared as a party politically driven response. He defended his Secretary of State Ed Balls, who he claimed had only just received the SCR. The reality was that Balls's department had seen several drafts of the SCR over a five-month period and the final draft some weeks earlier and raised no issues.[25] In the event Brown avoided Cameron's charge that the process of SCRs was flawed, which would have been a criticism of his own government policy, but claimed that the Haringey SCR showed 'failings and weaknesses in the system': which 'system' was unclear, but the statement had the effect of connecting any problems to Haringey Council.

Both Cameron's and Brown's comments were made under 'parliamentary privilege' which provides immunity from any legal challenge. Cameron had thrown down the gauntlet for Brown to act and he had deflected attention away from positive comments about the economy and Labour's recent achievement in the polls (see Chapter 4). Despite the many factual errors Cameron made in what he had to say, for example about the age of Peter Connelly's mother, the budget of my department, the performance of Haringey Council's schools and my role in managing the SCR which was well within government procedures, he had built dramatically upon the dominant narrative which was taking hold in the media. The performativity of the notion of a 'failed department' and the suggestion by Cameron of my alleged impropriety and dishonesty in how he questioned the 'independence' of the SCR positioned both as 'true'. As a result these two new and important strands in the narrative were established. It linked the story to both the government in terms of its social policies, its inspection regimes and processes for SCRs, and to the regulator Ofsted casting doubt on its many evaluations of Haringey Council's Children's Services as 'good'. Implicit in the attack was 'the slide of metonymy' in the false assumption that if a child dies in a particular local authority then their children's services must be failing.

Much of what David Cameron said could have been challenged, but it was as if the horror of familial child homicide and the shocking realities of what happened to Peter, represented by the images of his injuries and his blood-stained clothes, were too much to comprehend. The power of the performativity of the statements by David Cameron, and these images, suggested that social workers had been witness to the 'torture' of Peter and had failed to intervene. The denial of the risk of familial child homicide and the shock and disbelief of Peter's life and death was the basis of the blaming of those who 'failed to save him'. It seems that there was no other schema and no other discourse to defend any other position.

Ed Balls reacted

Events at PMQs had put Brown and Balls in a weak position politically and in the media. According to Aaron Davis (2009) there was much antagonism and mistrust between Opposition politicians and the Labour politicians during this period. I suggest that such turbulence may have contributed to the perceived need for the Labour government's 'robust' response to defend its position. My suspension was immediately sought by government officials, but refused by Haringey Council.[26] Consequently Balls took two actions which were both announced in the press. First, John Coughlan, Director of Children's Services in Hampshire, was sent to Haringey

Council to 'help ensure that proper procedures for safeguarding children were in place and are being properly applied' (High Court Judgment 23/04/10, para. 142) despite Peter Connelly having been dead for 15 months, during which time no issue had been raised about the safety of Haringey Council's children or the adequacy of the Serious Case Review. Second, an emergency Ofsted Joint Area Review (JAR) inspection of child protection services provided by Haringey Council, Great Ormond Street Hospital and other health services, and the Metropolitan Police Service was ordered to begin immediately together with a simultaneous Ofsted evaluation of the SCR into Peter's death. These developments were in stark contrast to the Labour government's press statement less than 24 hours earlier (see page 136).

For Ed Balls and the Labour government the politics of this case of familial child homicide were complex. First, a challenge to Haringey by the Conservatives was a challenge to Labour's own social policies and more especially Ed Balls's flagship policy *Every Child Matters* (DfES 2004), which had been presented as a response to Victoria Climbié's death. Second, Haringey's 'troublesome' past had impacted negatively on Labour politics before (see Chapter 1). This time, I suggest, the Labour government had to bring Haringey 'on-side'. Third, during Labour's time in government Haringey had changed. The leadership of the council had supported and endorsed Labour policies and had embraced many Labour initiatives with some vigour, for example its welfare to work policies and the building of 17 children's centres, several opened by government ministers, in particular Labour Children's Minister Beverley Hughes. In refusing to suspend me, Labour-led Haringey Council, in my view, risked being perceived as uncooperative with its own government, putting its 'recovered reputation' in jeopardy.

David Cameron's article in the Evening Standard

Cameron kept up the attack. In an article in London's *Evening Standard* (12/11/08, p.3), Cameron took a strong populist, moral, emotional and gendered stance. He drew upon his roles as a husband

and father of three young children so he had appeared to have much in common with other families. He was the morally responsible and upstanding father, asking 'how three people could inflict such pain on such a small child'. He was 'sickened' by the crime and protective of his wife, who 'couldn't watch [the TV news coverage] and left the room' (*Evening Standard* 12/11/08, p.3). His description signified a domestic scene of caring parents who knew their responsibilities in such contrast to the family of Baby P. Cameron expressed 'gendered emotion'; he was the husband angry on his wife's behalf. His anger was directed not at those who committed the crime, but at 'no one [who] is willing to hold their hand up and take responsibility'. Sociologist and academic Joanne Warner (2013b, p.1644) suggests that Cameron's engagement in the story provoked anger at social workers which led to moral rhetoric, or moralising talk.

The death of Baby P 'caused or allowed' by his mother and other known adults who were supposed to care for him had produced extreme moral disturbance. In the emerging narrative of accusation and blame it was social workers who had come to represent the moral failure in their inability to protect the child. That made them morally responsible for Peter's death themselves. In the same *Evening Standard* article Cameron argued that the way to stop further deaths was to 'reinforce professional responsibility'. He added criminality to the emerging positioning of me and the social workers, 'in the case of actions which are criminal, as they clearly were with the killers of this baby boy, the consequences must be clear – prison. But the same is true for professional negligence.'

The connotative meaning implied that the social workers and I were guilty of 'professional negligence' and that a prison sentence was not an unreasonable outcome. To support his position Cameron referred to the Labour government's 'child protection legislation', presumably the role of the DCS as the lead professional accountable for child protection services in a local authority, discussed in Chapter 4. Finally, Cameron challenged Balls's actions suggesting that: '[t]hey've [the government] got to come up with some answers fast'.

Cameron had in effect positioned himself as the 'hero of the people' standing up to the government for what had happened to Baby P.

Two further points are of note. First, Cameron in his article accuses the social workers but protects the police. He quotes from newspapers and asks, 'why when police expressed strong suspicions to social services was the child not taken into care?' Cameron overlooks the powers that police have to remove a child if they thought it necessary. But Cameron's defence of the police is in common with that of the Labour government. Cameron's attack was on social workers alone, especially me as Director of Children's Services, even though the published summary of the Serious Case Review indicated that Great Ormond Street Hospital and police had made serious errors. Second, Cameron made no mention of the role of Great Ormond Street Hospital.

Cameron, Brown and Balls, I suggest, were all by this stage trading in untruths. This was not a case of Steiner's 'knowing and not knowing', which suggests an unconscious 'not knowing', but I argue that they each chose to 'turn a blind eye' (see pages 79–81) to the complexity of what they were dealing with given the coverage of the case in the media and the impact on the public. More important for them, I argue, was the party political battle they were each involved in, complicated by their respective interdependence with some parts of the media. For example, Cameron's comments at PMQs had echoed the reporting in the *Sun* the same morning in relation to the SCR, in particular that I was guilty of leading an investigation of my own department when I was in fact complying with government policy.

Later in the same edition as Cameron's article, London's *Evening Standard* (12/11/08, p.3) reflected Balls's decision to send inspectors to Haringey: '[h]it squad will assess if staff should be sacked' and 'Tory Leader David Cameron today demanded sackings at Haringey after officials at the Labour-run council failed to apologise for their conduct', with images of me and Peter's social worker and portraying Cameron as the person driving the government's actions.

That evening, Mark Easton on BBC *News at 10* added to the intensity of the circulating affect, especially in relation to me, positioned as the uncaring bureaucrat. Against the backdrop of Haringey's Civic Centre, Easton told viewers that 'Haringey Council has consistently refused to apologise for the mistakes they made in protecting Baby P'; and that at a media briefing the Head of Children's Services [me] 'refused to say sorry to the child's father' and 'instead she handed out graphs showing how her department achieves high performance', and he held graphs up to the camera (BBC *News at Ten*, Wednesday 12 November 2008).

These claims were untrue and I made a formal complaint to the BBC some months later which they failed to uphold. To justify that, in their response published on their website, the BBC informed me that in relation to the first claim, 'refusing to say sorry', they were referring to Haringey Council (whom they had rung several times the same day) as consistently refusing to apologise, not me, but they could see how this might be mistaken as referring to me. Despite that, they had scrutinised my use of apologetic words, including several uses of the word 'sorry' at the press briefing and in subsequent interviews, and the BBC Complaints Director informed me in a letter that preceded their judgment that 'the distinction between expressions of sympathy or sadness and words which could be properly termed apologetic is that they give no indication of accepting a *degree of culpability*' (my italics).

My view is that the BBC wanted an expression of *guilt* from me, as opposed to sorrow about a case of familial child homicide. On the second claim, in the fast flow of questions at the press briefing I had not properly answered a question about whether I would apologise to Baby P's father. I had no concerns about how my department had worked with the father. Social workers had supported Peter's father and his siblings and I had written to Peter's father to offer our condolences and support with Peter's funeral. Peter's father had thanked social workers at the time and in the media he stated that they had 'acted with professionalism and courtesy' (BBC News 14

November 2008).[27] He was clear that he did not blame Haringey and that 'those who systematically tortured Peter and killed him kept it a secret...[n]ot just from me but from all the people who visited the house...even after he died, they lied to cover up their abuse' (*Daily Telegraph* 15/11/08, p.11; *Guardian* 15/11/08, p.14).

But the BBC, seemingly in their drive to reject my complaint, went as far as retrieving from Haringey Council a letter I had written to Peter's father shortly after Peter's death. The BBC judged that I had not expressed the kind of apology they thought appropriate and so it upheld its position. I return later in this chapter to the 'culture of apology'. On the third claim, the BBC agreed that no graphs had been given out or held up by me since it was Haringey's press team that had provided journalists who attended the press briefing with background information about Haringey and its in both written and graphical form as is routine in press briefings. But the BBC regarded this as a minor issue in my overall complaint which was rejected.

BBC *News at Ten*, by virtue of having the highest number of viewers of any news programme, had significant influence on the narrative. Easton's report added dramatically to the negative positioning of me in the media. The narrative of my 'refusing to apologise' and my behaviour characterised as being 'unrepentant' took on great significance the next day and in the weeks, months and years that followed. For example, Michael Gove, Conservative MP, claimed that I should not be compensated, given that I had taken to 'waving graphs in people's faces' (*Daily Telegraph* 2/12/08, p.6).

The BBC's report the night before (Tuesday 11 November) had not contained any manifest criticism of me, and I argue that Cameron's article, events at PMQs, the *Evening Standard* articles and Easton's report demonstrated a degree of 'institutionalised dependency' between the politicians and the media, or 'mediated reflexivity' (see page 91) in which each was both cause and effect of the 'bounded reality' they were forming (Davis 2009). For example, the *Sun's* reporting on the morning of 12 November was reflected in Cameron's claims in the House of Commons and in the stance the

Evening Standard took that evening. Similarly I argue that without Cameron's intervention in particular, Easton would not have made such a report to camera on the BBC *News at Ten*.

The public was beginning to be shaped as 'ill-informed spectators' (Davis 2003). But public opinion began to interact with the misinformation flowing from the interdependence of the media and the politicians and rapidly created a dynamic three-way interdependence. At its centre was the familial homicide of a child in which the circulation of negative emotion was escalating among members of the public. This public emotion in turn was beginning to drive the responses of the media and politicians.

The responses of members of the public on day 2

The initial responses of some members of the public began mainly on Wednesday 12 November on websites and in blogs and, in the main, were expressions of shock and disbelief about Baby P's death, particularly about the involvement of his mother. Most comments came from women, mostly mothers, but a few fathers also contributed. They made no reference to any politician, any party political conflict, or any newspaper, but they shared expressions of sorrow and grief. For example: '…they [those convicted] should al get the death penalty…' (Contributor 1, Facebook Group 2, 12/11/08),[28] 'I am a proud parent of 3 and reading this at lunchtime almost had me in tears. Just how or why the child's mother could let this happen is beyond me…' (Contributor 2, Group 2, 12/11/08), 'it makes me feel sick just thinking about it i have a 18 month old and i would kill anyone who harmed him in anyway. that poor little man how could she let it happen…' (Contributor 3, Group 2, 12/11/08), 'my little one was born on the exact day as baby p and it really makes me sick when sick people can do that…hang the bastards' (Contributor 4, Group 2, 13/11/08), and:

> hearing today what this little boy had to endure in his short life has reduced me to tears, to a point where I have had to turn the tv off…I'm a mum of 2 little girls and cannot comprehend how little boy's mum could let it happen… *(Contributor 5, Group 2, 12/11/08)*

But these members of the public were simultaneously being misled and misinformed as a consequence of the mediated reflexivity between the *Sun* and party politics, and also they were being misled by the police. In particular, the images in the media representing the injuries to Baby P, especially his blood-stained clothes, caused enormous distress (see page 139). For example: 'we do not need to see such horrible evidence' (Contributor 5, Group 2, 12/11/08), 'this image is disturbing' (Contributor 1, Group 3, 12/11/08), '…its not fair that his blood stained clothes should be on parade for all to see. I personally feel sick from seeing that t-shirt especially when ive got 2 children…' (Contributor 6, Group 2, 12/11/08), and 'the photos… make me sick to my stomach how anyone can do that to a poor defensless baby is beyond me there's some downright evil people in this world' (Contributor 2, Group 3, 14/11/08).

Further, connecting these images with suggestions that social workers had not only failed to save Baby P, but ignored this abuse, projected even greater hostilities towards social workers, suggesting answers to my earlier question as to why the police published such material: the anger towards social workers and me escalated and drew attention away from the police. For example: 'Sharon Shoesmith look in shame [at the bloodstained clothes] you bitch' (Contributor 1, Blog 2, 12/11/08), 'I hope these people can live with themselves knowing they let this little boy die' (Contributor 2, Blog 2, 12/11/08), 'how can the council rep come on TV and say no-one will be sacked? 60 times that child was seen by social services, the mother arrested twice, they must be fucking stupid' Contributor 7, Group 2, 12/11/08), 'this is a fuking disgrace how can anyone be so fuking evil, they should get there fuking life taking away…its a discrace how social services never took that poor boy away from them evil bastards…' (Contributor 3, Group 3, 12/11/08), 'something has got 2 b done that's 2 babies in the last couple of months' (Contributor 1, Group 2, 12/11/08), 'CHILD HAS SUFFERED at the hands of the f***ing social services…' (12/11/09, capitals in original).

What began as a small number of abusive emails, texts and letters sent to me personally, and to Haringey Council generally, grew during the next ten days to several hundred, putting significant pressure on the council and on me in particular. Many expressed distress about what had happened to Peter, but some were abusive, threatening and often obscene in expressing the harm they wished to do to me and the social workers.

These reactions suggest that the initial responses of members of the public were of sorrow about the loss of a young life, especially shock and disbelief about the involvement of the mother. But these emotions of sorrow were shaped as anger and given expression as blame. Cooper (2014b) suggests that society lacks a discourse to manage the emotionally indigestible facts of child torture and murder which may reflect the decline in public mourning rituals. For example, some members of the public may have been denied a form of expression that mourned the death of such a young child. From a Kleinian perspective discussed in Chapter 3, the responses of members of the public were different degrees of defence which reduced the 'psychic discomfort' inherent in the reporting of the familial homicide of Baby P.

Warner (2013b, p.231), in the case of Baby P, suggests that public anger was mobilised by politicians in conjunction with the press. Further, I argue that the public was responding to a dynamic network of misinformation moving between the media, politicians and the police, who in turn responded to the public's response. In particular, their interactions portrayed social workers as ignoring the 'torture' of Baby P. Such a portrayal made some members of the public, especially mothers and their children who depended upon social worker support, feel more vulnerable. The responses of the public were not simply a cause and effect relationship between the public's repulsion and the media's reporting, but the public's responses were being shaped by the media and the politicians in a complex process of interactions characteristic of Entman's 'cascade activation network', discussed in Chapter 3.

Thursday 13 November 2008

By Thursday this dynamic process had intensified towards the social workers and me, not only creating us as objects of hate and resentment but also placing us in danger. The effects of Mark Easton's BBC news report were immediate: '[t]he woman who puts performance graphs before a baby's life', '[s]he boasted of Council's 3 star services' (*Daily Mail* 13/11/08, p.11). Others focused on whether I should be sacked: '[c]hildren's chief faces calls to quit' (*Daily Telegraph* 13/11/08, p.8); and on Haringey politicians: 'investigation into brutal death of 'baby P' increases the pressure on council chiefs' (*The Times* 13/11/08, p.10).

Reports on events at the previous day's PMQs were extensive: '[s]pat was shameful' (*Daily Star* 13/11/08, p.9), '[h]ouse shamed by row over political corpse of baby P' (*Guardian* 13/11/08, p.2), '[t]he question that threw Brown off his learning curve' (*Daily Telegraph* 13/11/08, p.8), 'grubby scenes in parliament' (*Daily Mirror* 13/11/08, p.7). But Cameron's performance at PMQs was lauded by some: '[his] vehemence was spontaneous and magnificent' (*Daily Mail* 13/11/08, p.10); while Brown was accused of using 'procedural stuttering, bumbling and mumbling' and he was challenged 'to show he cares by being decisive' (*Daily Express* 13/11/08, p.12).

Several elements of this media reporting were evidence of more complex evaluations. Notably, the media's use of the words 'shameful' and 'grubby' to describe the behaviour of the politicians seems to separate the politicians' behaviour from the media's own reporting of the story; for example, events at PMQs were 'a spat' or bitter party political conflict, *even* over the death of a child which the media judged as shameful. But despite that, the demonstration of emotion became important, with Cameron positioned as the victor as he was seen to be more in tune with his feelings, in contrast to Brown who was positioned as 'not caring' or being unemotional, reinforcing existing stereotypes of him. This criticism of Brown may have reflected the antagonism and distrust between Labour MPs and journalists that existed at this time (Davis 2009).

David Cameron's letter published in the Sun

The *Sun*, in particular, was vitriolic, promoting Cameron and publishing a short letter from him in the same edition of the newspaper (*Sun* 13/11/08, p.9). In his letter headlined '[e]xcuses won't do', Cameron reiterated his claims: '[w]e've heard countless excuses but no apology', 'Britain's sickened and we're angry too', 'another child slips through Haringey's safety net'. His words suggested that Peter and Victoria were the 'only' cases of familial child homicide and that both died in Haringey. Cameron refers to 'Britain' being 'sickened' and he refers to 'we', giving a sense of speaking on 'our' behalf and uniting 'us' in grief and determination: 'we won't let [Peter] down in death', he told readers. Those professionals he accused had been positioned outside 'the sentiment of the nation' and Haringey outside all that was decent 'Britishness'. It was as if Haringey, its social workers, and especially me as the face of both, did not and could not share the nation's shock and distress about what happened to Peter Connelly and therefore the nation needed to act: 'professionals who let Peter down must pay the price with their jobs'. At the same time Cameron challenged other newspapers, claiming 'it's not about politics' and 'all of us should be angry', in effect suggesting that Brown should show his anger too.

That evening, an image of me at the Royal Ascot racecourse taken from my daughter's Facebook pages and published on the front page of London's *Evening Standard* (13/11/08, p.1) became significant in the further positioning of me. It was reproduced in many newspapers and attracted extensive comment. In the wake of Peter's death I was positioned as 'living it up' in a high-salaried privileged lifestyle, and with my daughter's travels in the USA attributed to me it created a great contrast with Peter's life. Building upon suggestions of deceitful behaviour and criminality, London's *Evening Standard* in an article published several months later (10/12/08, p.12) suggested that my visit to Ascot was linked to a building contract, which provided me with substantial financial gain, but no such evidence existed, nor was it the case. Haringey Council informed them that I had contributed to a charity as part of this event but this was not reported, given its incongruence with the narrative.

I argue that by now the *Sun* and Cameron in particular were locked in 'mediated reflexivity', each dependent upon the other to act. Cameron's words were rhetorical but I suggest that they supported the *Sun* to be much bolder. For example, '[i]diots who betrayed baby P must go now', '[p]rice of a life', 'have you no shame', 'demand for justice' appeared alongside 'mugshots' which 'criminalise' me, my four colleagues and the GOSH paediatrician (*Sun* 13/11/08, p.9). In particular, the *Sun* was confident enough to launch its petition. In line with Cameron's view that those named in the media should pay with their jobs, the petition invited readers to agree that they should all be sacked under a banner of false information that claimed that social workers made sixty visits to Baby P and his family. The petition cast the social workers, the paediatrician and I as 'criminally incompetent', I was 'smug' and stated 'if Sharon Shoesmith had used common sense a baby might be alive', picking up Cameron's theme of common sense used in his article in London's *Evening Standard*.

This notion of common sense suggested a faulty sense of realism, that is, that the abuse was so real, so evident, there for anyone to see, so obvious that anyone with any degree of intelligence would have acted to save Peter. Such a position reinforced the view that social workers either ignored the 'torture' or were too incompetent to see it, a position that can only have served to distress readers. Finally, a pledge: that '[a] price must be paid for his little life, and we will not rest until that price has been paid by those responsible' (*Sun* 13/11/08, p.8). In effect it was as if, along with those convicted, we were also guilty of 'causing or allowing' Peter's death.

The apparent interdependency of the *Sun* and Cameron may have been direct or indirect. But undoubtedly the *Sun* was attractive to Cameron given the political power of its allegiance. The size of its reach estimated in March 2008 by the *Guardian* was in excess of seven million, mainly in the 'C2DE' social classes (which includes skilled, semi-skilled, unskilled and manual workers) and with 45 per cent of the readership being female. The *Sun* at the time supported the Labour party, having switched its allegiance to the Labour party and its then-leader Tony Blair six weeks before the general election in 1997. The support of the *Sun* had been significant in Labour's return to government in 1997, having previously been regarded as destroying its chances in 1992. But more recently, under its editor at the time, Rebekah Brooks, the *Sun* had been more ambivalent in its support for Blair's successor, Prime Minister Gordon Brown. In July 2007, with Brooks's recommendation, Cameron had recruited News International's *News of the World* (*NoW*) former editor Andy Coulson as his Head of Communications. Coulson had replaced Brooks as editor at the *NoW* when she took up the editorship of the *Sun* in 2003. Before becoming Cameron's Head of Communications Coulson had resigned from his editorship at the *NoW* in the aftermath of convictions of *NoW* journalists for phone-hacking in 2007. In 2014 Coulson was convicted for conspiracy to hack phones and given a prison sentence.

The story of Baby P had different but interrelated investments for Cameron, Brooks and Coulson. Politically for Cameron, as leader of the Opposition, the story was a rich source of challenge to Labour's policies, most of them represented by Labour-led Haringey Council past and present. It was also a human drama of familial child homicide with high 'news value' (Stanley and Manthorpe 2004) and the kind of 'populist' news story that Davis (2009) claims Opposition politicians use to gain attention in the media. Cameron was already 'wooing' the Murdoch press given his visit to Murdoch's yacht only a few months before in August 2008 (Elliot and Hanning 2012). For Brooks, as the *Sun's* editor, presumably the familial homicide of Baby P was not only an important news item, but it lent itself to the kind of moral campaigns the tabloid had pursued previously. For example, the petition to lengthen the sentence of the two boys who murdered James Bulger; and after ten years of campaigning, 'Sarah's Law', which was linked to the murder of Sarah Payne and enabled parents to check if a person had a history of child sex offences. Coulson had a dual role. First, as Cameron's new Head of Communications he could assist Cameron to challenge Brown at the precise moment that Brown had something to vaunt in his handling of the economy, with a story of the utmost sensitivity which would sell newspapers. Second, Coulson could facilitate the much-coveted relationship between Cameron and his former colleague Brooks.

The context of this triad of mutual interest became even more significant later when just before the 2010 election the *Sun*, having supported Labour since 1997, switched its allegiance to the Conservatives. During the Leveson Inquiry it was revealed that Cameron, Brooks and Coulson enjoyed close professional and personal relationships during this period (Leveson 2012a), confirmed in the hacking trial (Davies 2014), and discussed in Chapter 4. In effect there were already established relationships between Rebekah Brooks and the head of Cameron's communications unit, Andy Coulson, and Cameron himself which I suggest facilitated both Cameron's and the *Sun's* stance on the story.

Ed Balls changed his position

I have argued that the relationship between the *Sun* and Cameron was characteristic of 'mediated reflexivity' but both the *Sun* and Cameron were also engaged in 'mediated populism', discussed in Chapter 3. That is, they were drawing in public support. Given the events of the previous two days, in particular the confrontation of Brooks and Cameron with Brown and Balls, Cameron's stance in two newspapers, his challenge to Brown at PMQs, and his support of the *Sun* to undertake the 'moral task' of getting rid of those 'responsible' through its petition, Brown and Balls were in an increasingly vulnerable position. Brown's political legitimacy, especially his ability to connect on an emotional level with the British people, was at stake. I argue that if 'loony-left' Haringey Council and its 'incompetent' social workers and 'unfit' director were positioned 'outside all that was decent', then Balls and Brown could not risk being positioned in the same place themselves. They had to wrestle themselves in the eyes of the media, and the British public, onto the 'same side' as everyone else. And they had to prevent any clash with their old adversary Haringey Council by ensuring that it was also 'on-side', to which I return.

For Brown and Balls, achieving consensus with the Conservative Opposition would mean not only that they were on the 'right' side of the moral argument, but also in a process characteristic of 'indexing'

(Bennett 2011; Schlosberg 2013), discussed in Chapter 3, the media would be more likely to cease to probe. With the two political parties on the same 'side', the media would therefore neglect its 'purported role...as a last line of public interest defence' (Schlosberg 2013, p.3) in preference to selling newspapers with a high-profile 'human story'. In that context, and at that moment, I suggest that any challenge to the emerging narrative or a probe into the conduct of the Metropolitan Police and GOSH was much less attractive for the media or the politicians, and too complex for this simplistic account of what happened to Peter Connelly.

Mediated populist engagement became the focus also for Brown and Balls. They each addressed the British public through the print and broadcast media. Brown gave an interview to the *Metro* (13/11/08, p.2), a free newspaper estimated to reach three million readers each day. Using similar language to Cameron, Brown was 'outraged when he first heard about the "sickening" abuses of Baby P'. He had 'made it his aim to never let such cruelty towards a child happen again and had ordered an *inquiry*'. Only two days previously in an email on 11/11/08 to Permanent Secretary David Bell, Director of Safeguarding, Janette Pugh describes references in the media to 'an inquiry' as 'irritating spins,' but here the Ofsted JAR inspection is cast as *the inquiry*, probably to satisfy these demands. With a reference to his perceived lack of emotion in contrast to Cameron's, Brown told the readers that 'it is important for me to act in a proper way and not allow the anger and emotion...to get in the way'. Possibly Brown sought to position himself as a Prime Minister who is decisive and in control.

On the same day on BBC Radio 4, Ed Balls acknowledged that the SCR *was* conducted in line with government procedures and thereby rejected Cameron's claims of impropriety on my behalf. But Balls repeated the misleading claim Brown made at PMQs that Balls had only seen the SCR on 12 November. This may have been the case, but senior officials in Balls's department had seen the SCR at various stages in its drafting and the final document had been provided to his team some weeks before these events at PMQ. Officials raised no concerns about the SCR. In effect Balls makes the SCR the proxy or the rationale for the government's change of direction from the more benign stance evident in its press release only the day before.

Using the SCR in this way solves some problems and creates others. To strengthen cross-party consensus, Balls invited Michael Gove (Conservative Opposition spokesperson for children), local MPs David Lammy (Labour) and Lynne Featherstone (Liberal Democrats), and Barry Sheerman (chair of the Select Committee) to read the full SCR. In line with government policy the full report of an SCR remained confidential to protect the family and only a summary was published. Usually SCRs were evaluated by Ofsted and never read by politicians. So it is possible that none of these politicians had ever read an SCR before. Balls declared that the SCR contained 'clear evidence that agencies had failed, singly and collectively', and Gove declared that it was a 'manual' for improving services as it disclosed in narrative detail what went wrong (*Daily Telegraph* 2/12/08, p.6).

It was Ofsted's role to evaluate the SCR, and since Balls's view was that the SCR 'raised serious concerns about the wider systems and management of services for safeguarding children in the borough' (Hansard 20 November 2008, Column 372), Ofsted was compromised in relation to its forthcoming evaluation of the SCR. Further, the SCR, in line with government policy, was intended to act as a learning tool. But SCRs had become an example of Beck's (1992) 'organised irresponsibility' in which child protection agencies, while preventing the risk of harm to most children, are unable to attribute 'errors', that is, abuse or homicide of children, to the system or risk framework that governs their work and which cannot guarantee the elimination of risk (see Chapter 4). SCRs were increasingly used to give an account of what went wrong and to condemn and to blame individuals.

Despite the challenges of PMQs a few days earlier and the many issues in the press, mostly led by Cameron and the *Sun*, I argue that Balls effectively built consensus with the Opposition (and by implication the *Sun*). This consensus is evident in the first debate in the House of Commons the following week on Monday 17 November in which Balls 'thanks' the Opposition for their support: 'I am grateful to the Hon. Member for Surrey Heath [Michael Gove] and to other Opposition Members for the support they have given me over the past eight days' (Hansard 20 November 2008, Column 372).

Haringey Council politicians

A turning point was also evident in relation to Haringey politicians. The Leader of Haringey Council, George Meehan, had refused to suspend me. By Thursday 13 November he expressed his confidence in the social workers and me and had that message conveyed to the staff, schools and others.[29] I also received emails from several other elected councillors, particularly from Claire Kober, who later succeeded George Meehan as Leader after he resigned. It read:

> Sharon, The last few days have been dreadful for everyone, I wanted to say that I have the utmost respect for you as a public servant, and whilst there are service improvements that we must deliver, I have every confidence that you are the individual to get us where we need to be. Keep your chin up.[30]

But on the same day the Labour government provided Haringey Council with a press officer to work only with Haringey politicians and not its officers, which in hindsight signalled the change in Haringey Council's stance. A televised apology by Labour Councillor Liz Santry followed that evening. Her apology was highly damaging to me given that my alleged 'refusing to apologise' [for the death of a child] had become the most dominant 'soundbite' in how I was characterised. Santry's apology reinforced the positioning of me as 'hard-faced' in the sense that I had *still not* apologised, '[b]ut Sharon Shoesmith…still refused to offer any public apology or to resign', and it became juxtaposed with my visit to Ascot: '[w]e're sorry…but no remorse from race-going head of child services…or sackings…' (*Evening Standard* 13/11/08, p.1).

Santry's apology was a collective impersonal apology or corporate apology, part of the new 'culture of apology' (Mills 2001) or 'commodification of apology' (Taft 2000) which began to emerge during the first decade of the twenty-first century as symbols of responsibility and accountability. I had expressed the sorrow and devastation of all those in Haringey Council services who had known Peter. I had also expressed my personal sorrow at the loss of life. But these expressions were not enough. The apology has something in common with the religious confession which leads to contrition and achieves forgiveness and reconciliation (Brooks 2000 cited by Mills 2001).

But the demand for an apology from me in the media was different. My expression of personal sorrow about Peter's death was not enough. What was required of me, represented by the BBC's position, was a personal admission of culpability. That is, bearing the *responsibility* for 'the brutal killing of a young child'. It was, in effect, not an apology that was being requested, but a resignation presented as an apology. An apology was in effect a resignation; one would follow the other. Such an apology was positioned as public accountability, which I return to. Such an apology was not about forgiveness or reconciliation.

For my part, I could not countenance ever taking responsibility for the killing of a child. My personal and professional life had been one about educating, caring for, and protecting children. But the absence of an apology from me began to dominate the narrative. It may have been that Haringey politicians thought erroneously that a more corporate apology from Santry, masterminded by the Labour government press officer, might have freed them from the cycle of accusation and that things might have settled down by the weekend. They were wrong.

The responses of members of the public on day 3

Expressions of sorrow by members of the public began to escalate into anger and retribution. Comments on the Old Holborn Blog in particular were characteristic of the loss of boundaries and unrestrained foul-mouthedness described by Holland (1996). For example, the televised apology by Santry drew extreme comment on the Old Holborn Blog: 'Liz Santry, you are incompetent, dangerous

and a deadly threat to children. Resign, Fuck Off and do it sharpish'
(Contributor 1, 14/11). Significantly, in the same blog Ed Balls also
received direct criticisms, for example:

> Good to see the shitstorm is beginning to reach the in-tray of Ed 'So
> weak' Balls. Pass the fucking parcel and tick the fucking boxes whilst
> doing fuck all substantive that could make a fucking difference,
> well Eddie boy, the fucking buck is coming home, and it large and
> steaming and isn't going to be hidden away (Contributor 2, 14/11).

On Facebook Group 1, the most regular contributor, a Conservative
councillor from another council, posted Santry's email address, and
urged the members to send her the message '[t]oo little too late'
(Contributor 1, Group 1, 13/11/08). Next day he made derogatory
comments: 'There's a lot of arse-covering going on in Haringey', and
reiterated the false claim that I had 'twice refused to apologise for the
council's role in Baby P's death' (Contributor 1, Group 1, 14/11/08).

But the comments that dominated Facebook Group 1 were once
again not matters of politics or politicians but matters related to the
overwhelming sadness and grief that the members felt about the life
and death of Baby P. The very deep sorrow expressed about Baby
P supports the view that some respondents, especially mothers,
needed an opportunity to express grief, or to mourn. Their sorrow
began to reveal a degree of vulnerability which had no other means
of expression. For example: 'I want to cry every time I think about
this poor little boy and the pain and suffering he endured in his short
life' (Contributor 8, Group 2, 13/11/08), 'I just cant stop crying
yesterday and today cos of this is sooo sad! I feel gutted' (Contributor
4, Group 3, 13/11/08), and:

> i am a mother myself and i carnt imagine ever doing anything like
> that to my son, they are sick twisted bastards who should never be
> allowed to walk free again i hope they rott in hell baby p will be in
> heaven now were he belongs his so called 'PARENTS' will go to
> fuking hell, RIP baby p you will NEVER be hurt again god bless this
> child xxx. *(Contributor 9, Group 2, 13/11/08)*

But anger was also rising in relation to the social workers in response to the misinformation that social workers knew of the abuse Peter was being subjected to and failed to intervene to save him: '[s]ocial workers have FAILED again... They should all get the sacked for not taking that baby out of there' (Contributor 10, Group 2, 13/11/08), '[a]s for social services they need a good kick up the arse I mean look at what happened to that poor girl Victoria and the same thing has happened AGAIN only younger they are a DISGRACE' (Contributor 11, Group 2, 13/11/08).

Neubaum *et al.* (2014, p.30), in their study of the uses of social media discussed in Chapter 3, found that despite criticism taking place in the media, people engaged in a process of social sharing of emotion online; in particular there was a specific need for people to express their internal states to others following an emotional event, to have a feeling of not being alone, and the efficacy to cope with the extreme situation. The Facebook groups in this study were characteristic of 'affective groups' (Hinshelwood 1989, p.77) in which feeling states were rehearsed and moved around, or groups that operated without a leader (Hoggett 2009). The groups were an amalgam of passions (Hoggett 2009) which were unable to contain the emotion that the individuals were unable to contain themselves. Some members argued with each other as some postings caused confusion and triggered past distress. For example, some members of the group were clients of social workers and the criticisms of social workers caused them particular distress. These members defended social workers either because the member had a family member who was a social worker or because they were helped in the past:

> I was helped by social services when I was younger coz my mam was seen unfit to look after me...they saved my life' [and the next day from the same woman], 'the social workers n child protection saved me so they aren't all crap. *(Contributor 3, Group 3, 13/11/08 and 14/11/08)*

I argue that these responses were an amalgam of sorrow, grief and a need to mourn for some, for others an expression of vulnerability, and for others expressions of anger and retribution mainly represented by comments on the Old Holborn Blog. Overall, the public was being provided with serious levels of misinformation exacerbated by the absence of anyone who could act as a stabilising influence. I argue that by this stage any opportunity to take another approach to managing the familial homicide of Baby P was lost.

Friday 14 November 2008

Just as Brown had done on Thursday (*Metro* 13/11/08, p.2) and Cameron had done the day before (*Evening Standard* 12/11/08, p.3), Balls effectively engaged with the growing emotional response to the story by expressing his own emotions (*Wakefield Express* 14/11/08). In doing so Cameron, Brown and Balls had reinforced the consensus between them and they each had an opportunity to express a degree of grief, especially as fathers. But also explicit was their criticism of social workers and the paediatrician whom they positioned outside of this sense of grief. The effect on the social workers and the paediatrician who had seen Peter and not realised the danger he was in was never considered. The only 'rational' explanation was that they didn't care, didn't bother, lacked common sense, or social workers with their dubious 'welfare' role weren't up to the task.

The press on the morning of Friday 14 November was unrelenting in its targeting of me and the social workers. The narrative about me was elaborated: '[d]ay at the races for scandal boss', 'Ascot luxury – a portrait of a modern social services chief' (*Daily Express* 14/11/08, p.21), juxtaposing a luxury lifestyle with those of social care clients, especially Peter's and his family, which was commented on in the media. The *Daily Mail* (14/11/08, p.1) described me as a 'hatchet-faced harridan…washes her hands of the death, refuses to resign and boasts of providing a three star service, backed by pie charts, graphs and a perfect paper trail of criminal incompetence and wilful neglect'.

The untruths, the misogynist use of language and positioning of me as an overpaid female bureaucrat enjoying luxury holidays, living in a posh flat in London's West End, having 'done very well for herself' (*Daily Mail* 13/11/08, p.8), despite being 'an ordinary

[Northern Irish] girl who went to an ordinary school' (*Belfast Telegraph* 14/11/08, p.1), accompanied with pictures of my local primary school) was relentless. It was notable that my being a mother of two daughters was rarely reported as it was incongruent with the narrative.

Similarly, a letter from almost seventy headteachers in Haringey was reported in many newspapers and on BBC News but failed to change the narrative that had taken hold. In their letter the heads describe me as 'an outstanding public servant', referring to my commitment and leadership and suggesting that if I should have to leave Haringey 'then our children and young people will lose one of their most effective, determined and committed champions'. They referred to my role in transforming 'a demoralised education service' and to the 'exceptional rate of improvement of many of the borough's schools [which] would not have been possible without the support of the service that I rebuilt, revitalised and led'.[31] These contributions were characteristic of Schlosberg's (2013) 'additional frames' which are unable to shift a narrative that has taken hold even when they are articulated by other elites.

Headlines in the press continued to suggest that the briefing against social workers by police continued. For example, reports that the police were inhibited in their work on the case of Baby P by decisions of social workers: '[p]olice claim that they were overruled by social workers', 'social workers wanted the mother to care for the baby she had in prison' (*Daily Mail* 14/11/08, p.18; *Daily Telegraph* 14/11/08, p.7) (yet joint plans to take the new baby into the care of the local authority were agreed well before the birth), and criticism of Haringey Council lawyers who it was claimed had to be ordered to release material to the murder trial (*Sun* 13/11/08, p.9; *Independent* 13/11/08, p.13).

In the *Sun*, for the first time the image of a baby's head representing Peter's injuries was positioned alongside the images of the social workers, the paediatrician and me (14/11/08, p.5). This image had a very strong connotative effect of positioning us as the culprits, those responsible for these dreadful injuries and who needed to be punished, hence promoting the need to sign the petition. The *Sun*'s petition was reported to have 75,000 signatories and it included an invitation to 'tell Ed Balls what you think by signing the petition' (p.6) and, with reference to me and the others, suggested 'JUST GO NOW' on the front page (*Sun* 14/11/08, capitals in the original).

At the same time the *Sun* (14/11/08, p.6) kept up its attack on Haringey Council. It claimed that the council was run by 'politically-obsessed zealots', that it was 'the last bastion of what used to be called the Loony Left', and should 'put innocent babies before the wheelie bins' (14/11/08, p.31). The same edition had an image of Councillor Santry in which she was dubbed as 'incompetent, politically correct and anti-white' (p.4). These words were a powerful example of Haringey's 'stickiness'. The use of 'anti-white' is a twist on the multicultural nature of Haringey which might appeal to the *Sun*'s readers, and a reference to the ethnicity of Peter as a 'white' boy and his assumed lack of status in Haringey Council.

My home, as well as my office, was under siege by many journalists and camera crews both national and international, so I planned to go elsewhere that evening. Journalists had yet again followed me from work onto London's underground. I repeatedly changed carriages at different stops to keep away from them. I got off at London's King's Cross (which is not my stop) and as I ran through the station to catch a bus and get away from the journalists I saw for the very first time the image of Baby P published on the front of the *Evening Standard* (14/11/08, p.1). Once again an image was central to an unfolding narrative. It was the image that has become iconic, the beautiful blue-eyed blond little boy. In an earlier edition the *Sun* had urged the public to tell them the whereabouts of those they had named, and to provide photos or information (13/11/08, p.9). This seemed to lead to the fictitious story that my in-laws had urged me to go [to resign] published in the *Sun* (14/11/08, p.14). On the bus from King's Cross as I attempted to escape from the media I was photographed by members of the public so I got off and walked the rest of the way.

The responses of members of the public on day 4

By Friday 14 November I had been positioned as a cold and calculating bureaucrat, a woman lacking in emotion, who was incompetent and dishonest. Douglas (1984) might suggest that I had become the scapegoat that provided a cultural function enabling a form of social order or social cohesion of like-minded people to emerge. I argue that the degree of distress that some people felt made it more serious. I was positioned as guilty of a crime by the circulating affect and deserving of punishment.

Each of the Facebook groups shared the electronic link to the *Sun*'s petition. In the *Sun* all ten letters from readers (14/11/08, p.71) communicated extreme views which reflected Cameron's stance on criminality: 'they should face prosecution for criminal negligence', 'they should be tried for aiding and abetting killing'. These were potentially very serious views which put me, and the others named, increasingly at risk if we were identified in public spaces. The emotion was heightened, and the degree of risk intensified, when faulty perceptions about what social workers might have known about the danger that Baby P was in were circulated on Facebook: 'they possessed the facts of the torture but decided NOT to help the child' (Contributor 1, Blog 2, 14/11/08); '[t]hey have no idea how to safeguard children I was revolted and feel physically sick' (Contributor 2, Blog 2, 14/11/08); 'everyone who touched this case is as guilty as the parents for the death of this child. They chould all be sacked and locked up themselves' (Contributor 2, Group 1, 14/11/08); 'its time to start a push to get her [Sharon Shoesmith] prosecuted' (Contributor 3, Blog 2, 14/11/08); and:

> the social services and the other members involved are as bad as the sick evil parents themselves they were well aware of the horrific extent of all incidents yet they turned a blind eye. How could they hand the baby back to such evil parents in the first place baffles me! It can only be for financial reasons... *(Contributor 3, Group 3, 14/11/08)*

The comments reflected a serious level of misinformation and the escalation of a drive for retribution. This drive was further reflected in comments about the absence of convictions for murder for Baby P's mother, her boyfriend and his brother. Failing a murder conviction, the expectation was that long sentences should be given to those convicted of causing or allowing Peter's death. Several petitions sprang up demanding harsh sentences and one which was demanding the death penalty attracted almost 5000 signatures between 14/11/08 and 07/07/13. The Old Holborn Blog was again extreme in its views; for example, President Obama (2006, p.57) was quoted, who, in the context of capital punishment, opined that some crimes, for example mass murder, the rape and murder of a child, 'are so heinous, so beyond the pale, that the community is justified in expressing the full measure of its outrage by meting out the ultimate punishment'. And the writer adds: 'If only we had the option' (Passer-by, 14/11/08). In direct response to Obama's comment another Old Holborn Blog post demonstrated a sense of fear or danger in the Other: 'I think special hatred should also be reserved for Sharon Shoesmith. She felt she and her department had nothing to apologise for. What a callous evil bitch' (14/11/08).

The iconic image of Baby P as a blue-eyed blond-haired beautiful boy brought new waves of emotion. Public reaction represented by letters to newspapers, responses on media websites, in blogs and social media sites (especially Facebook), emails and text intensified. Responses from the public expressed aggression against those who were convicted, intense anger towards social workers, and shock, distress and disbelief about the death of Baby P. The Other who evoked fear and a sense of danger is a different person for different people; for example, with reference to the mother: 'eat shit and dye u fucking bitch u don't deserve to breath the same air as me' (Contributor 7, Facebook Group 3, 12/11/08). And to the mother, her boyfriend and his brother: 'let the fuckers rot in hell and even that's too good infact I don't think there is a punishment that I concider bad enough for these bastards' (Contributor 12, Group 2,

12/11/08). While posts on Old Holborn Blog were more threatening, for example:

> Get the addresses of the people who do things against children when they get out of prison, and torture them. Cant we do something instead of just always words, I will do whatever it takes. Does anyone agree or am I deemed a thug??? *(Old Holborn Blog, Anon, 16/11/08)*

In relation to the social workers: 'its descracful they way they treated that bairn I think that they should all be sacked for it they should protect the kids more and should be able to tell if they are being abused!!!!!' (Contributor 8, Group 3, 15/11/08). With reference to me: 'evil fucking bitch, i swear if i seen her i would have deck her one,, she is evil through and through that one...not much better than the 3 scum that did this' (Bebo, 10/12/08). One member summed up the impressions of many. If such allegations about me made by the media were true it would be entirely possible to agree with these sentiments:

> she [Sharon Shoesmith] is responsible for making sure these individuals [referring to Tracey Connelly, her boyfriend and his brother] are identified and dealt with swiftly which would have saved this little boy's life. She didn't which was bad enough but then to refuse to apologise point blank and to then produce graphs and pie charts...is unforgiveable and completely inappropriate in these circumstances. *(Contributor 3, Group 1, 15/11/08)*

Saturday 15 and Sunday 16 November 2008

On Saturday 15 November 2008 the iconic image of Baby P was published in many papers (*Daily Mirror, Daily Telegraph, Guardian, Sun*). It was as if the reality that Baby P was a beautiful blue-eyed blond boy made him the object of even greater affection. For example: 'heart-breaking first pictures of baby P are a stark reminder of the innocent young life so brutally snuffed out' (*Daily Mirror* 15/11/08, p.8), 'how could anyone kill this lovely boy?' (*Sun* 15/11/08, p.6), and 'heart-breaking picture of the little angelic tot' (*People* 15/11/08, p.11). Baby P's image reinforced all the anger that had been emerging in the last few days, the most dominant being that the social workers, paediatrician and myself were to blame and should be sacked. For example, the *Sun* appealed directly to the emotion of its readers: 'look at that face on page one today, and then if you haven't already, please fill in our petition on this page or online'.

The petition, entitled 'Beautiful Baby Campaign', reached 130,000 and included images of me, the social workers and the paediatrician and silhouettes of other unnamed staff. The *Sun* (15/11/08, p.25) told its readers: '[b]oy's plight clear to anyone with a brain'. This article continued Cameron's idea that spotting the abuse was simply 'common sense', and it compared spotting child abuse with having your gas boiler fixed and suggested 'it's easy'. The *Daily Mirror* (15/11/08, p.21) printed my image alongside the iconic image of Peter with the headline '[a]nger at tragedy, heart-breaking first pictures [of Peter]', 'an act of pure evil'. The juxtaposition of the two images suggested the evil unfeeling woman who not so much failed to save this beautiful boy, but is responsible for his death. Similarly the *People* (15/11/08, p.11) reported, 'criminal charges could be brought against the professionals involved in [Peter's] care' and the *Sunday Express* (15/11/08, p.29) asked, '[h]ow did baby P's *other* killers get away with it' (my emphasis) suggesting that social workers were also killers and should be prosecuted and jailed.

At the same time the message in these images was so stark and the growing public opprobrium so strong that the submerged reality only came briefly to the surface when a journalist reminded her readers that '[social workers] didn't kill the tragic toddler' (*Daily Mirror* 15/11/08, p.21). Similarly, *The Times* (13/11/08, p.3) found it necessary to remind readers, 'it is important to remember that 'Baby P' was not killed by social workers...he died at the hands of sadists...' And in a letter to the *Guardian* (14/11/08, p.41), '[l]et's not forget, in the inevitable hue and cry for scapegoats following the tragic life and death of Baby P, that the social workers and medical practitioners killed no one'.

During the weekend, party politics raged in two respects. First, a social worker who had worked for Haringey Council some years previously told the press that she had written to government ministers about her concerns in Haringey Council.[32] They had referred her concerns to the Commission for Social Care Inspection (CSCI) who investigated and reported that Haringey Council had considered her complaint properly and there were no outstanding issues. These details were reported to Members of Parliament during a debate on 20 November 2008.[33] But newspaper headlines implicated government ministers; for example: '[m]inisters were warned before baby P's death' (*Daily Express* 13/11/08, p.21), 'Baby P and the Ministers' (*Daily Mail* 13/11/08, p.1), '[m]inisters warned babies were at risk' (*Daily Telegraph* 13/11/08, p.1) and '[b]uck passing but ministers could have cost child his life, claim Tories' (*Evening Standard* 13/11/08, p.5). Cameron accused the government of bureaucratic buck-passing and Liberal Democrat MP Lynn Featherstone called for the action of ministers to be scrutinised (*Independent* 15/11/08, p.2; *Daily Mail*, pp.8/9; *The Times*, p.6). A letter to the *Sunday Mirror* (16/11/08, p.40) called for Balls's resignation and the *Independent* (15/11/08, p.7) suggested that Balls should expect 'a rough ride' [at the House of Commons debate] on Monday night [17/11/08].

Second, the 'moral underclass' (Roseneil and Mann 1996) was the subject of political comment in several newspapers. This 'moral underclass' was for Conservative MP Iain Duncan Smith (*Guardian* 13/11/08, p.32) and the *Sun* a symbol of their theme of 'broken Britain' which was developing in the rhetoric of the Conservative Opposition throughout 2008. With high levels of poverty in Haringey and the need for welfare support by many of its residents, the death of Baby P in Haringey was for the Conservatives the embodiment of 'broken Britain'. Conservative MP Michael Gove in the *Sunday Express* (16/11/08, p.7) suggested that Peter was a '[v]ictim of a moral wasteland' in 'New Labour's Britain'. *The Times* (16/11/08, p.18) claimed that '[t]his wel-feral state abandoned Baby P.' The *Observer* (16/11/08 p.18) suggested the existence of 'families that were straight out of nightmares...an underclass...untouched by the affluence of modern Britain'. Others took a more empathic stance, casting Tracey Connelly as a victim herself: '[o]ur first step towards understanding the death of [Baby P] should be not to blame social workers but to face the mother's experience of childhood' (*Guardian* 15/11/08, pp.31/32).

Despite this, the 'broken Britain' stance suggested that Tracey Connelly was part of this moral underclass that threatened the decent British way of life and values. Her own childhood was reported to have been dysfunctional and it was the subject of many media articles (for example, *London Lite* 13/11/08, p.5; *Daily Telegraph* 15/11/08, p.25; *The Times* 15/11/08, pp.6/7). Stories in the media created disgust, repulsion and inevitably anger towards her; for example:

> how is it that this disgusting piece of humanity, in the shape of the mother, was ever allowed to have the child in the first place? She came from a family of drunks, never worked and watched porn all day. Her council house – she had to have one didn't she? – stank. Why wasn't the child taken from her at birth? *(Sun 13/11/08, p.9)*

Tracey Connelly was the failed mother unworthy of motherhood, she 'cries sham tears' (*News of the World* 16/11/08, p.4) and 'cared more about pups than son's death' (*Sunday Express* 16/11/08, p.11), the home she provided for Baby P was an 'earthly hell...stinking of human waste' (*Daily Mail* 15/11/08, pp. 8/9). In terms of Labour's 'social investment state' discussed in Chapter 4, Tracey Connelly had little 'human capital' and hence little value to the state. She belonged to a group that was demonised by the Conservatives but also by Labour as part of a 'dependent underclass' which created moral concerns. *The Times* (13/11/08, p.2) summed it up: 'the unspeakable case of baby P which raises profound questions about the state of Britain today...[t]he welfare state has created some communities with no morality...[whose] adults were part of the dependency community'.

The implication was that social workers had, in effect, failed in their moral duty to save Baby P from such a dysfunctional family. Tracey Connelly was simply 'too irresponsible' to even be blameworthy and somehow the responsibility for her actions was transferred to social workers. It was as if social workers had failed to protect decent British people from the realities of some people's lives and strengthened the sense of the culpability of social workers which Cameron had given voice to. This blaming of social workers revisited the 'profound, unresolved moral disturbance about social work's necessary propinquity to the underclass' (Warner 2013b, p.216).

Further, Ofsted, which was first criticised at PMQs, came under scrutiny in the media. Ofsted's evaluations of Haringey Children's Services as 'good' consistently in six inspections in three years were questioned. Cameron and the media had equated a case of familial child homicide with a failing department. The assumption was that if a child is killed and an SCR is necessary, then services must be poor and so Ofsted had got it wrong. This claim was made despite many 'good' Children's Services in England having had a case of familial homicide. Ofsted was positioned as either in collusion with Haringey or incompetent: 'a three star report – a tortured child – Haringey's social services were lauded by inspectors despite the killing of baby P' (*Independent* 15/11/08, p.6). The *News of the World* (16/11/08, p.17) called for me and Ofsted officials to be sacked: 'they're all guilty', and '[s]ack them for sake of all kids'.

During Sunday afternoon the press reported that the ruling Labour Group of Haringey Council was in an emergency meeting. Little is known about the content of this meeting. Anecdotal reports from Labour group support staff suggested that there was much discussion, debate and angry disagreement. With the benefit of hindsight it is likely that the Leader of Haringey Council, George Meehan made clear his intention to resign and possibly an expectation that I should also resign. In effect, I suggest that Haringey Council made no fight-back against the many untrue claims being made in the media which could have been rebutted. The council may have been disturbed by the widening of the story to include their Head of Legal Services, who became the subject of the weekend press following the reporting of the questionable advice given by a solicitor in his team that there was insufficient evidence for a care order requested by Peter Connelly's social worker the month before Peter died. Also several aggressive demonstrations had already taken place outside Haringey Council offices including during council meetings and residents had threatened to withhold their council tax (*Belfast Telegraph* 17/11/08, p.3). I suggest that Haringey Council was now dependent upon the Labour government to help it out of the crisis. It is arguable that by Friday 14 November 2008 the (absent) 'voice' of Labour-led Haringey Council with a seconded government press officer was also the 'voice' of the Labour government. The lack of any dissenting comment from Haringey politicians supports this suggestion.

Lastly, some newspapers had begun to focus on the lack of a conviction for murder for Tracey Connelly, her boyfriend Steven Barker and his brother Jason Owen, yet there was no in-depth probing in these newspapers as to why there was no evidence to support a murder conviction. In the absence of a murder conviction the *News of the World* demanded that the maximum sentence of 14 years for causing or allowing a death should be handed down to those convicted (16/11/08, p.17) and *The Times* (13/11/08, p.3) suggested that 'there must be real questions about why they face only a maximum of 14 years...[h]ad they treated an adult in that way the verdict would surely have been murder and the sentence would surely have been higher'.

The responses of members of the public on day 5

Most readers of the *Sun* were in social classes C2DE and almost half were women. These readers are likely to have included recipients of welfare benefits and possibly also those who required the support of social workers. I argue that at least some of those who responded on social media sites were vulnerable themselves. By the weekend the many expressions of shock and distress continued: 'how could this have happened I have 3 kids of my own and I could never hurt any of them I don't understand how someone could hurt a child like that...' (Contributor 6, Group 2, 13/11/08); the degree of distress was profound in many cases: 'this makes me so angry...I lost my daughter she was born asleep' (Contributor 13, Group 2, 14/11/08). Also:

> when I heard this on the news, I cried, I then went into the room where my baby girl sleeps and felt this over whelming, desperate need to hold her close to me, she herself is 14 1/2 months old and the thought of someone hurting her makes me feel sick. *(Contributor 14, Group 2, 15/11/08)*

And:

> i have a little boy whos exactly the same age as baby p, wen i look at my son and see how much he needs his mummys love it breaks my heart to know wot baby p was going through wot went on in that little boys head wot can a little boy that age do so wrong to deserve that kind of punishment. i hope that the people who did this to him get beaten the shit out in prison, these people dont deserve 2 b on this earth wot gives them the right. and as for social services it is dicusting that they missed this little 1 having a broken back what pain he must have he been going through. its about time we did something about these kind of people like torture them and let them know wot this baby boy went through forget human rights they took this little boys human rights away when they started beating him, i could go on forever but it wouldnt bring him back r.i.p little baby p your in a better place now. and comeon gordon brown do something about this make sure it dosent happen again!! *(Contributor 15, Group 2, 14/11/08)*

This degree of distress and the anger, hatred and moral condemnation of social workers by the public was reminiscent of the behaviour of the women protesters in Portsmouth who attacked homes assumed to be those of paedophiles (Evans 2003, discussed in Chapter 3). In similar ways, these extreme outward expressions may not have explained the inner meaning of Baby P's death for some of these women. Their outward expressions may have been in Kleinian terms a projection of their own anxieties as mothers. One mother, for example, along with her young children, appears to address Baby P directly. Taken at 'face value' it is a mother telling her young children about a child who has been killed by his mother. In doing so she projects herself both as a good mother, and the good mother that Baby P never had:

> baby p my little boys and i read a book to you today and leo 2, he said she was a bad person wasnt she mummy and i said yes sweetie she was and he asked why she made baby p fall asleep and i had no answer for him, but he said that you would like it if you could live with him because you would be happy and you could play with his toys. good night baby peter and sleep well we are all thinking about you. *(Contributor 16, Group 2, 14/11/08)*

The postings on social media sites showed that the object of emotion was different for different individuals. For some it was grief for Baby P and a need to mourn. For others, from an object-relations perspective (discussed in Chapter 3), the circulation of affect may have brought back memories and insecurities that caused distress, for example for a child stillborn, a child never conceived, of their own childhood experiences of abuse, of going into the care of the state, of adoption from a childhood they knew as abusive or had no knowledge of, and for some the uncomfortable reality of their own parenting, and finally a dependency on the support of social workers who were being so heavily criticised in the media.

I argue that many of the actors in the aftermath of the news of Peter's death, including the public, will have had their own specific life experiences that the emotional object of the homicide of a young child may have 'attached to'. For example, Gordon Brown had suffered the loss of his baby daughter, David Cameron was experiencing the life-limiting medical condition of his young son who died a few months after these events, and Rebekah Brooks gave a moving account from the witness box of her own trial about her deep sadness at not being able to give birth to her own child (she had recently celebrated the arrival of her surrogate daughter). Many of those who posted on social media sites related the death of Baby P to their own life experiences and for some that caused varying degrees of stress. For my own part, with a self-perception of someone who cared deeply about children I found it impossible to bear the nation's blame for Peter's death.

The many expressions of anger and hostility directed at the social workers may have been a defence against other meanings. For example, for some these projections of anger may have enabled them to disown their own maternal ambivalence towards their own children which they could never consciously 'own', thereby relieving their anxiety. Following Evans (2003), who suggested that the Portsmouth protesters may have unconsciously identified with the paedophile, it may be in the case of Baby P that some of the women who felt so angry and aggressive towards the social workers identified with Peter's mother. Paraphrasing Evans (2003, p.177) (quoted in Chapter 3), it is possible that some of these women were 'disowning the aggressive and destructive anxieties about their own capacities and bad inner objects as mothers by projecting them onto the figure of the social worker'.

In grieving for Baby P, especially taking part in the vigil at his graveside may have been for some an expression of grief and an opportunity to mourn the loss of a young life. For others there may have been a degree of moral integrity which, in a similar way to the Portsmouth protesters, allowed some mothers to feel more in control. But at the same time they were injecting their vulnerability as mothers into their own children through the notion of the bad mother who let Baby P die.

In this way diverse patterns of meaning and feelings for a wide range of people were attached to the emotional object of the familial homicide of Baby P, but these emotions were displaced onto the figure of the social worker. These included a need to mourn, expressions of anger, vulnerabilities about their own parenting, or their own sense of loss. For some the story of Baby P will have been traumatic. But in all cases the public was responding to misleading information. Their responses had been shaped by the interdependencies of the tabloid media and politicians.

From virtual to actual presence on the streets

On Friday 14 November 2008, Facebook Groups 2 and 3 referred to the possibility of a protest march to Downing Street to seek justice for Baby P. This was reported in *London Lite* (14/11/08, pp.1/5), indicating that the suggestion may have come from the 'grassroots' rather than the media per se.

The move from the virtual to an actual presence on the streets was a significant development and by 16 November 2008 some of the plans had been published online. A vigil was planned for 4 December 2008 at the place where Peter's ashes had been scattered with a headstone provided by the *Sun*. A rally was to take place on Saturday 13 December 2008 at Trafalgar Square followed by a march to 10 Downing Street.

The shift from a 'virtual to actual' presence was potentially threatening and dangerous. Characteristics of 'virtual crowds' (discussed in Chapter 3) were emerging, with their complex fusion of passions and their inability to reason things out with forms of attachment which are primitive, shallow and persecutory (Bird 2003; Young 1995). For example, Bebo 1 (14/11/08): 'they [social workers] must have known this was going on'; Bebo 2 (15/11/08): 'you fucking bitch I hope you die' directed at me, and the next day, 'break her back see how she likes it'. Blog 2 (15/11/08): 'fuck off and die, you bitch' directed at me; and Blog 1 (14/11/08): 'she [Sharon Shoesmith] should have made these events impossible'.

The presence on the streets of mothers and children seeking justice for the death of Peter Connelly, I argue, was characteristic of the 'punitive populism' seen in the Portsmouth protests (Evans 2003, see Chapter 3) in which the government had become absorbed into a potentially highly volatile situation. At the core of events in Portsmouth and the aftermath of Baby P's death is the denial of crimes against children; in the case of Portsmouth it was paedophilia, and in the case of Baby P it was familial child homicide.

The date of Saturday 13 December 2008 for the march was significant since those convicted of causing or allowing Peter's death were due to be sentenced on 15 December 2008 and there had been questions about the absence of murder convictions and views about the possible leniency of the sentences. By 29 November, the date for sentencing had been postponed (*Sun* 29/11/08, p.9). Sentencing finally took place on 22 May 2009 after Tracey Connelly's boyfriend Steven Barker received a life sentence for the rape of a two-year-old, a subject I return to in Chapter 6.

The shift from a virtual to an actual presence on London's streets is likely to have been of serious concern to the government. What may have begun as 'punitive populism' now had the potential to spiral out of control. Jeanette Pugh, Director of Safeguarding for the DCSF at the time, gives some indication of these concerns when she described Ed Balls's perception of the level of public concern to be 'overwhelming and unprecedented'.[34]

But the interpretation of this public response as hostile may have been in error. The demonstration on 13 December became an expression of sadness and grief, and an opportunity to mourn that had been prevented in the media coverage, rather than any challenge to social workers or government. Albeit I had already been sacked, the demonstration was peaceful with approximately 300 mainly women and children who released doves and balloons. The anger expressed online was not in evidence on the street, suggesting that they were different groups or that the aggressive virtual behaviour was not transferred to actual behaviour. It may be that the march was dominated by a need to mourn rather than a need to seek retribution. This interpretation was borne out in the months to come when several YouTube videos were produced as tributes to the memory of Baby P.[35]

Uncertainty, power and familial child homicide

Government statistics cited earlier show that Peter Connelly had been one of 57 children who died as a result of familial child homicide in 2007. Between the deaths of Victoria Climbié and Peter Connelly, 416 children were victims of familial child homicide, and in the thirteen years that the Labour government was in power 612 children were victims. In the aftermath of Baby P's death the media reporting gave the public the impression that 'only' two children had died, Victoria and Peter.

My answer to the media question on 11 November, 'can you guarantee no more deaths?', had been the 'wrong' answer. Brown, Cameron and Balls gave the 'right' answer. Brown, from his economic summit in Washington, USA, answered, 'I'll make sure this never happens again' (*Daily Express* 15/11/08, p.15). Balls told the public, 'it is our duty to take whatever action is needed to ensure that such a tragedy does not happen again, that lessons are learned and that children in *Haringey* are safe' (*Evening Standard* 13/11/08, p.1, my emphasis), comments that implied that children were safe everywhere else and that Haringey was the exception. Finally, Cameron claimed, 'my biggest concern is how we stop this from ever happening again…it is an outrage that less than 10 years after the murder of Victoria Climbié – and more than three decades since the case of Maria Colwell – *another child* was left to slip through the safety net to their death' (*Sun* 13/11/08, p.9, my emphasis). His statement implies that familial child homicide should have ceased to be a problem. Since Maria Colwell died in 1973, using government statistics cited in Chapter 2, an estimated 2000 children have been victims of familial homicide.

Politicians (and others) talk about 'never events' and 'zero harm' but rarely acknowledge that these terms can only ever be aspirational. Never letting another child die are reassuring words, because harm to children touches most people so profoundly. Reassurance fortifies a human desire for certainty (see the discussion on p.117). Paradoxically, during this six-day period some of the realities of familial child homicide had appeared in the press but never came to prominence. For example, *The Times* on the day of the convictions (11/11/08, p.27) described the child protection system as 'a lethal mixture of bureaucracy, blame culture and fear of violence [which] blinds us to the horror that is staring us in the face'.

The *Daily Telegraph* (13/11/08, p.13) cited Brandon *et al.*'s (2008) research into 161 cases of abuse in which two-thirds of the children died, half of whom were under five years. But the journalist of the article is resigned to the developing narrative: 'as in the case of baby

P, governments call for reviews, Opposition politicians posture and declaim while citizens recoil in horror'. The *Observer* (16/11/08, p.33) suggested that 'people...find it hard to accept the realities of child abuse in the family'. The *Guardian* (15/11/08, p.1) considered the 29,200 children across the country on child protection registers, and the *Sunday Times* (16/11/08, p.18) told its readers that 'two children a week are killed as a result of physical abuse in the home' but despite that it continued to cooperate with the vilification of social workers by providing a link to the *Sun*'s petition.

In effect, the realities of familial child homicide are denied and blame is projected onto social workers. By Sunday 16 November 2008, six days after the public learned of the familial homicide of Peter Connelly, a simple narrative was in place. The death of Baby P was portrayed erroneously as the result of incompetent social workers, a rogue director and a hopeless local authority, in an otherwise sound system.

Conclusion

The narrative that social workers were to blame for the familial homicide of Baby P emerged in six days. The narrative was not a simple cause-and-effect relationship between the public's disavowal or denial of harm to children, and media reporting. Blaming social workers was defined, developed and exacerbated through the dynamic interaction of the media, politicians and members of the public. Together with a range of other historical, social, cultural and political influences discussed in previous chapters, blaming social workers had become embedded in cultural responses.

But the public was misled and misinformed by a network of knowledge that produced diverse patterns of meaning and feelings for different individuals. For some, the narrative denied an opportunity to express grief and to mourn for Baby P; for others, from an object-relations perspective discussed in Chapter 3, the narrative evoked insecurities that caused distress, including projections of anger and hostility towards social workers which defended their own parenting; and confusion for those reliant on the support of social workers, or whose lives had been transformed by social workers who were being so heavily criticised in the media. In some cases there was a discourse of retribution which, without a steadying influence, was potentially dangerous. The narrative placed the paediatrician, and especially the social workers and me, in personal danger.

A space of potential reasoning between 'knowing and not knowing' the realities of familial child homicide was increasingly denied. Knowing and not knowing is a defensive process of denial of the reality of what is seen or has come to be known. It is a reluctance or inability to know the shocking truth. From such a position a person can use 'perverse arguments' to deny or avoid the facts, in this case that social workers had stood by and watched the torture of Peter Connelly. The space between knowing and not knowing the reality of familial child homicide had become entirely inaccessible given the interactions of the media, the politicians and the shaping of the public response. By the weekend of 15 and 16 November the increasingly distressed, angry and vengeful responses of the public on social media sites, strengthened by the growth of the *Sun*'s petition, I argue, began to drive political responses.

Ed Balls had been well-positioned by the function of the 'cascade activation network', which describes the power of the complexities of the interactions between politicians, the media and the public, as the person who must act to bring the perceived public opprobrium to a close. In the next chapter I consider the implications of that process.

Chapter 6

The Identification of a Cultural Trope that Blames Social Workers for Harm to Children

Introduction

In the previous chapter I demonstrated the complexity and the potency of the narrative that developed in six days between 11 and 16 November 2008 which blamed Haringey social workers and me for the death of Baby P. In this chapter I identify the blaming (mainly) of social workers as 'a cultural trope' which I explain in more detail below. I argue that the cultural trope is both the cause and the effect of the interactions between the media, politicians and the public.

The cultural trope led to the construction of the Haringey Joint Area Review (JAR) 2008 which was the result of the Ofsted-led inspection ordered by Ed Balls and the second Serious Case Review (SCR2), both designed to bring closure to the perceived public opprobrium. The cultural trope is forged psychosocially in the dynamic interaction of denial, fear, anxiety, loyalty and defensiveness, leading to blame with far-reaching consequences.

Mediated populist engagement

The responses to the familial homicide of Baby P were a complex multi-layered, dynamic and fast-moving process of investments and dependencies between many individuals and organisations influenced by both time and place.

I argue that by the time the Ofsted inspection was about to commence, three working days after the public learned of Baby P's death, Rebekah Brooks and Ed Balls were increasingly dependent upon each other to achieve a 'successful' outcome. For example, the *Sun* was promoting a high-profile petition and campaign, and in my view Ed Balls was positioned at risk of damaging exposure in public if he failed to take an authoritative stance. In particular he risked the scorn of party politics from David Cameron, the leader of the Conservative Opposition, and Lynne Featherstone, Liberal Democrat MP, who each had their own engagement with the media and with the public. Balls also risked losing the endorsement of the *Sun* which was so essential to electoral success. At the same time Ofsted was vulnerable, having failed to challenge the assumption that Peter's death meant that their past grades of 'good' for Haringey were faulty. Further, Peter had died in 'sticky' Haringey with all of its connotations at a time when the Labour government was vulnerable on multiple fronts.

But transcending all this complex elite interdependency and investment was the issue of the UK public with whom these 'elites' had sought to engage. Rather than a linear relationship in which the media and/or politicians responded to the emotion of the public, I argue that the responses of the media and politicians in a process of 'mediated reflexivity' had the effect of creating and structuring an emotional public sphere which defined social workers as objects of anger and hostility.

In a process characteristic of Entman's 'cascade network of activation' (see Chapter 3), (mis)information about the life and death of Baby P flowed to the public initially from interactions between Cameron and Brooks then on to Brooks and Balls, and finally from Brooks to Balls to resolve. What was communicated to Ed Balls was 'packaged into selected framed communications' (see Chapter 5), that social workers were to blame and had to be sacked. This was a very different position from that represented in his press release only a week earlier (see page 136).

The power of the media, in particular the *Sun*, was demonstrated in the flow from Brooks to Balls created by the *Sun*'s petition. During the inspection in Haringey's Children's Services department and the drafting of the JAR report, the *Sun* published new daily totals of the numbers signing its petition. That number was reported by the *Sun* to have reached 1.4 million within 14 days suggesting that, on average, 100,000 people signed the petition each day. Such numbers signing a petition were unprecedented both before and since.

The petition had a forceful performative effect in establishing (erroneously) that social workers made 60 visits and, in doing so, they not only failed to save Peter but also they ignored evidence of 'torture'. Such a shocking message gave the petition agency. At the same time Brooks as the editor of the *Sun* in her editorial was pressing for my resignation. She used the power of rhetoric to imply that children in Haringey were at risk under my leadership: 'resign today so that a new boss can set about protecting them' (*Sun* 17/011/08, p.8).

The interdependency of Brooks and Balls was evident in a phone call from Brooks to Balls which, during the Leveson Inquiry, Brooks agreed had taken place. Brooks was asked: 'Did you telephone Mr Balls during the week commencing 17 November 2008 telling him to get rid of Sharon Shoesmith or they would 'turn this thing on him'?' (Leveson Inquiry 2012b, p.45). Brooks agreed that the call took place but she denied she used these words. She did agree that the *Sun* was campaigning for my resignation and also that of others. Later, Nick Davies, the *Guardian* journalist who exposed phone hacking, reported that a government official heard the calls from Rebekah Brooks to Ed Balls in which Brooks was pretty blunt with Balls telling him that he had to sack me. The official told Davies that Brooks was quite threatening in telling Balls that 'we don't want to turn this thing on you' (Davies 2004, p. 223).

The effects of the phone call appear to be reflected in the urgency with which Balls informed the House of Commons, on the evening of 17 November 2008, the same day that the Ofsted-led inspection began, that he would 'not hesitate to act on the findings of the inquiry', and 'where serious mistakes are made, there must be accountability', and that the findings of the Ofsted inspectors would be immediately published, implying that none of the established Ofsted protocols for inspection and publication would be observed (Hansard 17 November 2008, Column 16).

Next day, headlines in the *Sun* newspaper became much more accusatory: 'Heads must roll. And the first must be Haringey's shameless Sharon Shoesmith, whose arrogance doomed Baby P to a needless death...300,000 *Sun* readers have now signed our petition, Ms Shoesmith. And counting' (*Sun* 18/11/08, pp.5, 6). The *Sun*'s challenge to Balls to deliver an outcome that satisfied the public was visible in its 'insider knowledge'. It reported that 'the government is acting swiftly over the killing of Baby P', 'an emergency hit squad will be sent in to run Haringey social services next month', and 'officials stressed that Ministers do not have the power to sack officials' (*Sun* 18/11/08, p.6).

Given that 'Ministers do not have the power to sack officials', articles in the *Sun* focused instead on 'councils' and, I suggest, on Haringey Council: '[w]e want councils to use common sense, humanity and the powers they already possess to act promptly and save children from such depraved cruelty' (*Sun* 19/11/08, p.8). The message bestowed upon Haringey Council was a moral issue of saving children.

With the use of vivid metaphors the British people were positioned as in pain and in anger: 'a howl of anger', a 'deafening roar' of protest 'sweeping' Britain. This was pain that the child protection workers portrayed in mugshots as criminals apparently failed to share: they 'cling on shamelessly', '[t]he voice of Britain 'CANNOT be ignored' and 'the *Sun* will not rest' (*Sun* 20/11/08, pp.1, 8, capitals in the original).

In effect, these interactions suggest that Balls had succumbed to a risky relationship with the *Sun* newspaper. The public emotion mediated by the interdependency of the media and politicians, and based on misinformation, rapidly *became* the problem that Balls needed to bring to a close. The growing force of the public protest, public emotion or, as Balls reportedly referred to it, 'the public enclosure'[36] was presenting as a compelling force.

Distortions of 'public accountability'

Familial child homicide is a persistent social problem and Haringey Council was not alone in experiencing the death of another child known to its social workers. But, unlike other local authorities, for 'sticky' Haringey Council the death was shaping up as a fourth major crisis (see Chapter 1).

Haringey Council's Labour Leader George Meehan and lead councillor for children Liz Santry met with Children's Minister Beverley Hughes MP twice between 19 and 26 November. Even before the inspection was complete, according to the feedback I received, Hughes emphasised that the report would be deeply negative and, echoing Balls's words, claimed that they were 'looking for closure'.[37]

In less than a week from stating their confidence in me and the social workers, Meehan and Chief Executive Ita O'Donovan, after these meetings with Hughes, each invited my resignation as the only way they could see to bring closure. The emotion that each displayed seemed to reflect personal conflict in that O'Donovan and Meehan insisted that my resignation had nothing to do with my 'competence' or my record as a DCS, but was simply a case of my 'public accountability' and they would help me find another job. Their confidence in me was communicated in a letter on 13 November 2008 to Haringey's headteachers and all staff, and their support for me *prior to the outcome of the Ofsted report* was referred to in the Judicial Review.[38]

From my perspective there was a mismatch between what I was experiencing with the Ofsted inspection and O'Donovan's insistence that the JAR report would be negative, since the inspectors had not been critical in their briefings to me. This mismatch between O'Donovan's insistence that the report would be negative was repeated in the days to come in the media and it began to overwhelm me. I took the unusual step of sending a text message to the lead inspector seeking reassurance that the report would reflect the feedback I had had and would therefore contain positive comment. The text had been sent late one evening from a cafe when I was unable to go home because of the press presence outside my home. Later in court the text was revealed and used to mock me in the media. More importantly at the time, the request from Meehan and O'Donovan to resign was profoundly troubling.

Having spent a lifetime working for children, I was unable to countenance being held responsible for the murder of a child. My resignation would most certainly have signified personal responsibility and the many distortions of what had been reported in the media would remain unchallenged. I was being invited to take the blame, or to be the scapegoat, for the killing of Peter Connelly, presented as my 'public accountability', a view later rejected by the Court of Appeal.

I suggest that Labour-led Haringey Council looked for what appeared to be the security and protection of the Labour government. Undoubtedly this act would lead to the blaming or scapegoating of social workers and myself but would safeguard Haringey Council's 'survival', and avoid putting its recovered position in jeopardy by casting out the 'polluting matter' (see page 83) (Douglas 1984/1966). To have done otherwise would have defied the Secretary of State, potentially with more substantial consequences. Minutes of a meeting between Balls and Meehan on 1 December 2008, showed that just before Meehan resigned and I was sacked, Balls told Meehan that he was 'grateful for their cooperation over the past few weeks', demonstrating that Haringey Council had been brought 'on-side'.[39]

Bringing closure

To bring closure to the public opprobrium, I argue that Balls was in effect dependent on either Ofsted to deliver a judgment of 'inadequate' that targeted me, or on Haringey Council's ability to secure my resignation given they had no evidence with which to dismiss me. The 'second batch' of evidence disclosed to the Judicial Review by Ofsted after they discovered that they had failed to discharge their duty of candour to the court contained 17 drafts of the JAR report, commentary by the deputy director and reflections by the lead inspector in which she describes the inspection as 'an extremely busy and disorganised process'.[40] The evidence included emails and minutes of meetings between civil servants and Ofsted officials and indicated that communications had taken place between the head of Ofsted Christine Gilbert, and the Permanent Secretary of State David Bell (Gilbert's predecessor at Ofsted), and the Secretary Ed Balls, concerned with the process of producing the JAR report through 17 drafts. This was highly unusual and inappropriate since Ofsted is an organisation supposed to be independent of government.[41]

The final Haringey JAR 2008 (Ofsted 2008a) judged services to safeguard children in Haringey as 'inadequate'. Similarly the grades for the first SCR and for Haringey's Annual Performance Assessment (APA) 2008 (Ofsted 2008e) were judged 'inadequate'. Six years later an anonymous Ofsted inspector told the BBC1 documentary *The Untold Story of Baby P* that the Haringey APA 2008 had been graded 'good' before the news of the death of Baby P was known, but once the news was known had been rewritten to reflect a grade of 'inadequate'.

Communications between the most senior civil servants in the DCSF and senior Ofsted officials continued throughout the inspection and during the week in which the report was written, evident in email exchanges. These include references to telephone calls between Ed Balls and Christine Gilbert, and in the minutes of two meetings.[42] For example, on day three of the four-day inspection, in an email exchange between David Bell (DCSF Permanent Secretary) and Jeanette Pugh (DCSF Director of Safeguarding), Bell was concerned to deflect the media's attention from three issues that would be supportive to Haringey.[43]

First, the SCR for Peter Connelly had been 'evaluated' by Ofsted as 'inadequate' but officials in Bell's department had seen several drafts, including the final draft, and raised no concerns.

Second, Bell appeared concerned that the names of 38 other local authorities which had had SCRs evaluated by Ofsted as 'inadequate' were due to be published on the same day as the Haringey JAR (Ofsted 2008b), making the grade of 'inadequate' for Haringey's SCR not unique to Haringey.[44] Further, one of the 38 belonged to Hampshire whose Director of Children's Services John Coughlan had just been sent to Haringey to 'secure child protection' (see Chapter 5).

Third, notwithstanding the fact that Haringey's SCR had been accepted by his officials, Bell was further concerned that many other authorities that had an 'inadequate' SCR were also evaluated by Ofsted in their inspections as 'good' (which was the case in Haringey). This apparent mismatch of grades is the crux of the criticisms of Ofsted by politicians and in the press in relation to Haringey. There was therefore the potential for a much greater 'crisis' particularly related to public confidence in Ofsted. Bell told Pugh:

> we feel weak on this one [the third point] so we'll need to do a bit more on this and decide whether there is further action that needs to be taken before a week on Monday/Tuesday (1/2 December 2008 when Ed Balls is due to publish the Haringey JAR and Ofsted publishes a report on other SCRs).

In effect, this evidence was incongruent with the developing narrative that Haringey Council's Children's Services were uniquely bad. Bell outlined in the email the 'lines to take' he had discussed with Jeremy Heywood, who was chief of staff to Prime Minister Gordon Brown. The plan was for Ed Balls to manage this *after* the Haringey JAR was published so that 'this issue can be dealt with 'defensively' [with the media] if required on the back of the oral statement [to be made by Balls]'.

Bell suggested that 'Ed may wish to phone Christine [Gilbert] to confirm that those areas [that have inadequate SCRs] would not be named (until later and after he had dealt with Haringey).' Finally Bell told Pugh with reference to his phone call to Christine Gilbert, that 'Christine remains in no doubt as to what Ofsted needs to do with the [Haringey] inspection.' In the minutes of a meeting between DCSF and Ofsted officials that took place on the last day of the inspection, conversations between Balls and Gilbert were discussed in which it was reported that Gilbert had been urged by Balls to ensure that 'the report must be clear in its judgments and attribution of responsibility' and it needed to deliver 'definitive evidence on which the Minister can act.'[45]

These interactions suggest that Ofsted's top team knew well before the inspection was complete that there could be only one outcome: a grade of 'inadequate' and a targeting of me as head of the service.

Aspects of the drafting of the Haringey JAR 2008 are referred to in the High Court judgment at paragraphs 424–476. The drafting not only reflected the developing narrative that social workers were to blame but it increasingly attached negative comment to me as leader of Haringey Council's Children's Services. The drafting progressed through 17 drafts over seven days with multiple contributors. The emails attached to different drafts showed that the majority of the contributors to the Haringey JAR 2008 had never been part of the inspection team and had never been to Haringey Council.

Emails attached to several of the drafts also showed that team inspectors who had been to Haringey objected to new negative judgments being added to the report by others and they complained that there was no evidence to support some judgments and in some cases they provided contradictory evidence. For example, in a response to an early draft a team inspector wrote in an email dated 25 November 2008 that comments on audits were, 'too harsh, they [Haringey] do have a system of themed audits and can show evidence of these findings being reported back.' By the next day both the team inspectors gave detailed feedback on a further draft, they commented on performance management saying, 'they also have these, for example, supervision, recording, themed audits and departmental audits.' But the published report read, 'performance management arrangements across agencies are insufficiently robust' (Ofsted 2008b para 40). The team inspectors objected to the deletion of a positive paragraph on supervision and on the negative comments on policy and practice stating, '[w]e are not clear that we found this', '[o]verall policies and procedures were OK'. Crucially they objected to criticisms of the working of the LSCB telling senior Ofsted officers that '[the LSCB] has taken an appropriate lead in identifying key safeguarding issues of concern to children, young people and their families and has worked across agencies to tackle these issues'. Finally they had much to say about a recommendation in the draft to 'urgently establish more secure assessment and intervention strategies' saying 'we are struggling to understand this recommendation, their [Haringey's] processes are OK.' They advised that these criticisms of the quality of assessments could not be evidenced and they gave examples of good assessments. On comments about the need for all elected members to have CRB (Criminal Records Bureau) checks, they raised the point that this recommendation was not in line with government policy and asked 'is this policy on the hoof?' But their objections were consistently disregarded.

Following this feedback on Wednesday 26 November, the team members, including the deputy lead inspector, did not see the report again until after it was published. The deputy lead inspector retained some parts of the draft report and in subsequent emails indicated her concern that they did not have the evidence to support the judgments in the management section of the report. Nevertheless, the drafting and redrafting continued to add unsubstantiated negative evidence and to remove positive comment. The negativity of the drafting escalated dramatically after the *Sun* delivered its petition to 10 Downing Street on Wednesday 26 November 2008, the same day that Balls secured the appointment of my successor,[46] and well before the report had been finalised.

The agency of the *Sun*'s petition was writ large in the image on national television of four men dragging heavy sacks along Downing Street to reach No. 10. The sacks were alleged to contain 1.4 million signatures. The image provided a powerful performative message of the symbolic weight of the 'voice of Britain'. In response, Ed Balls visited the *Sun*'s offices and was photographed looking at the petition under a headline of 'Power of your feeling is clear' in which he appeared to address the petitioners themselves, telling them:

> '[a]ll of us are finding it impossible to understand how adults could commit such acts of evil against a little boy', 'everyone is angry' ... 'I will not hesitate to act [when the report is received].' *(Sun 27/11/08, p.5)*

This was understandably a statement about the unbelievable nature of familial child homicide that most people, including social workers, could align with. But, in Kleinian terms (see Chapter 3), Balls could be described as 'splitting away' from the anguish and horror of Peter's death, to find some kind of 'rational explanation' by focusing the anger on someone, and I suggest this was Haringey Council social workers including myself.

In Cohen's (2001) terms (see Chapter 3) it may have been a case of 'interpretative denial' in which the reality of familial child homicide is accepted but the meaning is denied.

Or following Rustin (2005, p.17) (see Chapter 3), it may be that Peter's plight gave rise to a 'psychic retreat' given the 'intense feelings stirred up by exposure to human cruelty and madness', a suggestion Rustin made about those who had seen Victoria Climbié.

Or in Cooper's (2014b) (see Chapter 3) terms it may have been the absence of a discourse to communicate emotionally indigestible facts that led instead to blame. Undoubtedly familial child homicide stirred up unpalatable feelings for the public, but it did so also for social workers and other professionals, most especially for those who knew Peter.

I argue that blaming social workers was an easy response that had become habitual. Social workers were expected by the public to carry the anguish that no one else could face. Crucially, social workers seemed willing to take on this role in seeing themselves as 'containers' for the grief the public was unable to process (Cooper 2010).

The published version of the Haringey JAR (Ofsted 2008a) was constructed around three alleged set of findings: the vulnerability of children, the inadequacy of leadership and management, and the urgent need for DCSF intervention.

The performative effect of the redrafting positioned vulnerable children 'at risk' and in need of 'urgent and sustained attention' (Ofsted 2008a Summary Judgment, p.3). The use of rhetoric such as 'fail to identify' and 'immediate risk' gave a sense of children in grave danger and at urgent risk of suffering the same fate as Peter Connelly. As late as four hours before the end of the inspection senior civil servants had insisted that, even though the inspection had not looked at the case of Baby P, it was essential that the report made reference to his case in order to bring closure to the public opprobrium. To fulfil this requirement five paragraphs from the evaluation of the first SCR which had not been written by any of the inspectors on the team were added to the inspection report (Haringey JAR 2008, paras 8–12). Further, no inspector had ever spoken with Peter's social worker about his case, or any other case that inspectors looked at during the inspection.[47]

With a 'finding' that vulnerable children were 'at risk', the 'judgment' that leadership and management were 'inadequate' followed and created the 'need' for *immediate* government intervention explaining the urgency of Balls's action in removing me from post. Yet the DCSF knew that Peter Connelly had died 15 months earlier and saw no need for such action then. Joanne Warner (2015, p.113) in her discussion of 'emotional politics' argues that 'official documents can be understood as emotionally active in terms of the way they reflect and generate emotional responses'. The Haringey JAR was 'emotionally active'. The published Haringey JAR offered (entirely erroneously) an *explanation* to the public of how and why Peter Connelly died, and a justification of all the action taken designed to bring closure.

On live television on 1 December 2008 Ed Balls outlined the urgent and sustained attention needed to improve outcomes for children at risk in Haringey and referred directly to me by my job title as 'not fit for office'. The words used by Balls were not drawn from the published report or from Ofsted's Record of Inspection Evidence (ROE); the words were his own.[48] He had used them, I argue, to demonstrate his authority and to silence the perceived 'public enclosure'. Balls described the findings in the report as 'devastating' and the failures that led to Peter's death as 'unforgivable', implying that Peter's death was my fault. In doing so he referred to 'the force' of the *Sun*'s petition in bringing about this outcome.[49] I was removed from my statutory post by Ed Balls on 1 December 2008, dismissed by Haringey Council a week later, and lost my appeal to Haringey Council on 12 January 2009. Mr Justice Foskett suggested that the Appeal Panel of Haringey Councillors that dismissed me on that day:

> might not have been quite so confident in their decision to accept some aspects of the report without question and quite so confident in their decision to dismiss [me and others] without compensation had they known of the problems with the inspection and the process by which the final report assumed the form it did.[50]

My sacking delivered a strong message not only that children in Haringey were at risk and that I was incompetent, but also it confirmed all the (mis)information in the media about the conduct of social workers. At its extreme, social workers were wrongly accused of standing by while a child was tortured.

The case of Baby P became another watershed in the history of children's social care. The impact was far-reaching, for example: in the 'Baby P effect', which described the rise in the number of children brought into care (see Chapter 1); in the recruitment and retention of social workers, which became problematic; and in Haringey Council, where social workers left in such numbers that the new Director had to make an appeal to other London DCSs to 'lend' him staff.[51] None of these effects had been seen in the period between Peter's death in August 2007 and the reactions of the media and politicians which began in November 2008.

For members of the public, especially those who depended upon the support of social workers, the impact is likely to have been traumatic, especially given that social workers had been positioned as not acting to save Peter from 'known abuse'. My findings show that some members of the public who contributed to social media sites sought opportunities to express their sorrow and grief. This suggests that there may have been a space of reasoning between 'knowing and not knowing' the realities of familial child homicide that could have enabled a different way to manage the public emotion. Further, it suggests that the 'public enclosure' that Balls perceived, and which he sought ways to close down, may have been less cohesive and less threatening than it appeared. What is notable is that Ed Balls and his department, on the one hand, did not anticipate these effects, and on the other they appeared unable to take any other approach. Whilst Balls, in his initial press release, appeared to set out to take a different approach, the complexities of the interdependencies of the media and party politics were so powerful that any attempt to provide a steadying influence was lost.

Identifying and defining the cultural trope

At the core of this complex process of blaming social workers is the persistent denial or disavowal of familial child abuse and homicide, especially when it involves the mother. Blaming social workers for such harm to children is a defensive process of denial which provides individuals with a kind of 'psychic retreat' (Steiner 1993). Steiner's psychic retreat is a state of simultaneously 'knowing and not knowing' the reality of what is happening. But this psychic retreat of blaming social workers is not entirely characteristic of Steiner's psychic retreat or his notion of 'knowing and not knowing' as an *unconscious* psychological state (Steiner 1993).

This psychosocial process of denial is more characteristic of Cohen's (2001) threefold model of literal, interpretative or implicatory denial; and especially interpretative and implicatory denial as discussed in Chapter 3. I question the presence of the literal denial of the reality that mothers can inflict harm on their children such that the child dies. More often there is a realisation of the reality of crimes against children, but the information provided by the media and politicians, and the outcome of inquiries into cases of child abuse, contribute to a sense of interpretative denial. The use of justifications, rationalisations and evasions described by Cohen in the context of familial child homicide conveys the message that professionals, usually social workers, failed to save the child and are held responsible. Lastly, there might be awareness of the realities of crimes against children but the implications are denied, for example: the inability of social workers to protect all children; the negative effects of social policies; or the circumstances of each case of familial child homicide. The dynamic interaction of interpretative and implicatory denial suggests a 'knowing' about familial child abuse but a simultaneous denial or a 'need not to know'.

I argue that blaming social workers for harm to children has become a habitual process of denying the realities of familial child abuse and homicide. That social workers are to blame has been forged and embedded as a belief, a reality, a truism or 'trope'. A 'trope' in literature is a word or expression used in a figurative or symbolic sense. It refers to a theme that is important and recurrent. The theme becomes overused such that it becomes a motif or cliché. A trope, in effect, is devoid of thought or reason. Referring to the blaming of social workers as a trope draws attention to the recurring nature of the blame which has become habitual and devoid of reason.

This trope that blames social workers is embedded in the signs, symbols, meanings and values developed over many decades through the interaction with social, historical, cultural and political factors discussed in Chapters 2 and 4 and demonstrated in this chapter and Chapter 5. I argue therefore that the term 'cultural trope' captures the dynamic interaction of the persistent denial of familial child abuse and homicide with these broad cultural influences. The cultural trope is essentially a defence, a state of 'knowing and not knowing' about harm to children. It is a psychosocial entity, but it is not fixed. It is shaped and defined by time, place and circumstance. It is unpredictable. It clings most often, but not always, to social workers. In Chapter 1, following Ahmed (2004), I described Haringey Council as 'sticky' to describe how it attracted negative connotations which simply attached to it, and began to function as a form of 'common knowledge'. In similar ways social workers have become 'sticky'. Other professionals, especially health professionals, can be the subject of the cultural trope, but it is social workers who most often attract blame.

The cultural trope in the case of Baby P was so embedded that Ed Balls could not have told the public that 57 other children had also died in the same year as Peter Connelly, or that Peter had died some 15 months earlier when investigations found that no Haringey social workers should lose their job, or that Victoria and Peter were not the only victims of familial child homicide but that 416 other children had also been victims in the seven years between their deaths. Such shocking statistics, hitherto unknown by the public, including many social workers, may have challenged the integrity of the Labour government, by then in its third term, and Balls's role as Secretary of State for the Department for Children, Schools and Families (DCSF).

Instead, in an act of 'indexing', Ed Balls and Gordon Brown, alongside the Opposition leader David Cameron, chose to reassure the public that 'this would never happen again' and in doing so further contributed to the media's portrayal of Peter's death as an exception and the result of a rogue local authority, a rogue director and incompetent social workers. Many in the social work profession will have known the futility of these claims but few had the courage to publicly confront them. In the hostile climate that had developed, to have challenged the cultural trope that blamed the social workers for the death of Peter Connelly would have risked being accused of failing to condemn his 'brutal murder'.

The interaction of the country's most senior politicians and top civil servants with the senior team of the regulator Ofsted, in effect, demonstrated the power of the cultural trope in the degree to which these most senior officials in both the DCSF and Oftsed became engaged in steering the outcome of an inspection. Such collaboration was well outside their organisations' protocols, perhaps giving some sense of the strength of the dynamics between the media, politicians and the public. Civil servants and Ofsted officers, appear to have become absorbed into a process which focused on ways to present Haringey Council's Children's Services as 'uniquely bad': a position that found congruency with the media and hence with the public.

To accuse these actors of deceit, dishonesty or collusion would be both unhelpful and simplistic. Organisational culture, and especially the embeddedness of the cultural trope, were both the cause and the effect of their responses to the familial homicide of Peter Connelly. Some of these actors will not have questioned the processes their organisations will have drawn them into, others will have been uncomfortable with what was unfolding, and some will have blamed others. Some may have believed that social workers *were* to blame, or believed 'the evidence' that blamed them. It may be that for some there was a sense of not being responsible for, or in control of, what was taking place: of being a small player swept along in a bigger event, or a member of a group or organisation that could only defer to the leader. The likelihood is that the layers of complex denial were so great that few quite knew where reality lay.

The potency of the cultural trope

The cultural trope that blamed social workers in the case of Baby P was intoxicating, persuasive and deeply potent with far-reaching effects. Three examples illustrate this claim. The first concerns the continuing dilemma for Ofsted after it published the Haringey JAR 2008, in answering questions from politicians and the press about perceived discrepancies between its previous inspection grades for Haringey of 'good' and the more recent grade of 'inadequate'; the second concerns presentations in court by Ofsted inspectors almost a year after the inspection; and the third concerns the second Serious Case Review (SCR2) ordered by Ed Balls.

Ofsted's accusation of deceit

In an attempt to defend Ofsted, Christine Gilbert, in an interview which appeared as headline news on the front page of the *Guardian* ('We failed over Haringey', *Guardian* 6/12/08), explained Ofsted's previous grades of 'good' by claiming that 'officials in the local authority where Baby P died were able to 'hide behind' false data last year to earn themselves a good rating from inspectors', describing this as 'deceit'. The claim was challenged by the Society of Local Authority Chief Executives (SOLACE)[52] and the allegation against officers in Haringey Council was never evidenced despite demands from the Parliamentary Select Committee on 10 December 2008 and from my Counsel during the Judicial Review in 2009.

Psychosocially this is an example of the far-reaching effects that were both the cause and the effect of the cultural trope that blames social workers. This was the 'knowing and not knowing' the reality of Peter's brutal murder which had become so complex that these actions were examples of Cohen's (2001) justifications, rationalisations and evasions characteristic of denial. The claims of Ofsted, despite challenges from the Select Committee, were never rigorously questioned by the media, given that they had congruence with the public view. With all that had gone before, these accusations 'made sense'.

Presentations in court

The second example of the potency of the cultural trope concerns presentations to the court by Ofsted inspectors almost a year after the inspection. The team inspector and his colleague had made the following contemporaneous observation of systems in the Haringey 'duty room' which managed referrals of vulnerable children:

> [s]ound administrative processes in place giving good support to ensuring that all new referrals are inputted into the IT system in a timely way (same day), admin staff pass all new referrals and all notifications from the police to duty team managers for decision and allocation on the same day. Constant flow of work but no backlog of work and admin found workload manageable. *(Ofsted Record of Evidence no.554 written on 17 November 2008)*

These processes in the 'duty room' were judged 'good', but the team inspector told the court that he and his colleague were 'very concerned about what we had found in relation to the cases we inspected during the duty room inspection.'[53] The team inspector added that the 'duty-room' observations 'gave rise to extremely serious concerns', and inspectors 'raised cases of clear abuse that had apparently not triggered child protection procedures'. These statements were in contrast to the team inspectors' observations in the duty room and to the briefings given to me during the inspection which did not raise such serious concerns. Further, one of the team inspectors told the court that 'we did not consider that we had identified any cases of children in immediate danger, such that would justify urgent action to obtain immediate protection',[54] which seemed to contradict these earlier statements and the 'urgent' action that was taken at the time.

The difference between what the inspectors recorded at the time and their objections to the redrafting of judgments in the JAR, and their conflicting views expressed later in court are stark. This may have been a case of loyalty to Ofsted, a fear of losing their jobs, or a sense that given all that had been reported in the press and by politicians that they had made errors themselves. Psychosocially the differences may have represented an absorption into the compelling nature of the cultural trope that defined their responses, along with many others, to Peter's death. Whichever it was, I argue that the potency of the cultural trope was such that this evidence was neither a defence of Haringey Council and its social workers, nor their own findings. The media reporting and the government response represented by the actions of Ed Balls had the capacity to confuse what was real or imagined. Besides, almost a year later and in light of all that had occurred, could any position other than that social workers were responsible be defended? Borrowing from Kitzinger (2004, p.215), the cultural trope had the ability to 'alter the landscape inside [our] heads'.

The 'official' Serious Case Review (SCR2)

The last of the three examples of the potency of the cultural trope concerns the second Serious Case Review (SCR2), regarded as the official SCR, ordered by Ed Balls. On 30 April 2009 Peter's social worker, her manager and two more senior staff had been very publicly dismissed, following new investigations ordered by Balls. The next day, Graham Badman, Ed Balls's appointee as chair of Haringey's LSCB, announced to the media that SCR2 had found 'no new evidence but it had come to different conclusions...the death [of Peter Connelly] could and should have been prevented.'[55] Subsequently the summary of SCR2 was published on 22 May 2009. I argued in Chapter 4 that SCRs became a proxy for the blaming of social workers and this was a stark demonstration of invoking the notion of prediction and prevention.

However, by October 2010, in what could be seen as an act of mediated party politics, the incoming Conservative Minister for Children Tim Loughton decided to respond to the demands of the *Sun* newspaper which Ed Balls was resisting, and to publish the full version of SCR2 (usually kept confidential to protect children and families and to encourage dialogue between agencies). Haringey's Local Safeguarding Children Board also contested Loughton's decision and won the support of the Information Commissioner. But the publication of the full SCR2 went ahead and provided significant, new information. The full SCR2 ('the official' SCR) for Baby P, which presumably the panel would never have expected to be published, told a different story from what the SCR2 panel chose to tell the public in the SCR2 summary. For example, it became clear that a report (Sibert Report 2008) which was highly critical of Great Ormond Street Hospital (GOSH) had not been provided to the SCR2 panel (neither had it been provided to the first SCR). GOSH had held the paediatrician to account, but the Sibert Report contained many significant criticisms of GOSH services provided in Haringey. Significantly, the report indicates that the paediatrician was 'standing in' for an absent colleague in a clinic she was not qualified for (Sibert 2008, pp.5–7). The BBC London documentary, *Great Ormond Street: Too Important to Fail* explored the detail of the context of GOSH paediatric services in Haringey and the problems in the case of Baby P in particular.[56] Further, London's Metropolitan Police Service (MPS) had undertaken two investigations of the conduct of police in the case of Baby P reported to their Strategic and Operational

Policy Committee both written by the lead detective of the murder investigation and panel member for SCR2. Both have the same title, *MPS Response to the Death of Baby P*, the first dated 4 December 2008 and the second, more detailed, version dated 8 January 2009. The MPS also received a Police Inspection Report written by the HMIC inspector as part of the Haringey JAR 2008. All three reports identified serious failings by the police which were not fully reflected in the summary of SCR2 or the published Haringey JAR 2008. These police reports were referred to in a BBC London report in April 2009 which investigated the hitherto unknown errors made by the police in the case of Baby P.[57]

Crucially, I suggest that all this new evidence would have made a material difference to the social workers, the paediatrician and myself who all lost our jobs. The Sibert Report would have provided defensive evidence, especially for the paediatrician but also for the social workers; and the evidence in the three police reports exposed the police mismanagement of the case and importantly did not support the many claims made by police in the media about the conduct of social workers, especially in relation to events in June 2007, as detailed below.

On 1 June 2007 Peter's social worker had made an unannounced visit to the Connelly home. She saw bruises on Peter's face and made a referral to the police of suspected physical abuse. In their contribution to the SCR1 report the police suggested that the marks on Peter 'could easily appear to have been caused by normal child's play and could give credence to the mother's version' (SCR1 Police Internal Management Review, para. 6.32). That is, the police suggested that the injuries could have been accidental. This position was in stark contrast to the account in the *full* SCR2 which is critical of police conduct in relation to the same incident:

> [t]he police held strongly to the view that the injuries were *non-accidental* [in June 2007] but they did not do their duty by accepting the responsibility to investigate the injuries. They left it to the social worker who is not trained in criminal investigation work. Neither did the police undertake a joint investigation with the social worker. *(SCR2 Full Report, para. 3.16.2, my emphasis)*

Of the same incident, the Police Inspection Report states:

> there was evidence of social workers effectively carrying out initial investigations on behalf of the police. This appeared to be the case in the initial stages of the [investigation of the] allegation made on [Friday] 1/06/2007 when the social worker did the preliminary work, the investigation not being pro-actively pursued [by the police] until the following Monday (4/06/07).

But the SCR2 *summary* which was published takes a different stance. It stated that:

> [t]he police were informed and elected not to undertake a joint investigation but to allow the social worker to look into it and call them in if she felt that they [the police] had a role. *(SCR2, para. 3.53)*

Overall, the SCR2 summary prepared for public consumption presented a markedly different account of the police case. It gave no account of the negative evidence that was documented in the full SCR2 and stated:

> [t]he police were only informed and involved at two stages. At other times matters were assessed by the social worker alone or by the doctor alone, *denying* the police the opportunity to assess whether a crime had been committed and deciding whether to investigate it… [i]n relation to the 1 June visit, the police were informed but asked the social worker to assess the situation and inform them of the outcome, when they would decide whether an investigation was justified. *This helps to create an unhelpful culture in which other services use discretion about involving the police. (SCR2 Summary, para. 4.5.1, my emphasis)*

Further, Ofsted, in March 2009, long after the events of November 2008, evaluated SCR2 as 'good' and the police contributions as 'excellent' despite the differences between the SCR2 summary and SCR2 full report. Ofsted made no challenge to these discrepancies. The evidence suggests that SCR2 is so flawed that Ofsted's evaluation cannot be regarded as a reliable account. In Chaper 4 (page 113) I reported Laming's criticisms of the quality of Ofted's evaluations of SCRs.

Ed Balls's demands for a second SCR (SCR2) and Tim Loughton's decision to publish the full SCR2 had exposed the errors of GOSH and the MPS. But when the full SCR2 was published in October 2010, few in the media or politics paid it much attention. Reporting simply repeated earlier claims that social workers were to blame. The media had brought closure to the case and had in effect failed in its purported role to hold power to account by failing to consider other 'frames'. The process of 'indexing' discussed earlier made it unlikely that the media would challenge this 'official account'.

In the aftermath of Peter's death, both GOSH and the MPS should each have been concerned about their conduct in the case. GOSH had failed to provide a specialist medical appointment for Peter Connelly for over four months (Sibert Report 2008, p.14); and simultaneously the police failed to allocate Peter's case to a police officer for almost three months, resulting in a decision, taken only the day before Peter died, to drop all charges against Peter's mother. A close comparison between the SCR2 summary and SCR2 full report shows how these serious issues were deflected, tempered, altered, omitted and contradicted in the SCR2 summary which had been prepared for public consumption. Once again the power of the cultural trope that blamed social workers was sustained such that the shortcomings of the police and health could not only be suppressed but also did not attract significant attention in the tabloid media, which had focused its efforts on targeting social workers.

I believe that many of the individuals involved in producing the Haringey JAR and the SCR2 'turned a blind eye' (see page 79) to what was taking place. This 'turning a blind eye', whether conscious or not, was forged psychosocially in the interaction of denial, fear, anxiety, loyalty, defensiveness, and may later have given rise to guilt for some. These processes perpetuated the blaming and scapegoating of social workers and damaged the social work profession.

How far-reaching is the cultural trope?

Further in-depth scrutiny of the police reports raises questions about the far-reaching nature of the cultural trope. The police, I argue, had significantly influenced the responses of the media, politicians and the public to the death of Baby P in statements made to the media. Numerous examples are referred to in Chapter 5, including briefings by civil servants for ministers which overlooked the conduct of the police in the case, and of David Cameron supporting the role of the police using misleading 'evidence' appearing in the media.

The two police reports to the MPS Strategic and Operational Policy Committee and the Police Inspection Report raise concerns about the exchange of information and intelligence between the police, Haringey Child Abuse Investigation Team (CAIT) and also the police Violent Crime Directorate (VCD) which included the Multi-Agency Public Protection Arrangements (MAPPA), concerned with potentially dangerous persons. MAPPA in Haringey was chaired by the Borough Commander of police, who also sat on the panel for SCR2. The Police Inspection Report suggests that there were 'significant opportunities being missed to include the use of [MAPPA] processes to assist in the management of risks presented to children by individuals falling within these categories' (Police Inspection Report, p.7).

Inspection of the MAPPA had also raised issues for the lead Ofsted inspector at the outset of the inspection, evident in emails to her colleagues on 14 and 15 November 2008. The lead inspector was concerned that the police inspector was insisting that she need not interview anyone from MAPPA even though she thought that such a decision would 'provide limited evidence on the actual effectiveness on the ground of joint working in these areas from a police perspective'. The lead inspector commented to her colleagues that she was unsure as to why the police inspector was 'so reluctant to look at the MAPPA arrangements...this was clearly a sticking point in our meeting, and seems to continue to be one. It is a mystery.' Clearly this was of concern to the Ofsted lead inspector as she would rightly expect the MAPPA arrangements to be included.

The apparent reluctance of the police inspector to interview officers from the MAPPA, her subsequent concerns about communication between the MAPPA and officers in the CAIT and the evidence in the two police reports raise questions. For example, was the behaviour of the police, which was notable in consistently blaming social workers, a process of avoiding negative publicity? Did the MAPPA have knowledge of the men who were living in the Connelly household which was not communicated to the CAIT or, if it was, was its significance not understood?

A murder conviction had not been obtained for the death of Peter Connelly and the date of sentencing for 'causing or allowing' Peter's death was postponed from 15 December 2008 when press and public began to question why there was no murder conviction and therefore the potential leniency of the sentence for 'causing or allowing' his death. At the same time members of the public were suggesting a public demonstration (see Chapter 5).

Barker was convicted of rape on 1 May 2009, which was the same day as Graham Badman, chair of the Haringey LSCB, briefed the media about the findings of SCR2, and a day after four social work staff were sacked, making news headlines. Ten days later the Care Quality Commission published a highly critical report (CQC 2009) into the conduct of the health services, especially GOSH, in the case of Baby P, but little connection was made by the media between the CQC, their report and the events that had already taken place. By 22 May 2009 the summary of SCR2 was published and on the same day Tracey Connelly and Jason Owen each received indeterminate periods of imprisonment, Connelly for a minimum term of five years and Owen for three years. Steven Barker received 12 years for causing or allowing Peter's death to run concurrently with a life sentence for the rape of a two-year-old child. The minimum term was 20 years with 10 years before he could be considered for parole. The trial for rape had taken place under strict instructions of no press coverage.

I argue that the sentence had strong congruence with the public opinion and brought an end to questions of why there was no murder conviction in the case of Peter Connelly. In that context it had parallels with the process of 'punitive populism' which Evans (2003) argued enabled the public, the media and politicians to have a greater role in determining sentencing and penal policy.

The inquest for Peter Connelly

Lastly, there was no inquest for Peter Connelly. An inquest hearing had been opened on 10 August 2007, and during 2010 the coroner held three pre-inquest hearings to determine whether the inquest needed to proceed. The MPS, Haringey Council, GOSH and the family doctor all made representations against the inquest proceeding. Requests for an inquest from Peter's father, his mother and Steven Barker were all turned down. The MPS made extensive submissions consisting of 43 separate documents which they stressed demonstrated the range and quantity of reports that had already been written. The two police reports and the Police Inspection Report discussed above were not among the documents.

In their submission to the coroner of 18 October 2010, the police held that the case had been the subject of 'the most extensive and independent public investigation' and that 'those responsible for [Peter Connelly's death] have been identified and made subject to either criminal or professional disciplinary procedures'.[58] The list included the names of the individuals – the doctor, social workers, elected councillors and me – who had resigned, been disciplined and/or been sacked, detailing allegations and outcomes for each. No police officer was listed as no officer had been disciplined or lost their job.

In reality, there had been no independent public investigation of Peter Connelly's death. The Haringey JAR 2008 was not an investigation into Peter's death. The SCR1 and SCR2 reports were the only reviews of the conduct of public services into Peter Connelly's death made public at that time, and my analyses have raised issues about the integrity of these reports. Further, the pre-inquest hearing heard that police contributions to SCR1 and SCR2 had been judged 'good' and 'excellent' respectively by Ofsted, and that the SCR reports and the Haringey JAR 2008 had no recommendations for the police. This was not representative of SCR2 full or summary reports previously discussed.

In considering whether an inquest was necessary, senior coroner Andrew Walker outlined in his report the two questions he was required to answer: 'By what means did Peter Connelly come to his death?' and 'In what circumstances did he die?'[59] The police gave a very clear response to the two questions in their submission of 29 October 2010:

> [t]he direct cause of Peter's death is well established, as is the identity and roles of the immediate authors of his death. *The failures of State agencies and individuals preceding his death are equally well documented and public.* An inquest cannot expect to add materially to the sum of knowledge in these areas of causation and contribution. *(Para. 11, my emphasis)*[60]

This is an example of just how potent the cultural trope that blames social workers can be. The police held that 'state agencies', and, I suggest, mainly social workers, were to blame.

Despite all that has been written and reported about the life and death of Peter Connelly, he did not have an inquest. Without an inquest, no one knows when he died, how he died or who killed him.

Chapter 7

Transcending Blame, Fear and Denial

In this book I have taken a psychosocial approach to piecing together a range of factors that have accumulated over forty years or more and argued that they led to the extreme responses to the familial homicide of Peter Connelly. These factors, discussed earlier, include:

- the idealisation of motherhood and childhood

- our need for certainty

- the lack of knowledge about familiar child abuse and homicide

- the effects of class politics

- the impact of specific cases of familial child abuse or homicide made high-profile by politicians and the media

- emotional policy-making

- expectations of social workers to accurately predict and prevent

- the developing role of Serious Case Reviews as a proxy for blame

- the distortion of notions of public accountability

- gender politics

- political contexts.

I identified a deeply entrenched cultural process of blaming social workers in cases of familial child abuse and homicide. I characterised this process as a cultural trope to describe the habitual nature of blaming social workers which is devoid of reason, thought or understanding. That social workers are to blame where children known to them are harmed has become forged as a belief, a reality or a truism. The cultural trope is essentially a defence, a state of 'knowing and not knowing' about harm to children and I positioned the cultural trope as a psychosocial entity.

Earlier I described how the cumulative effects of the cultural trope have led to a 'fear of failure' among child protection professionals, and especially among social workers. As a consequence the social work profession has come to exist in a volatile and stressful culture. Compared with the vast numbers of children protected by social workers, the tragedy of familial child homicide is relatively rare, affecting approximately one in a quarter of a million children a year, or one each week, not all of whom are known to social workers. But the risk for social workers of becoming the subject of a high-profile case impacts upon their day-to-day practice and has led to a level of unavoidable anxiety. The profession has become characterised as uncertain, insecure and defensive, as exemplified by the greater numbers of children brought into care with each successive inquiry, including in the immediate aftermath of the news of Baby P's death. These effects of the cultural trope deny social work its professionalism to make reasoned decisions.

At the same time social workers have often positioned themselves as 'containers' for the public's emotion which may have given them a sense of moral value, which I argue has also led to a sense of resignation to, or acceptance of, the criticism, and an inability to challenge public criticism. It is interesting to make the observation of the similarities between this tendency of the social work profession to look inwards and to absorb the blame, and Kitzinger's women who introjected the media's projections and came to blame themselves (Kitzinger 2004). Such a position may leave social workers vulnerable as individuals and weak as a profession especially at times when their knowledge and leadership is most needed.

The case of Baby P could be regarded as an outlier, an unusual or unique event. Aspects of the case were unique, for example the connection with Haringey Council and events in relation to Victoria Climbié. But it is the cultural trope that blames social workers that is the common factor in cases that have come to public attention over several decades and it is this, rather than the unusual aspects of the Baby P case, that is instructive. Further, broad evidence suggests that the cultural trope affects other professionals, usually caring professions such as nurses, midwives and doctors.

Embedded in these complexities is the impact of the cultural trope on the nature of multi-agency working. My analysis raises questions about multi-agency working not only in terms of the different histories, systems and cultures of different professionals, but also in terms of the impact of blame on each profession. The evidence of over forty years suggests that each profession has become increasingly dependent upon the others to make a firm diagnosis of child abuse. I suggest that each is fearful of making the wrong decision given the potentially negative consequences. The different power dynamics between agencies makes social workers the most vulnerable of these welfare agencies to vilification by the media. Increasingly the social care profession has been positioned outside of 'proper' professions, occupying the lowest position in the symbolic order of welfare professions, compared with doctors, nurses and police. In the case of Baby P, Great Ormond Street Hospital and the Metropolitan Police Service were each able to wield much more power and influence not only to avoid blame when Peter Connelly died, but also to evade immediate publicity of their own errors in the case.

At the same time social workers themselves (as well as everyone else) are part of the signs, symbols, meanings and values that drive the cultural trope. Given my findings that the cultural trope is institutionalised, I argue that it is the social work profession itself that is best placed to counter the worst effects of the cultural trope.

The crime of familial child homicide

Earlier I identified the denial or disavowal of the crime of familial child abuse and homicide. Given these habitual responses of the denial of cases of familial child abuse and homicide and the consequent blaming that I have described as a 'cultural trope', there is no opportunity to develop any understanding of the nature of the crime, in particular the homicide of Peter Connelly. That Tracey Connelly was a 'murderous mother' and the social workers 'incompetent' were the depths of the 'knowledge' not only for the public but for many professionals too.

These arguments give rise to a series of questions, including:

- Did Tracey Connelly 'know but not know' about the abuse of Peter until he was dead?

- What was the context of her guilty plea that she 'caused or allowed' his death?

- Was she aware at the time of her efforts to deceive social workers and others which she expressed in court?

- Was her *presentation* as a loving mother concealing the abuse from herself, as well as the paediatricians, social workers and police?

- Why did she express anxiety to doctors that social workers might take her child into care?

- How did doctors respond to those pleas?

- Was her need not to lose her boyfriend greater than her need to protect her child?

- Did she fear losing her welfare benefits if her boyfriend became a member of her household?

What might we have learned, and applied elsewhere, if these questions could have been asked of her? What might have been learned by asking the professionals in a context of 'no fear' how they perceived the mother and her child? In the current responses to familial child homicide these opportunities do not arise. We don't ask these questions and we don't know the answers. No inquiry into a case of familial child abuse has attempted to provide any detailed understanding of the phenomenon of child abuse or about those who commit it; they have all focused on professional failures (Stroud 2008, p.484).

The original aim of Serious Case Reviews was to learn lessons from cases of abuse and homicide, but I argued that they have become a proxy for blaming social workers, illustrated by the second Serious Case Review into the death of Peter Connelly. Since the events that followed news of Peter's death, Serious Case Reviews have been reviewed and repositioned several times. My view is that enabling Serious Case Reviews to become effective learning tools is part of a complex process of shifting not only the perception of social workers but also the public's knowledge of familial child abuse and homicide.

Journalist Matthew Syed, in his book *Black Box Thinking* (2015), provides a compelling account of how organisations fail to learn, arguing that 'failure is rich in learning...[since]...it represents a violation of expectation'. He compares the aviation industry with health services in how they tackle error. At the core of the aviation industry is an intrinsic expectation to learn from errors rather than to blame. Syed (2015) compares this 'black box thinking' of the aviation industry with the 'closed loop' processes in health which he claims include denial, evasion and spin. Syed's analysis is instructive for health services but also for social care services. However, I argue that there are quite subtle differences between the context of failure or error in the aviation industry, health services and social care services. Given that pilot error usually kills the pilot(s), notions of neglect or wilfulness are not usually perceived although blame might still be present. In health services, errors that leads to death or serious injury bring notions of neglect or incompetence. Errors in social care services are similar to those in health services in that someone dies or is harmed. But the act or event in relation to social services is usually committed by a third party (usually a family member) and not in the presence of the social worker.

Further, the notion of 'failure', I argue, is performative; that is, it creates a state of affairs by the very act of being uttered. But there are differences between the professions. For example, the statement 'doctors failed to save a two-year-old child…' suggests that doctors applied all of their knowledge and skill but were unable to succeed. In contrast 'social workers failed to save a two-year-old child…' implies incompetence and perhaps wilful neglect. Importantly, Syed raises the inevitability of failure in a complex world and argues that until we alter how we think about failure, success will be elusive.

The work of all these services operates within a model of risk management. I argued in Chapter 2 that the very notion of managing risk implies that not all risk can be prevented. The result of such 'failure' is an aeroplane *accident* or an *unsuccessful* medical operation; but for the social worker it is a dead child in shocking circumstances with all the connotations of who is to blame. As a result, social workers work in a context that presupposes their own failure. Syed explores how health services might develop 'black box thinking'. For social workers I argue that the process is much more complex. The effects of the cultural trope must first be recognised, understood and tackled.

The cultural trope and the proposed crime of 'wilful neglect'

The Conservative government that was elected in 2015, in its first Queen's Speech, proposed the introduction of a criminal offence of 'wilful neglect' which would apply to social workers, educators and elected council members in England and Wales (Scotland already has similar legislation and Northern Ireland has not yet considered it).

The proposal for the new criminal offence of wilful neglect emerged from the government's response to the Communities and Local Government report into child sexual exploitation in Rotherham, in the north of England.[61] In its response, the government suggested the imposition of criminal sanctions for those who are found to be guilty of 'deliberate, wilful or reckless neglect or mistreatment of children'. The criminal sanctions would cover inaction, concealment and/or deliberate cover-ups, and would ensure that those 'responsible for the very worst failures in care' can be held accountable. Convictions would carry a maximum jail sentence of five years. I argue that the cultural trope, with its far-reaching consequences demonstrated in this book, sets the context not only for the crimes which were denied, but also for this proposal.

To some degree these proposals for a criminal offence might be regarded as political posturing, since proving 'wilful neglect' would be difficult and therefore unlikely to secure a conviction. At the time of the Queen's speech Isabelle Trowler, the government's chief social worker for children, posted a message on social media saying that the proposal to jail social workers 'comes with [the] territory of holding responsibility on behalf of the state' but added that she thought it would be very difficult to secure a conviction. More crucially, she described the government's proposal as matching 'the public [and] political mood', I assume in relation to their attitudes towards social workers. Simultaneously, social workers reacted against the government's proposals, launching a petition which by September 2015 had fewer than 12,000 signatures, falling substantially short of the 80,000 social workers in the UK. In response, writing in *Community Care* (03/09/15), Trowler suggested that the first reactions of social workers:

> should not be one of defence, but of concern for the people we serve. We must focus on the experiences of the victims of abuse, their families and local communities, who feel too often so failed by public services... As a profession we must therefore fully engage with the upcoming consultation.

These exchanges require some careful reflection. Given the attitude towards social workers, which I describe as a cultural trope, the positioning and the power of 'the public and political mood' is understood and has been demonstrated in the case of Baby P. As such it reinforces what Trowler is saying about defensiveness, that is, that the public and politicians are not likely to respond positively to defensive behaviour from social workers. However, embedded in Trowler's advice is a sense that social workers should engage with the consultation *because* public services are *failing* to support families and communities. This is an example of the cultural trope in the form of a simplistic assumption that social workers and other professionals are *failing* their clients and that blame, or worse, 'wilful neglect', via a legal process is a valid remedy.

At the time of writing the government's Home Office confirmed that the proposal for a criminal offence would be put out for public consultation by September 2016. For social workers, teachers and elected councillors in local government to argue *against* a proposal to call them to account for 'wilful neglect' is a non-sequitur, that is, such an argument simply doesn't follow. What does follow is that if child protection professionals *are* guilty of 'wilful neglect' then they should be convicted, a position that Trowler was possibly also communicating. If members of the public are asked whether child protection professionals should be charged in cases of 'wilful neglect' then there is only one answer, yes.

This book has spelt out the complexities of cases of familial child abuse and homicide, especially in the case of Baby P which could, if such a law had been in place, have led to custodial sentences for Peter's social workers. Health professionals and police are not part of the proposal for a custodial sentence, yet in the case of Baby P they had a case to answer; but, with the exception of the paediatrician, they were able to avoid scrutiny. Had Peter's social worker been found guilty, especially in the context of the public opprobrium, evidence emerging later may have led to a miscarriage of justice. The complexities of the case of Baby P are paralleled in the cases of sexual exploitation which took place in Rotherham and several other English cities where social workers were blamed and lost their jobs.

In the case of Rotherham, evidence of police misconduct in the cases of sexual exploitation was slow to emerge.

This potential criminalisation of child protection professionals does not extend to the police. They are subject to the Corporate Manslaughter and Corporate Homicide (CMCH) Act 2007 but with one significant difference. The CMCH Act can lead to companies and organisations guilty of corporate manslaughter as a result of serious management failures resulting in a gross breach of a duty of care. Crucially, prosecutions are of the organisation or corporate body including 'police forces' but not named individual officers as in the case of social workers.

Legal remedies inherent in the proposed legislation would therefore seem flawed. Further, prosecution would need to engage with the complexities of such cases, including the nature of the multi-agency working, and it would reach far beyond the public services that seek to protect (and do protect) children. For example, in the case of Baby P, who would have been the guilty party: the social workers, the paediatrician, the police or senior people in their organisations? What would the evidence have been and how would 'wilful neglect' have been proven? How would wider issues such as the impact of austerity on families and on the services that seek to support them be accounted for?

There are lessons that can be learned from the German experience. Researcher Linn Katharina Döring (forthcoming) has compared German and UK systems of 'holding social workers to account'. German child protection services are run by both government and non-government or private companies (a model being progressed in the UK). In Germany the government retains overall responsibility for child protection and is obliged to 'watch over' non-government services.

German social workers can be charged in cases of fatal child abuse/neglect with 'negligent manslaughter by omission'. It is almost only German government front-line social workers and not their managers, or professionals from private agencies or from other professionals such as health and police who have been charged for their involvement in a case. However, most cases are terminated, overturned, or they result in moderate administrative fines due to rules of 'diversion' or 'quasi-conviction' and social workers return to their jobs. Presumably 'quasi-conviction' is a case of not actually being guilty of directly causing the death. Unlike the UK, crucially there is no naming of professionals or media campaigns on the scale of those seen in the UK. Nevertheless, Döring lists the numerous side effects of the threat of criminal investigations or trials which echo many of the findings outlined in this book. For example, the impact on recruitment and retention, the negative impact on client and social workers relationships, how trials shape social policy, a culture of blame instead of learning, a tendency to protect professionals rather than a focus on what's best for children, the difficulty of assessing causality and predictability (foreseeability) when the outcome is already known, and the reluctance of professionals to reveal failures and therefore learn from mistakes.

The attribution of blame against social workers in Germany is in a different form to that of the UK. In Germany it is primarily legal and in the UK it is more informal and open to the complex interactions of the media, political opportunism and public perception such as I have demonstrated in relation to Baby P. Juxtaposing the different approaches in Germany and the UK, and the complex interactions between the media, politicians and the public, helps to engender a different perspective on the UK government's plans to introduce a criminal charge of 'wilful neglect' in England and Wales.

At present what occurs, and has occurred, in high-profile cases is pressure on the social worker to resign before the case becomes public. Social workers have had access to a professional regulator often of dubious quality, and if funds are available also access to the Employment Tribunal (ET) which deals with employment law but not the intricacies of social care. All these processes, with the possible exception of the ET, rely on quasi-legal processes, for example, conducted within local authorities or by school governing bodies against teachers or headteachers. Such processes have dubious processes of legal accountability and regulation, opening up the potential for abuses of power. I argue that these processes are themselves influenced by the cultural trope ensuring that obtaining a 'fair hearing' for a social worker is eminently difficult or, for the social workers in the case of Baby P, simply not possible. By a 'fair hearing' I refer to a judicial proceeding that is conducted in such a manner as to conform to fundamental concepts of justice and fairness. The 'trial by media' and by politicians in the case of Baby P and other cases give rise to a denial of natural justice and therefore a denial of the principle of the due process of the law being exercised.

New opportunities

For the first time the introduction of a criminal offence of wilful neglect could give social workers access to formal legal representation in a properly constituted court of law, as opposed to local quasi-legal proceedings and the 'court of public opinion' or 'trial by media'. What first appeared as a threat which drew a defensive reaction from social workers might be the best opportunity that the social work profession has had to communicate the challenges of the job and to mount a proper legal defence when social workers come under attack.

What might Peter Connelly's social worker have told us if she had been given a chance to give evidence in a court of law rather than being 'convicted' by the media? What might we have learned from the Great Ormond Street Hospital paediatrician judged as incompetent by the media if we had given her a fair opportunity to give evidence? She could have told us herself about 'standing in' for absent colleagues in a clinic she had never been trained for. What might she have said when she learned that Peter had had over 30 presentations to health professionals and she had not been provided with a single note on file?

Earlier I referred to the emotional pressures on the panel members of the Laming Inquiry in learning about the life and death of Victoria Climbié. More recently *The Times* (31/08/15) referred to the comments of Judge Patricia Lynch QC when she spoke about her own stress and that of the jury from hearing paedophilia cases, especially the detail of sex-abuse cases. But little to no attention has ever been given to the stress experienced by lone social workers visiting homes to make critical decisions about the welfare of children, most often 'without clear evidence'. Instead, with the benefit of hindsight they are condemned. Perhaps in a court of law social workers would find an opportunity to speak about the unspeakable aspects of their jobs. Perhaps senior managers, without the pressures of the cultural trope, might choose fairness in the actions they feel *able to take*. Haringey Council's most senior officers and politicians initially chose fairness; but in the light of the responses to Peter's death chose to sack those named in the media, labelling their actions as 'public accountability'.

In common with all other high-profile cases of familial child abuse or homicide, much government 'emotional policy-making' followed the death of Peter Connelly. For example, the Social Work Task Force recommended the establishment of an independent and strong organisation which would represent and support the social work profession. In response, by January 2012 the College of Social Work was launched but survived less than four years. The College had been established as something of a hybrid. It was not a professional association, or a trade union, or an organisation equivalent to the medical royal colleges, which are independent professional bodies for various medical specialists. The College of Social Work was situated too close to government and attracted only 20 per cent of UK social workers and was dependent on government and employer funding. Its independence was challenged and eventually it was no longer prioritised for government funding, rendering it financially unsustainable.

In contrast, the British Association of Social Workers (BASW) is an independent member-led professional association for social work in the UK, established in 1970. It includes an arm's-length trade union, an advice and representation service and a publishing company. It claims to be the voice of social workers, speaking up for the profession in the media, and lobbying and campaigning for social work in political circles. Its membership is, however, also low in comparison to the number of social workers nationwide, with approximately 18,500 compared with 80,000 social workers nationwide, although there has been an unprecedented increase in recent months with the numbers reaching over 20,000. This low level of engagement of social workers in their professional organisations that strive to support them suggests a fragmentation of the profession, partly driven by perceptions of hierarchies, that is, front-line social workers as different from managers, perhaps leading to a lack of a sense of professional unity and purpose. As such it builds upon the vulnerabilities of social workers and their profession.

With the demise of the College of Social Work, BASW is set to take on many of its functions including: the running of the professional capabilities framework which sets out expectations of social workers at every stage in their career; the continuing professional development (CPD) endorsement framework; and a range of publications, reports and policy documents.

Taken together, the proposal for a criminal offence of 'wilful neglect' and the closure of the College of Social Work could have given the social work profession the best possible chance in recent history of establishing a strong national independent professional body.

However, the Children and Social Work Bill (2016) is set to overhaul social work regulation. It is proposed that a new government agency will replace the current regulating body, the Health and Care Professionals Council (HCPC) and will be accountable to the Secretary of State for Education. Such a move marks a significant shift given that the HCPC is operationally and financially independent of government and is accountable to parliament rather than the government of the day. These proposals are highly controversial as they would make the social work profession the only professional body directly regulated by government. Further, the proposals underline the failure of the social work profession to form its own strong independent professional body.

Where next?

Whether or not the proposals in the Children and Social Work Bill and a criminal offence of 'wilful neglect' become law, in the context of the cultural trope I have put forward a series of actions.

First, the social work profession at all levels of seniority must unite under one strong independent representative body.

Second, that professional organisation must develop the wherewithal to support social workers through litigation and with strong membership be able to fund that litigation.

Third, employers will need to more thoroughly consider professional indemnity arrangements.

Fourth, social workers who are accused will need formal support networks to prepare for a 'fair hearing'.

Fifth, the profession must lead on developing and promoting new discourses that improve knowledge and understanding, drawing in influential social commentators who can provide support.

Sixth, drawing upon the views of Newman (2010, p.273) that social workers should take on new roles of 'engaging, disciplining and responsiblising the public' I argue that communicating with the public should be a core part of every social worker's job.

With this in mind at the BASW Wales 2015 conference I led a workshop with social workers focused on developing ideas for communication with the public on multiple levels. Here are our suggestions:

- Approach local press and arrange for positive material about the work of social workers – 'day in the life of...'

- Be proactive in correcting items in the media when they get them wrong – write to newspapers in small groups and with identities withheld.

- Contribute to local fora that the council may already run or seek other local groups where contributions could be made.

- Research how to influence TV scripts to improve the portrayal of social workers.

- Encourage, support and expect your representative body to speak out against misleading items about social workers – you don't need to know the facts, simply lobby for a 'fair hearing' for social workers.

- Attend community events and give information about social work, for example Red Cross, Royal National Lifeboat Institution (RNLI), types of events that other services such as the Fire Service attend.

- Improve and encourage media coverage of events such as 'Fostering Fortnight', ideally coordinated across the country.

- Ensure a steady supply of press releases to local newspapers about the successes of your service.

- Use social media to communicate successes.

- Support service users if they wish to link with the local media to 'tell their story'.

- Explore social work links with schools – this was a successful partnership in the past and could have a role again.

- Get together more often with police and health to share learning and to ensure that the social work role is understood.

- Think about taking part in high-profile documentary (fly-on-the-wall) programmes.

- Use Facebook to communicate good and more difficult messages.

- Consider a 'supporting parents with parenting' column in a local newspaper with different weekly contributors – approach the local paper and discuss how this might work.

- Think about a 'drop-in' centre – something more accessible where families meet.

- Think about some more serious pieces – for example, the stress about missing a child being harmed. Develop this on the theme of 'looking out for children is everyone's business' – perhaps work with a local journalist to do this.

- Think about writing children's books: find local authors and illustrators, approach university art/literature departments for their help; for example, 'My social worker', 'My foster mum' (see ideas in *Letterbox Library* at www.letterboxlibrary.com).

- Find out how social work is portrayed in careers lessons (is it featured at all?); go and speak to year 10 students and sixth formers who are thinking about career choices – go back to your old school and to local schools.

- Put information about children into the council's communication with their residents. For example: we have x number of children, x% attend early years, x% primary schools, x% secondary schools and x% go to university/college; we look after x% of our children who cannot be supported in their own families and we have the services of x foster carers and x qualified social workers.

- Explore how social work might have a better 'professional footing', for example the 'Royal College of...' as in the medical profession.

- Be proactive about being a social worker – speak up and tell people you meet socially – be proud of your profession!

- Finally, find the right context and develop the courage to *speak about what is unspoken*.

Social work is an enormously challenging profession. It is very successful in protecting children. But it is also easily scapegoated. The responses to the familial homicide of Peter Connelly were in part driven by processes of scapegoating. In developing the notion of a cultural trope that blames social workers for harm to children known to them, the processes of scapegoating might be better understood.

Learning from the case of Baby P is vitally important. Knowledge of how the complexities of the politics of blame, fear and denial functioned in the case is instructive. Blame, fear and denial need now to be replaced by knowledge, awareness and understanding to achieve a renewed focus on how cases of familial child homicide are managed. I believe that it is only the social work profession itself that can transcend the blame, fear and denial that characterised the responses to the familial homicide of Peter Connelly.

To do so the social work profession must be stronger and more united, led with much greater determination at all levels in order to teach the media, the politicians and the public how to make child protection their business too. In essence the social work profession must find the strength to stay with the emotional challenges of mediated politics and the effects on the public, by ensuring that its voice is heard and, more importantly understood. I believe that these are tasks of vital importance to the profession in its work to protect children.

Appendix 1

Who's Who?

Baby P Peter Connelly, deceased 3 August 2007

Graham Badman CBE Former Director of Children's Services in Kent and Ed Balls's appointee to the Chair of Haringey's LSCB in November 2008

Ed Balls MP The Labour government's Secretary of State for Children, Schools and Families, 2007–2010

Steven Barker Boyfriend of Peter Connelly's mother sentenced to twelve years for causing or allowing his death to run concurrently with a life sentence for the rape of a two-year-old girl

Sir David Bell Permanent Secretary of State, DCSF

PC Keith Blakelock Police officer murdered in riots at Broadwater Farm, Haringey, in 1985

Rebekah Brooks Editor of the *Sun* newspaper, 2003–2009

Gordon Brown MP Labour Prime Minister, 2007–2010

David Cameron Leader of Conservative Opposition, 2005–2010

Victoria Climbié Victim of familial child homicide who died in Haringey in 2000

Jane Collins Chief Executive, Great Ormond Street Hospital, 2001–2012

Peter Connelly Known as Baby P, see above

Tracey Connelly Mother of Peter Connelly, convicted of causing or allowing his death

John Coughlan CBE Director of Children's Services (DCS) at Hampshire Council, appointed by Ed Balls interim DCS in Haringey, December 2008 – January 2009

Mark Easton Home Affairs Editor, BBC

Sir Paul Ennals Former Chief Executive of the National Children's Bureau

Lynne Featherstone Liberal Democrat MP for Hornsey and Wood Green, 2005–2015

Mr Justice Foskett Judge who heard the Judicial Review 2009–2010 brought to the High Court by Sharon Shoesmith

Christine Gilbert CBE Her Majesty's Chief Inspector at Ofsted, 2006–2011

Michael Gove Shadow Secretary of State for Children, Schools and Families, 2007–2010

Bernie Grant Labour MP for Tottenham, 1987–2000

Jeremy Heywood Downing Street Chief of Staff, 2008

Beverley Hughes Labour MP and Children's Minister at DCSF, 2005–2010

Jeremy Hunt Conservative Secretary of State for Health, from 2010

Cllr Clair Kober Leader of Haringey Council December, from 2008

Marie-Thérèse Kouao Great-aunt of Victoria Climbié, given a life sentence for her murder in 2001

Lord Laming Former Chief Inspector of the Social Services Inspectorate and author of two Laming Reports, 2003 and 2009

David Lammy MP Labour MP for Tottenham, from 2000

Tim Loughton MP Conservative Parliamentary Under-Secretary of State for Children and Families, 2010–2012

Carl Manning Boyfriend of Marie-Thérèse Kouao who was also given a life sentence for the murder of Victoria Climbié

Cllr George Meehan Labour Leader of Haringey Council 2006–2008

Ita O'Donovan Chief Executive of Haringey Council, 2006–2010

Jason Owen Brother of Steven Barker, the boyfriend of Baby P's mother, convicted of causing or allowing the death of Baby P

Jeanette Pugh DCSF's Director of Safeguarding at the DCSF

Cllr Liz Santry Haringey Council's Lead Member (LM) for Children and Young People, 2006–2008

Barry Sheerman Labour MP and Chair of the Education and Children's Social Care Select Committee

Sharon Shoesmith Director of Education and then of Children's Services in Haringey, 2003–2008

Professor Jo Sibert Professor of Child Health and Consultant Paediatrician and lead author of the Sibert Report

Isabelle Trowler The government's chief social worker, from 2014

Andrew Walker Senior Coroner, North London Coroners' Court

Ian Willmore Labour Deputy Leader of Haringey Council at the time of Victoria Climbié's death in 2000

Stuart Young Assistant Chief Executive of Haringey Council, responsible for People & Organisational Development, 2006–2013

Appendix 2

Glossary

APA Annual Performance Assessment

BAE British Aerospace Systems

BASW British Association of Social Work

BBC British Broadcasting Corporation

CAFCASS Children and Family Court Advisory Service

CAIT Child Abuse Investigation Team of the London Metropolitan Police

CE Chief Executive

CMCH Corporate Manslaughter and Corporate Homicide Act 2007

CPA Comprehensive Performance Assessment (of Local Authorities)

CPD Continuing Professional Development

CPS Crown Prosecution Service

CQC Care Quality Commission

CRB Criminal Records Bureau

CSCI Commission for Social Care Inspection

CYPS Children and Young People Service

DCS Director of Children's Services

DCSF Department for Children, Schools and Families

DES Department for Education and Science

DfE Department for Education

DfES Department for Education and Skills

DH Department of Health

DHSS Department for Health and Social Services

DVCVA Domestic Violence, Crime and Victims Act 2004 (amended in 2008 and 2012)

DWP Department of Work and Pensions

ECM Every Child Matters

E-enabled electronically enabled/computer software

ET Employment Tribunal

FOIA Freedom for Information Act

G20 An international forum for governments and central banks from 20 major economies, previously the G8

GCSE General Certificate of Secondary Education

GMC General Medical Council

GOL Government of London Office

GOSH Great Ormond Street Hospital

GP General Practitioner (of medicine)

GSCC General Social Care Council

HCC Health Care Commission

HMCI Her Majesty's Chief Inspector (Ofsted)

HMIC Her Majesty's Inspector of Constabulary (police)

ICS Integrated Children's System

IDeA Improvement and Development Educational Agency

JAR Joint Area Review, a form of Ofsted inspection

LBH London Borough of Haringey

LM Lead (Elected) Member for Children (Local Authority)

LSCB Local Safeguarding Children Board

LSOA Lower-layered Super Output Area

MAPPA Multi-Agency Public Protection Arrangements

MPA London's Metropolitan Police Authority

MPS London's Metropolitan Police Service

NHS National Health Service

NMUH North Middlesex University Hospital

NSPCC National Society for the Prevention of Cruelty to Children

OFSTED Office for Standards in Education, Children's Services and Skills

ONS Office of National Statistics

PC Police Constable

PCT Primary Care Trust (NHS)

PDP Potentially Dangerous Persons

PMQ Prime Minister's Question's

PSSPAF Personal Social Services Performance Assessment Framework

QC Queen's Counsel

SCR Serious Case Review

SOLACE Society of Local Authority Chief Executives

TOR Terms of Reference

VCD Violent Crime Directorate

VISOR Violence and Sex Offender Register

Appendix 3

The Research Materials and Their Uses

In the introductory chapter I referred to the materials used in the research for this book. These materials were all documents in five categories:

- media coverage

- views and opinions of members of the public who posted on social media and wrote to newspapers

- utterances by politicians and private views conveyed by senior civil servants in emails;

- documents related to the Haringey Joint Area Review (JAR)

- the Serious Case Reviews into the death of Peter Connelly and related reports.

The five categories of documents provided a breadth of evidence across the many actors who responded to the familial homicide of Peter Connelly. More importantly they enabled the analyses of the intertextuality between the different categories of documents which allows me to grasp the dynamic interaction between key players. The five categories of documents and how I have used them are set out below. Materials mainly in categories 1–3 were used for the analysis in Chapter 5 which is concerned with the narrative that emerged in the six days between 11 and 16 November 2008. The materials in categories 4 and 5 plus the media analysis for the time period 17 November to 1 December were used for the analysis in Chapter 6.

Finally, the extensive nature of the documentary evidence was such that I had to 'process' it initially into three very lengthy 'source documents' to support the analysis stage. These source documents are purely descriptive and mainly factual and an outline of the contexts follows my description of each category of research materials.

Category 1: Media coverage

Media coverage during two time periods was analysed using articles obtained from the online database Nexis, using the search term 'Baby P'. The first time period is 11–16 November 2008, which was from the day that the convictions of those responsible for Peter Connelly's death were announced until the day before the emergency Ofsted inspection (the JAR) began. The second time period is from Monday 17 November to 1 December 2008 and includes the inspection of Haringey's Children's Services, the delivery of the *Sun*'s petition to Downing Street, the final draft of the Haringey JAR Inspection being submitted to the Secretary of State, and my 'sacking' on live television.

For the first time period, 11–16 November, using the search term 'Baby P', on 12 May 2012 I identified 476 articles in UK newspapers and journals. I concentrated on national newspapers and journals so excluded 160 references in regional newspapers, reducing the sample to 316 media articles in UK national tabloids and broadsheets and nine journals representing local government or social work.[62] I sorted the articles into date order from 11–16 November. I was particularly interested in the iterative or incremental development of the narrative over the six days rather than searching for themes across the sample. I read and reread the articles several times and identified the dominant theme for each of the six days in a process characteristic of Neuman's (2011) 'open coding' method. That is, coding or identifying themes by what is presented in the text rather than by predetermined categories or themes.

The themes identified included 'no sacking of social workers', 'Shoesmith's complacency', 'comparisons with Climbié', negative 'references to Haringey Council', 'torture of the child', 'events in the House of Commons', 'reactions of Cameron, Brown and Balls', 'criminalising of the social workers', 'failure to say sorry', 'positioning of Shoesmith', 'briefing by the police', 'length of sentencing', 'the iconic image', 'marches and demonstrations' and 'the moral underclass'.

The themes were repeated in the different newspapers, allowing me to exclude some of the articles and all the journals given their delay in publishing the media stories. Simultaneously I had regard for the different political orientations of both broadsheets and tabloids and included the range in the sample. The *Sun* had the most dominant role in the unfolding narrative and I included articles from the *Sun* for each of the six days. I also included all articles or letters written by the Prime Minister, the Secretary of State and the leader of the Opposition, and television and radio broadcasts that were prominent in focusing on a particular theme. Finally, I included articles that took up a different position, although these were an exception. This process reduced the sample to 26 articles across 19 newspapers.[63] I then included a news broadcast from the BBC and an interview from BBC Radio 4 during the six days that contributed to the unfolding narrative.

For the second time period, 17 November to 1 December 2008, using the same search term 'Baby P', 785 articles appeared in UK newspapers, with 86 in the *Sun*. Given the dominance of the *Sun*'s petition my analysis at this stage concentrated almost exclusively on the themes in articles in the *Sun*, including all editorials. Following the same process as in the previous time period, I sorted the 86 items in the *Sun* chronologically across the 15 days and drew upon the themes for each day. The themes were fewer than in the first time period and concentrated on 'the strength of the petition', 'sacking of Sharon Shoesmith', 'appeals to Ed Balls', 'take-over of Haringey' and 'the swell of public anger'.

Quotes from newspaper articles in Chapters 5 and 6 are referenced using the name of the newspaper, the date and the page number in the printed copy rather than the name of the author of each article so that the breadth of the sample of newspapers could be identified.

Category 2: Views and opinions of members of the public

Views and opinions of members of the public about the case of Baby P from 11–16 November 2008 were in the form of letters or texts printed in newspapers, and comments posted on social media sites, in blogs and on the internet video site YouTube. During the target six days, 81 letters or texts from the public appeared between nine newspapers. Three-quarters concerned the case of Baby P and of those 90 per cent were critical of Haringey Council, the social workers involved in the case, and/or me. The remaining ten per cent commented on the family of Peter Connelly or on politicians. From these I created a sample of 12 letters, two from each day, chosen to represent the dominant themes, and any dissenting views, and to ensure that all newspapers were represented.

Facebook and Bebo were the social networking sites and in March 2013 using the search items 'Baby P', twelve Facebook groups were still accessible and four in Bebo. Three Facebook groups in particular began either the day of the news of Peter's homicide, or the day after, and continued until 16 November (and beyond), and had a substantial number of postings. Two of the four Bebo sites also covered the time period 11–16 November 2008 but had many fewer postings. Using the same search terms, ten blogs were accessible and three covered the target days 11–16 November 2008. I chose Old Holborn Blogspot on the basis that it was by far the most active with 398 comments starting a few days into my target timeframe on 14 November with 339 postings in the three days up to 16 November. I included the two most active blogs, Peter Reynolds' Blog and The Square Ball Blog, for comments during the weekend 15 and 16 November 2008 when anger had built up and demonstrations were being planned. Both Bebo and Old Holborn Blogspot were much more extreme in their comments than Facebook, often expressing violence.

The vast majority of participants in the three Facebook sites overall were women, judging by the names and images used. Approximately 81 per cent were women compared with 19 per cent men, substantially above the ratio of Facebook users of 67 per cent women but lower for men at 33 per cent generally in 2008.[64] Judging by the images used, with only two exceptions, the women were almost exclusively white, they appeared to be mainly in their late twenties and thirties[65] and they often referred in their postings to being mothers. Many contributors to Old Holborn Blogspot used nicknames and it was not possible to provide any reliable estimate of gender or age. The postings on Facebook, Bebo and Old Holborn Blogspot, formed my social media sample.

The three Facebook groups are:

- **Facebook Group 1,** was created originally with the stated aim of forcing my resignation (and later blocking compensation) and was active from 12 November 2008 to 7 June 2011. During that period the site had 115 postings with 52 by men, making it more male dominated than Facebook users generally and much more male dominated than Groups 2 and 3. Of the 52 postings from men, 21 were from one man. Further, the Chair of the Haringey Conservatives in Tottenham in 2008, which was in political opposition to Labour-led Haringey Council, was recorded as the 'administrator' or creator of this group although he made no postings himself. This suggests that the group may have been covertly politically led. Between 12 and 16

November, 30 postings appear from 16 women and seven men, one of who posted on eight occasions.

- **Facebook Group 2,** had 212 postings from 11 November 2008 to 22 April 2010. Only 28 postings were from men, making it considerably female dominated. From 11–16 November, there were 154 postings with 69 posted on 12 November 2008, the day after the death of Baby P was reported, with all but five from women. Of the 28 postings from men, seven were from one man.

- **Facebook Group 3,** had 204 postings, 40 from men. Between 12 and 16 November, 125 comments were posted with only 32 from men.

Category 3: Utterances by politicians or other powerful 'elites'

Utterances by politicians or other powerful 'elites', especially senior officials in Ofsted, were made either in press releases, in debates in the House of Commons and the House of Lords (published in Hansard), in the print and broadcast media, or in approximately 200 emails exchanged during the target time between civil servants, and between civil servants and Ofsted officials, and released to the Judicial Review in the High Court.

Category 4: Documents related to the Ofsted JAR inspection

Documents related to the Ofsted inspection of Haringey's included emails and documents that were disclosed to the Judicial Review process by Ofsted in two 'batches'. The first 'batch' provided a number of emails between Ofsted employees and between Ofsted and DCSF employees, and the Record of Evidence (ROE) from the inspection. The ROE is a collation of a summary of every interview or document read or observation made with an attached judgment represented by 1 to 4 (1 being outstanding, 2 good, 3 adequate and 4 inadequate). For the Haringey JAR the ROE consisted of 797 ROEs. The Judicial Review was the first time a ROE had ever been seen publicly.

The second 'batch' was produced under order from Mr Justice Foskett when it became clear that Ofsted had not discharged its duty of candour to the court. The legal duty of candour in Judicial Reviews requires a public authority, when presenting its evidence, to set out fully and fairly all matters that are relevant to the decision that is under challenge, or are otherwise relevant to any issue arising in the proceedings. This second 'batch' added significantly to the evidence. It included 17 drafts of the JAR inspection report, a document and PowerPoint presentation containing reflections on the inspection by the lead inspector, and detailed notes of the inspection made by the deputy lead inspector, as well as further email correspondence.

It is important to note that the judgments in the Haringey JAR report were not the focus of the Judicial Review and so this material was never systematically analysed or presented to the court.

Category 5: Serious Case Reviews 1 and 2

This category includes the first and second Serious Case Reviews (SCR1 and SCR2) and their executive summaries into the death of Peter Connelly completed by Haringey's Local Safeguarding Children Board (LSCB) all publicly available, and the evaluations of those SCRs completed by Ofsted and disclosed to the Judicial Review. The Sibert Report (2008) was published on the GOSH website in June 2011, and two internal police investigation reports and a police inspection report (from HMIC) were made available to me.

Three source documents

The following three source documents were produced to manage the extensive nature of the documentary evidence. The three documents then provided the basis from which I developed my analysis. The first source document focused on the Ofsted inspection and provided a chronological description of the processes Ofsted undertook in collaboration with the DfES to produce the Haringey JAR from its announcement on 14 November 2008 to the published report on 1 December 2008. Parts of this chronology were minute-by-minute and hour-by-hour communications by email between combinations of different actors in the DCSF and Ofsted. The source document included the chronology of the production of the final draft of the JAR report through 17 drafts. The 17 drafts had emails attached, enabling me to see the order in which they were produced and who was sending copies to whom, and with what instruction. Words and phrases in successive drafts of the JAR were altered and I had to track these changes made by different actors using a colour coding process. At times a single draft was altered simultaneously by different actors and on one occasion two different drafts were in circulation. This source document is reflected mainly in the analysis in Chapter 6.

The second source document concentrated on the two Serious Case Reviews (SCRs), the Ofsted evaluations of the SCRs, the two police reports produced by the police inspector and the Sibert Report. There were no prior themes as the analysis focused on different accounts that were produced at different stages. This source document consisted of four parts: a comparison of the SCRs and a comparison of the second SCR summary with its full report; an analysis of Ofsted's evaluations of each SCR; an analysis of the two police reports and how the findings were reflected in the SCR2 summary and the police inspector's report; and an analysis of the Sibert Report and how it was reflected in the SCR2 summary and full report. The material was cross-referenced with the overall chronology of media themes and political interactions described below in the third source document. The material in the second source document is reflected mainly in the analysis in Chapter 6.

The third document was the most lengthy and provided an overall chronology of events from the birth of Peter Connelly in March 2006 to October 2014. The most detailed part was the period from 11 November 2008 to the end of 2009, which includes the target time frame for this book. The chronology also captured the day-by-day development of media reports across numerous newspapers, political reactions published in newspapers and available in emails, public responses mainly in social media, police briefings to the public and the activities of Ofsted. This document emphasised the iterative nature of the interactions of the various actors. The importance of the impact of different historical, social, political and cultural contexts also began to emerge in the data. The analyses and findings of this process are reflected in Chapters 5 and 6.

Bibliography

Ahmed, S. (2004) *The Cultural Politics of Emotion*. Cambridge: Cambridge University Press.

Altheide, D.L. (1996) *Qualitative Media Analysis*. Thousand Oaks, CA: Sage.

Ariès, P. (1962) *Centuries of Childhood: A Social History of Family Life*. London: Vintage Books.

Ashenden, S. (2004) *Governing Child Sexual Abuse: Negotiating the Boundaries of Public and Private, Law and Science*. London and New York: Routledge.

Atmore, C. (1998) 'Towards 2000: Child Sexual Abuse and the Media.' In A. Howe (ed.) *Sexed Crime in the News*. Melbourne: Federation Press.

Atmore, C. (2003) 'Feminism's Restless Undead: The Radical/Lesbian/Victim Theorist and Conflicts Over Sexual Violence Against Children and Women.' In P. Reavey and S. Warner (eds) *New Feminist Stories of Child Sexual Abuse: Sexual Scripts and Dangerous Dialogues*. London: Routledge.

Audit Commission (2008) *Every Child Matters – Are We There Yet?* Press Release, 29 October 2008.

Audit Commission (2009) *Annual Review and Accounts*. London: The Stationery Office.

Bailey, R. and Brake, M. (1980) 'Contributions to Radical Practice in Social Work.' In M. Brake and R. Bailey (eds) *Radical Social Work and Practice*. London: Edward Arnold.

Baldwin, N. and Spencer, N.J. (2004) 'Economic, Cultural and Social Contexts of Neglect.' In J. Taylor and B. Daniel (eds) *Child Neglect – Practice Issues for Health and Social Care*. London: Jessica Kingsley.

Bauman, Z. (1992) *Intimations of Postmodernity*. London: Routledge.

Bauman, Z. (1993) *Liquid Times: Living in an Age of Uncertainty*. Cambridge: Polity.

Beck, U. (1992) *Risk Society: Towards a New Modernity.* New Delhi: Sage.

Beck, U. (1994) 'The Reinvention of Politics: Towards a Theory of Reflexive Modernization.' In U. Beck, A. Giddens and S. Lash (eds) *Reflexive Modernization: Politics, Tradition and Aesthetics in the Modern Social Order.* Cambridge: Polity.

Beck, U. (1999) *World at Risk.* Cambridge: Polity.

Beck, U., Giddens, A. and Lash, S. (eds) (1994) *Reflexive Modernization: Politics, Tradition and Aesthetics in the Modern Social Order.* Cambridge: Polity.

Behlmer, G. (1982) *Child Abuse and Moral Reform in England 1870–1908.* Stanford: Stanford University Press.

Behn, R.D. (2001) *Rethinking Democratic Accountability.* Washington D.C.: Brookings Institute.

Bennett, W.L. (1990) 'Towards a theory of press-state relations in the United States.' *Journal of Communication 40*, 2, 103–125.

Bennett, W.L. (2011) *News: The Politics of Illusion* (Ninth edition). New York: Longman.

Bennett, W.L. and Entman, R.M. (eds) (2001) *Mediated Politics, Communication in the Future of Democracy.* Cambridge, New York, Melbourne, Madrid: Cambridge University Press.

Bion, W. (1961) *Experience in Groups and Other Papers.* London: Tavistock.

Bion, W. (1962) *Learning from Experience.* London: Heinemann.

Bird, J.F. (2003) 'I wish to speak to the despisers of the body: the internet, physicality and psychoanalysis.' *Journal of Psychoanalysis, Culture and Society 8*, 1, 121–126.

Blair, T. (1996) Speech given at Ruskin College, Oxford University. Available at www.leeds.ac.uk/educol/documents/000000084.htm, accessed on 22 March 2016.

Blair, T. (2007) Lecture on Public Life, at Reuters, Canary Wharf, London. Available at http://image.guardian.co.uk/sys-files/Politics/documents/2007/06/12/BlairReustersSpeech.pdf?guni=Article:in%20body%20link, accessed on 22 March 2016.

Blanden, T., Dekker, P. and Evers, A. (eds) (2010) *Civicness in the Governance and Delivery of Social Services.* Baden Baden: Nomos.

Borins, S. (2001) *The Challenge of Innovating in Government.* Available at www.strategie-cdi.ro/spice/admin/UserFiles/File/CA%20The%20Challenge%20of%20innovating%20in%20government.pdf accessed on 22 March 2016.

Bortolaia-Silva, E. (ed.) (1996) *Good Enough Mothering? Feminist Perspectives on Lone Motherhood.* London and New York: Routledge.

Bovens, M. (2005) 'Public Accountability.' In In E. Ferlie, L.E. Lynn Jr. and C. Pollitt (eds) *The Oxford Handbook of Public Management.* Oxford: Oxford Handbooks Online. Available at www.oxfordhandbooks.com/view/10.1093/oxfordhb/9780199226443.001.0001/oxfordhb-9780199226443-e-9, accessed on 22 March 2016.

Bovens, M., Schillemans, T. and Hart, P.T. (2008) 'Does public accountability work? An assessment tool.' *Public Administration 86*, 1, 225–242.

Bowlby, J. (1969) *Attachment and Loss. Vol. 1: Attachment.* London: Hogarth Press.

Bradshaw, J. (2001) *Poverty: The Outcomes for Children.* London: Family Policy Studies Centre.

Brake, M. and Bailey, R. (eds) (1980) *Radical Social Work and Practice.* London: Edward Arnold.

Brandon, M. (2009a) *Understanding Serious Case Reviews and Their Impact: A Biennial Analysis of Serious Case Reviews 2005-7.* London: DCSF.

Brandon, M. (2009b) 'Child fatality or serious injury through maltreatment: making sense of outcomes.' *Children and Youth Services Review 31*, 10, 1107–1112.

Brandon, M., and Thoburn, J. (2008) 'Safeguarding Children in the UK: a longitudinal study of services to children suffering or likely to suffer significant harm.' *Child and Family Social Work 13*, 4, 365–377.

Brandon, M., Bailey, S., and Belderson, P. (2010) *Building on the Learning from SCRs: A 2 year Analysis of Child Protection Database Notifications 2007-2009.* London: DfE.

Brandon, M., Belderson, P., Warren, C., Howe, D., *et al.* (2008) *Analyzing Child Deaths and Serious Injury through Abuse and Neglect: What Can We Learn? A Biennial Analysis of Serious Case Reviews 2003-5.* London: DCSF.

Brennan, T. (2004) *The Transmission of Affect.* Ithaca, London: Cornell University Press.

Brinton Perera, S. (1985) *The Scapegoat Complex: Towards a Mythology of Shadow and Guilt.* Toronto, ON: Inner City Books.

Broadhurst, K., Grover, C. and Jamieson, J. (eds) (2009) *Critical Perspectives in Safeguarding Children.* Chichester: Wiley.

Broadhurst, K., Hall, C., Wastell, D., White, S. and Pithouse, A. (2010a) 'Risk, instrumentalism and the humane project in social work: identifying the informal logics of risk management in children's statutory services.' *British Journal of Social Work 40*, 4, 1046–1064.

Broadhurst, K., Wastell, D., White, S. Hall, C., *et al.* (2010b) 'Performing initial assessment: identifying the latent conditions for error at the front-door of local authority children's services.' *British Journal of Social Work 40*, 2, 352–370.

Brockman, F. and Nolan, J. (2006) 'The dark figure of infanticide in England and Wales.' *Journal of Interpersonal Violence 21*, 7, 869–889.

Burton, J. and Broek van den, D. (2009) 'Accountable and countable: information management systems and the bureaucratisation of social work.' *British Journal of Social Work 39*, 7, 1326–1342.

Butler, I. and Drakeford, M. (2005) *Scandal, Social Policy and Social Welfare.* Bristol: Policy Press.

Butler, I. and Drakeford, M. (2011) *Social Work on Trial: The Colwell Inquiry and the State of Welfare.* Bristol: Policy Press.

Butler-Sloss, Lord Justice, E. (1988) *Report of the Inquiry into Child Abuse in Cleveland 1987*. London: HMSO.

Bynner, J. (1999) *Risks and Outcomes of Social Exclusion, Insights from Longitudinal Data*. Available at www.oecd.org/edu/school/1855785.pdf, accessed on 22 March 2016.

CAFCASS *Annual Reports and Accounts 2008/9, 2009/10, 2010/11, 2011/12*. Available at www.cafcass.gov.uk, accessed on 22 March 2016.

Campbell, B. (1988) *Unofficial Secrets: Child Sexual Abuse, the Cleveland Case*. London: Virago.

Cartwright, D. (2010) *Containing States of Mind: Explaining Bion's 'Container Model' Psychoanalytic Psychotherapy*. London: Routledge.

Centre for Public Scrutiny (2009) *Public Accountability*. Obtainable from Centre for Public Scrutiny, 77 Mansell Street, London E1 8AN.

Chapman, J. (2004) *System Failure: Why Governments Must Learn to Think Differently*. DEMOS. Available at www.demos.co.uk/files/systemfailure2.pdf, accessed on 22 March 2016.Children and Families Act 2014, c.6, available at www. legislation.gov.uk/ukpga/2014/6/contents/enacted, accessed on 7 June 2016

Children and Families Act 2014, c.6, available at www.legislation.gov.uk/ ukpga/2014/6/contents/enacted, accessed on 7 June 2016.

Chodorow, N.J. (1978) *The Representation of Mothering: Psychoanalysis and the Sociology of Gender*. Berkeley: University of California Press.

Chodorow, N.J. (1989/2012) *Feminism and Psychoanalytic Theory*. New Haven, CT: Yale University Press.

Chodorow N.J., and Contratto S (1989/2012) 'The Fantasy of the Perfect Mother.' In N.J. Chodorow *Feminism and Psychoanalytic Theory*. New Haven, CT: Yale University Press.

Civin, M. (2000) *Male, Female and Email: The Struggle for Relatedness in a Paranoid Society*. New York: Other Press.

Clapton, G., Cree, V. and Smith, M. (2013) 'Moral panics and social work: towards a sceptical view of UK child protection.' *Critical Social Policy 33*, 2, 197–217.

Cloke, C. (2001) Out of Sight: Report on Child Deaths from Abuse 1973–2000. London: NSPCC.

Cohen, S. (2001) *States of Denial: Knowing About Atrocities and Suffering*. Oxford: Polity.

Cooke, H.F. (2007) 'Scapegoating and the unpopular nurse.' *Nurse Education Today 27*, 3, 177–184.

Cooper, A. (2005) 'Surface and depth in the Victoria Climbié Inquiry Report.' *Child and Family Social Work 10*, 1–9.

Cooper, A. (2007) 'Surface Tensions: Emotion, Conflict and the Social Containment of Dangerous Knowledge.' In Perri 6, S. Radstone, C. Squire and A. Treacher (eds) *Public Emotions*. Hampshire: Palgrave Macmillan.

Cooper, A. (2010) *Deep Down They're Really Good People: Social Work Now – The State of Mind We're In,* Unpublished discussion document compiled by Professor Cooper, The Tavistock Institute of Human Relations.

Cooper, A. (2014a) 'History as tragedy, never as farce: tracing the long cultural narrative of child protection in England.' *Journal of Social Work Practice 8,* 3, 251–266.

Cooper, A. (2014b) 'A short psychosocial history of British child abuse and protection: case studies in problems of mourning in the public sphere.' *Journal of Social Work Practice 8,* 3, 271–285.

Cooper, D. (1994) *Sexing the City: Lesbian and Gay Politics within the Activist State.* London: Rivers Oram Press.

Corby, B., Doig, A. and Roberts, V. (1998) 'Inquiries into child abuse.' *Journal of Social Welfare and Family Law 20,* 4, 377–395.

Corby, B., Shemmings, D. and Wilkins, D. (2012) *Child Abuse: An Evidence Base for Confident Practice* (Fourth edition). Maidenhead: Open University Press.

CQC (2009) *Review of the Involvement and Action Taken by Health Bodies in Relation to the Case of Baby P.* Newcastle upon Tyne: Care Quality Commission. Available at http://dera.ioe.ac.uk/10510/1/Baby_Peter_report_FINAL_12_May_09_%282%29.pdf, accessed on 31 May 2016.

Crawford, C. and Conn, L. (1997) 'Female child sexual abuse: unrecognised abuse and ignored victims.' *Counselling,* November 1997, 278–281.

Cree, V. (1995) *From Public Streets to Private Lives.* Aldershot: Avebury.

CSCI (Commission for Social Care Inspection) (2006) *Making Choices: Taking Risks.* Newcastle and London: HMSO.

CSCI (Commission for Social Care Inspection) (2007) *Social Services Performance Assessment Framework Indicators.* Available at http://webarchive.nationalarchives.gov.uk/20141124154759/http://www.ofsted.gov.uk/resources/social-services-performance-assessment-framework-indicators-2003-06, accessed on 22 March 2016.

Cunningham, H. (1991) *The Children of the Poor: Representations of Childhood since the 17th Century.* Oxford: Blackwell.

Dally, A. (1982) *Inventing Motherhood, the Consequences of an Ideal.* London: Burnett Books.

Daly, M. (2010) 'Shifts in family policy in the UK under New Labour.' *Journal of European Social Policy 20,* 5, 433–443.

Davies, N. (2014) *Hack Attack, How the Truth Caught Up With Rupert Murdoch.* London: Chatto and Windus.

Davis, A. (2003) 'Whither mass media and power? Evidence for a critical elite theory alternative.' *Media, Culture and Society 25,* 5, 669–690.

Davis, A. (2007) *The Mediation of Power.* London: Routledge.

Davis, A. (2009) 'Journalist-source relations, mediated reflexivity and the politics of politics.' *Journalism Studies 10,* 2, 204–219.

DeMause, L. (1974) *The History of Childhood: The Untold Story of Child Abuse*. New York: Psychohistory Press.

Demos (2014) *Ties that Bind*. Available at www.demos.co.uk/files/TiesthatbindREPORT.pdf?1390241705, accessed on 22 March 2016.

Denney, D. (2005) *Risk and Society*. London: Sage.

Denzin, N.K. and Lincoln, Y.S. (eds) (2000) *Handbook of Qualitative Research*. Thousand Oaks, CA: Sage.

DES (2007) *Local Authority Circular 25: Future Arrangements for the Statutory Notifications Previously Sent to the Commission for Social Care Inspection*. London: DES

Devaney, J., Lazenbatt, A. and Bunting, L. (2011) 'Inquiring into non-accidental deaths.' *British Journal of Social Work 4*, 2, 242–260.

DfE (2010) *Preventable Child Deaths in England: Year Ending 31 March 2010*. London: DfE.

DfE (2010) *Working Together to Safeguard Children: A Guide to Interagency Working to Safeguard and Promote the Welfare of Children*. London: DCSF

DfE (2010) *Children in Need in England, Including their Characteristics and Further Information on Children who were the Subject of a Child Protection Plan (2009–10 Children in Need census)*. London: DFE.

DfE (2011) *Child Death Reviews: Year Ending 31 March 2011*. London: DfE.

DfES (2003) *Keeping Children Safe – A Response by Government to the Victoria Climbié Inquiry and the Joint Chief Inspectors' Report 'Safeguarding Children'*. London: TSO.

DfES (2004) *Every Child Matters: Change for Children*. London: DfES.

DfES (2005) *Statutory Guidance on the Roles and Responsibilities of the Director of Children's Services and the Lead Member for Children's Services*. London: DfES.

DH (1995) *Child Protection: Messages from Research*. London: HMSO.

DH (1996) *Childhood Matters: The Report of the National Commission of Inquiry into the Prevention of Child Abuse*. London: HMSO.

DH (1998) *Modernising Social Services: Promoting Independence, Improving Protection and Raising Standards*. London: Stationery Office.

DH (2001) *The Children Act Now: Messages from Research*. London: Stationery Office.

DH (2002a) *Safeguarding Children: A Joint Chief Inspectors' Report on Arrangements to Safeguard Children*. London: DH Publications.

DH (2002b) *Complex Child Abuse Investigation: Inter-Agency Issues*. London: HMSO.

DH (2002c) *Learning from Past Experience: A Review of Serious Case Reviews*. London: DH.

DH (2007a) *Independence, Choice and Risk: A Guide to Best Practice in Supported Decision-Making*. London: DH.

DH (2007b) *Best Practice in Managing Risk*. London: DH.

DHSS (1974) *Report of the Committee of Inquiry into the Care and Supervision Provided in Relation to Maria Colwell.* London: HMSO.

DHSS (1988a) *Working Together: A Guide to Inter-Agency Co-operation for the Protection of Children from Abuse.* London: HMSO.

DHSS (1988b) *Protecting Children: A Guide for Social Workers Conducting a Comprehensive Assessment.* London: HMSO.

Dickens, J. (2011) 'Social work in England at the watershed – as always: from Seebolm Report to the Social Work Taskforce.' *British Journal of Social Work* 41, 22–39.

Dingwall, R. (1986) 'The Jasmine Beckford affair.' *Modern Law Review* 49, 4, 488–518.

Dingwall, R., Eekelaar, J. and Murray, T. (1983 / 2014) *The Protection of Children.* New Orleans: Quid Pro Books.

Döring, L. (forthcoming), *Negligent Criminals or Negligent Criminalisation?* Unpublished PhD Thesis, Department of Criminology, Max Planck Institute for Foreign and International Criminal Law, University of Freiburg.

Douglas, M. (1996) *Thought Styles, Critical Essays on Good Taste.* London: Sage.

Douglas, M. (1984 / 1966) *Purity and Danger: An Analysis of the Concepts of Pollution and Taboo.* London: Routledge and Kegan Paul.

Douglas, M. (1986) *How Institutions Think.* Syracuse, NY: Syracuse University Press.

Douglas, M. (1992) *Risk and Blame: Essays in Cultural Theory.* London: Routledge.

Douglas, M., and Wildavasky, A.B. (1982) *Risk and Culture: An Essay on the Selection of Technical and Environmental Dangers.* Berkeley, CA: University of California Press.

Douglas, T. (1995) *Scapegoats: Transferring Blame.* London: Routledge.

Downes, D., Rock, P., Chinkin, C. and Gearty, C (2007) *Crime, Social Control and Human Rights, from Moral Panics to States of Denial, Essays in Honour of Stanley Cohen.* Cullompton: Willan.

Drakeford, M. and Butler, I. (2010) 'Familial homicide and social work.' *British Journal of Social Work* 40, 5, 1419–1433.

Driver, S. and Martell, L. (2002) 'New Labour, work and the family.' *Social Policy and Administration* 36, 1, 46–61.

DWP (1998) *New Deal for Lone Parents.* London: HMSO.

Dykman, J. and Cutler, J. (2003) *Scapegoats at Work: Taking the Bull's Eye off Your Back.* Connecticut: Praeger.

Edelman, L. (2004) *No Future: Queer Theory and the Death Drive.* Durham and London: Duke University Press.

Elliot, A. (2002) 'Beck's *Sociology of Risk*, a critical assessment.' *Sociology* 36, 2, 293–315.

Elliot, F. and Hanning, J. (2012) *Cameron: The Rise of the New Conservative.* London: Harper Collins.

Ellis, C. (2004) *The Ethnographical I: A Methodological Novel about Autobiography.* Walnut Creek, CA: Rowman Altamira.

Ellis, R.J. (1994) *Presidential Lightning Rods: The Politics of Blame Avoidance.* Lawrence, MI: University Press of Kansas.

Entman, R.M. (2004) *Projections of Power: Framing News, Public Opinion and US Foreign Policy.* Chicago and London: The University of Chicago Press.

Ericson, R.V. Baranek, P.M. and Chan J.B.L. (1989) *Negotiating Control: A Study of News Sources.* Milton Keynes: Open University Press.

Esser, F., Carsten, R. and Fan, D. (2000) 'Spin doctoring in British and German election campaigns.' *European Journal of Communications 15*, 2, 209–239.

Evans, J. (2003) 'Vigilance and vigilantes: thinking psychoanalytically about anti-paedophile action.' *Theoretical Criminology 7*, 163–189.

Fawcett, B., Featherstone, B. and Goddard, J. (2004) *Contemporary Child Care Policy and Practice.* Basingstoke: Palgrave.

Featherstone, B. (1997) "I Wouldn't Do Your Job!': Women, Social Work and Child Abuse.' In W. Hollway and B. Featherstone (eds) *Mothering and Ambivalence.* London: Routledge.

Featherstone, B. (2006a) 'Why gender matters in child welfare and protection.' *Critical Social Policy 26*, 2, 294–314.

Featherstone, B. (2006b) 'Rethinking family support in the current policy context.' *British Journal of Social Work 36*, 1, 5–19.

Featherstone, L. (2008) *Baby P Verdict.* Available at www.lynnefeatherstone.org/2008/11/baby-p-verdict.htm, accessed on 22 March 2016.

Ferguson, H. (2004) *Protecting Children in Time: Child Abuse, Child Protection and the Consequences of Modernity.* Basingstoke: Palgrave Macmillan.

Ferguson, H. (2009) 'Performing child protection: home visiting, movement and struggle to reach the abused child.' *Child and Family Social Work 14*, 4, 471–480.

Fitzgibbon, D.W. (2007) 'Risk analysis and the new practitioner: myth or reality.' *Punishment and Society 9*, 1, 87–97.

Fitzgibbon, W. (2012) *Probation and Social Work on Trial.* London: Palgrave.

Foley, P., Roche, J. and Tucker, S. (eds) (2001) *Children in Society: Contemporary Theory, Policy and Practice.* London: The Open University.

Foucault, M. (1995) *Discipline and Punishment.* New York: Vintage Books.

Freeman, M. (1997) *The Moral Status of Children: Essays on the Rights of the Child.* The Hague: Kluwer Law International.

Freeman, M. (2009) *Hindsight: The Promises and Perils of Looking Backward.* New York: Oxford University Press.

Freud, S. (1975/1915) *A Case of Hysteria, Three Essays on the Theory of Sexuality.* Trans. J. Strachey. London: Hogarth Press.

Frosh, S. (2002a) *After Words: The Personal in Gender, Culture and Psychotherapy.* London: Palgrave.

Frosh, S. (2002b) 'Characteristics of Sexual Abusers.' In K. Wilson and A. James (eds) *The Handbook of Child Protection* (Second edition). Edinburgh: Balliere Tindall.

Frosh, S. (2002c) *Key Concepts in Psychoanalysis*. London: British Library, Science Reference & Information Service.

Frosh, S. (2003) 'Psychosocial studies and psychology: is a critical approach emerging?' *Human Relations 56*, 1547–1567.

Frosh, S. (2010) *Psychoanalysis Outside the Clinic*. London: Palgrave.

Frosh, S. and Baraitser, L. (2008) 'Psychoanalysis and psychosocial studies.' *Psychoanalysis, Culture and Society 13*, 346–365.

Furedi, F. (2008) 'Fear and security: a vulnerable-led policy response.' *Social Policy and Administration 42*, 6, 645–661.

Gadd, D. and Dixon, B. (2011) *Losing the Race: Thinking Psychosocially About Racially Motivated Crime*. London: Karnac.

Garrett, P.M. (2009a) 'The case of Baby P: opening up spaces for debate on the 'transformation' of Children's Services?' *Critical Social Policy 29*, 3, 533–547.

Garrett, P.M. (2009b) *Transforming Children's Services: Social Work, Neoliberalism and the Modern World*. Berkshire: OUP.

Gibbs, A. (2001) *Contagious Feelings: Pauline Hanson and the Epidemiology of Affect*. Available at http://australianhumanitiesreview.org/archive/Issue-December-2001/gibbs.html, accessed on 22 March 2016.

Giddens, A. (1990) *The Consequences of Modernity*. Cambridge: Polity.

Giddens, A. (1991) *Modernity and Self and Identity: Self and Society in the Late Modern Age*. Cambridge: Polity.

Giddens, A. (1994) 'Living in a Post-traditional Society.' In U. Beck, A. Giddens and S. Lash (eds) *Reflexive Modernisation: Politics, Tradition and Aesthetics in the Modern Social Order*. Cambridge: Polity.

Giddens, A. (1998) *The Third Way*. Cambridge: Polity.

Giddens, A. (1999) 'Risk and responsibility.' *Modern Law Reviews 62*, 1, 1–10.

Giddens, A. (2002) *Where Now for New Labour?* Cambridge: Polity.

Gilbert, C. (2008) 'Questions 296–300.' In *Uncorrected Transcript of Oral Evidence Taken Before the Children, Schools and Families Committee: the work of Ofsted – 10 Dec 2008*. London: House of Commons Children, Schools and Families Committee.

Girard, R. (1986) *The Scapegoat*. Baltimore: The Johns Hopkins University Press.

Goddard, C. and Liddell, M. (1995) 'Child abuse fatalities and the media: lessons from a case study.' *Child Abuse Review IV*, 355–364.

Goldson, B. (2001) 'The Demonization of Children: From the Symbolic to the Institutional.' In P. Foley, J. Roche and S. Tucker (eds) *Children in Society: Contemporary Theory, Policy and Practice*. Milton Keynes: Open University Press.

Gordon, K. (2007) 'Theorising emotion and affect.' *Feminist Theory 8*, 3, 333–348.

Gordon, L. (1988) 'The politics of child sexual abuse.' *Feminist Review Special Issue* *28 (Spring)*, 56–64.

Greenland, C (1987) *Preventing Child Abuse and Neglect Deaths.* London: Routledge.

Griffiths, D. and Moynihan, F.J. (1963) 'Multiple epiphyseal injuries in babies (Battered Baby Syndrome).' *British Medical Journal 11*, 1558–1561.

Gyford, J., Leach, S. and Game, C. (1989) *The Changing Politics of Local Government.* London: Unwin Hyman.

Hammersley, M. and Gomm, R. (2000) 'Introduction.' In R. Gomm, M. Hammersley and P. Foster (eds) *Case Study Method.* London: Sage.

Hannon, C., Wood, C. and Bazalgette, L. (2010) *In Loco parentis – A Demos Report Commissioned by Barnardo's.* Available at www.barnardos.org.uk/resources/research_and_publications/in-loco-parentis--a-demos-report-commissioned-by-barnardos/publication-view.jsp?pid=PUB-1470, accessed on 22 March 2016.

Harris, J. (2008) 'State social work: constructing the present from moments in the past.' *British Journal of Social Work 38*, 662–679.

Hay, C. (1995) 'Mobilisation through interpellation: James Bulger, juvenile crime and the construction of a moral panic.' *Social and Legal Studies 4*, 197–223.

Haydon, D., and Scraton, P. (2000) 'Condemn a little more, understand a little less: the political context and rights implications of the domestic and European rulings in the Venables-Thompson case.' *Journal of Law and Society 27*, 3, 416–448.

Hier, S. P. (ed.) (2011) *Moral Panic and the Politics of Anxiety.* London and New York: Routledge.

Hills, J. and Waldfogel, J. (2004) 'A 'third way' in welfare reform? Evidence from the United Kingdom.' *Journal of Policy Analysis and Management 23*, 4, 765–788.

Hills, J., Sefton, T. and Stewart, K. (2009) *Towards a More Equal Society: Poverty, Inequality and Policy Since 1997.* CASE Studies on Poverty, Place and Policy. Bristol: Policy Press.

Hinshelwood, R.D. (1989) 'Social Possession of Identity.' In B.E. Richards (ed.) *Crisis of the Self: Further Essays on Psychoanalysis and Politics.* London: Free Association Books.

Hinshelwood, R.D. (1994) *Clinical Klein.* London: Free Association Books.

Hitlin, S. and Vaisey S. (eds) (2010) *Handbook of Sociology of Morality.* New York: Springer Science and Business Media.

HM Government (2006) *Working Together to Safeguard Children: A Guide to Inter-agency Working to Safeguard and Promote the Welfare of Children.* London: TSO.

HM Government (2011) *A New Approach to Child Poverty: Tackling the Causes of Disadvantage and Transforming Families' Lives.* London: TSO.

HM Treasury (2008) *Ending Child Poverty: Everybody's Business.* London: HM Treasury.

Hoggett, P. (2000) *Emotional Life and the Politics of Welfare.* Basingstoke and New York: Macmillan Press/St. Martin's Press.

Hoggett, P. (2008) 'What's in a hyphen? Reconstructing psychosocial studies.' *Psychoanalysis, Culture and Society 13*, 379–384.

Hoggett, P. (2009) *Politics, Identity, and Emotion.* Boulder, CO: Paradigm Publishers.

Holland, S. (1996) *The Internet Regression: Psychology of Cyberspace.* Available at http://users.rider.edu/~suler/psycyber/holland.html, accessed on 22 March 2016.

Hollway, W. (2004) 'Psycho-social research. Editorial introduction to Special Issue on psycho-social research.' *International Journal of Critical Psychology 10*, 1–5.

Hollway, W. and Featherstone, B. (eds) (1997) *Mothering and Ambivalence.* London: Routledge.

Hollway, W. and Jefferson, T. (1997) 'The risk society in an age of anxiety: situating the fear of crime.' *British Journal of Sociology 48*, 2, 255–266.

Hollway, W. and Jefferson, T. (2013) *Doing Qualitative Research Differently – A Psychosocial Approach.* London, California, New Delhi, Singapore: Sage.

Home Office (1999) *Supporting Families.* Available at http://webarchive.nationalarchives.gov.uk/+/http://www.nationalarchives.gov.uk/ERORecords/HO/421/2/P2/ACU/SUPPFAM.HTM, accessed on 22 March 2016.

Hood, C. (2002) 'The risk game and the blame game.' *Government and Opposition 37*, 1, 15–37.

Hood, C. (2007) 'What happens when transparency meets blame-avoidance.' *Public Management Review 9*, 2, 191–210.

Hook, D. (2008) 'Articulating psychoanalysis and psychosocial studies: limitations and possibilities.' *Psychoanalysis, Culture and Society 13*, 397–405.

Hopkins, G. (2007) *What Have We Learned? Child Death Scandals Since 1944.* Available at www.communitycare.co.uk/2007/01/10/what-have-we-learned-child-death-scandals-since-1944, accessed on 22 March 2016.

Horlick-Jones, T. (2005) 'Informal logics of risk: contingency and modes of practical reasoning.' *Journal of Risk Research 8*, 3, 253–272.

Howe, A. (ed.) (1998) *Sexed Crime in the News.* Melbourne: Federation Press.

Hunt, A. (2011) 'Fractious Rivals? Moral Panic and Moral Regulation.' In S.P. Hier (ed.) *Moral Panic and the Politics of Anxiety.* London and New York: Routledge.

Ince, D. and Griffiths, A. (2011) 'A chronicling system for children's social work: learning from ICS failure.' *British Journal of Social Work 41*, 8, 1497–1513.

Index of Multiple Deprivation (2010) *English Indices of Deprivation 2010.* Available at http://data.gov.uk/dataset/index-of-multiple-deprivation, accessed on 22 March 2016.

Iphofen, R. (2009) *Ethical Decision-making in Social Research: A Practical Guide.* Basingstoke: Palgrave Macmillan.

Jackson, L.A. (2000) *Child Sexual Abuse in Victorian England.* London and New York: Routledge.

James, A. and Prout, A. (eds) (2005) *Constructing and Reconstructing Childhood: Contemporary Issues in the Sociological Studies of Childhood*. London: Falmer.

James, A., Jenks, C. and Prout A. (1998) *Theorising Childhood*. London: Polity.

Jeffrey, V. (1992) 'The search for the scapegoat deviant.' *Humanist 52*, 5, 10–14.

Jenkins, P. (1992) *Intimate Enemies: Moral Panics in Contemporary Great Britain*. New York: Aldine de Gruyter.

Jenks, C. (2005) *Childhood* (Second edition). London and New York: Routledge.

Jervis, M. (2009) *Misconceiving the Evidence – Competence and Context in Child Abuse Trials*. Available at www.chrissaltrese.co.uk/wp-content/uploads/Misconceiving-the-evidence.pdf, accessed on 31 May 2016.

Johnston, R. and Pattie, C. (2006) *Putting Voters in Their Place: Geography and Elections in Great Britain*. Oxford: Oxford University Press.

Johnston, R. and Pattie, C. (2011) 'Where did Labour's votes go? Valence politics and campaign effects at the 2010 British General Election.' *The British Journal of Politics and International Relations 13*, 3, 283–303.

Jones, O. (2012) *Chavs*. London and New York: Verso.

Jones, R. (2014) *The Story of Baby P: Setting the Record Straight*. Bristol: Policy Press.

Kempe, C.H., Silverman, F.N., Steel, B.F., Droegmuller, W. and Silver, H.K. (1962/1985) 'The battered child syndrome.' *Child Abuse and Neglect 9*, 143–154.

King, M. (1995) 'The James Bulger murder trial: moral dilemma and social solutions.' *International Journal of Children's Rights 3*, 2, 167–187.

Kitzinger, J. (2003) 'Creating Discourses of False Memory: Media Coverage and Production Dynamics.' In P. Reavy and S. Warner (eds) *New Feminist Stories of Child Sexual Abuse: Sexual Scripts and Dangerous Dialogues*. London: Routledge.

Kitzinger, J. (2004) *Framing Abuse, Media Influence and Public Understanding of Sexual Violence Against Children*. London: Pluto.

Klein, M. (1946/1975) *The Writings of Melanie Klein, Vol. 3*. London: Hogarth Press.

Klein, M. (1952) 'Some Theoretical Conclusions Regarding the Emotional Life of the Infant.' In M. Klein, P. Heimann, S. Isaacs and R. Riviere (eds) *Developments in Psycho-analysis*. London: Hogarth Press.

Klein, M., Heimann, P., Isaacs, S., and Riviere, R. (eds) (1952) *Developments in Psycho-analysis*. London: Hogarth Press.

Klein, M., Heinemann, P. and Money-Kyrle, R.E. (1955/85) *New Directions in Psychoanalysis: The Significance of Infant Conflict in the Pattern of Adult Behaviour*. London: Tavistock.

Kuhn, R. (2007) *Politics and the Media in Britain*. Basingstoke: Palgrave Macmillan.

La Fontaine, J.S. (1994) *The Extent and Nature of Organised and Ritual Abuse Research Findings*. London: HMSO.

La Fontaine, J.S. (1998) Speak of the Devil: Tales of Satanic Abuse in Contemporary England. Cambridge: Cambridge University Press.

Labour Party (2001) *New Ambitions for Our Country (Election Manifesto)*. Available at http://labourmanifesto.com/2001/2001-labour-manifesto.shtml, accessed on 22 March 2016.

Laming Report (2003) *The Victoria Climbié Inquiry: Report of the Inquiry by Lord Laming*. London: TSO.

Laming Report (2009) *The Protection of Children in England: A Progress Report*. London: TSO.

Latour, B. (2005) *Reassembling the Social: An Introduction to Actor-Network Theory*. New York: Oxford University Press.

Laughey, D. (2007) *Key Themes in Media Theory*. Berkshire: OUP.

Law, J. (2009) 'Actor-network Theory and Material Semiotics.' In B.S. Turner (ed.) *The New Blackwell Companion to Social Theory* (Third edition). Oxford: Blackwell.

Lees, A., Meyer, E. and Rafferty, J. (2013) 'From Menzies Lyth to Munro: the problem of managerialism.' *British Journal of Social Work 43*, 3 542–558.

Leveson Inquiry (2012a) *Transcript of the Afternoon Hearing 10 May 2012*. Available at www.levesoninquiry.org.uk/wp-content/uploads/2012/05/Transcript-of-Afternoon-Hearing-10-May-2012.pdf, accessed on 22 March 2016.

Leveson Inquiry (2012b) *Transcript of the Afternoon Hearing 11 May 2012*. Available at www.levesoninquiry.org.uk/wp-content/uploads/2012/05/Transcript-of-Afternoon-Hearing-11-May-2012.pdf, accessed on 22 March 2016.

Leveson Report (2012) *An Inquiry into the Culture, Practice and Ethics of the Press*. Available at www.gov.uk/government/uploads/system/uploads/attachment_data/file/270939/0780_i.pdf accessed on 22 March 2016.

Levitas, R. (2005/1998) *The Inclusive Society? Social Exclusion and New Labour*. Basingstoke: Macmillan.

Lewis, J. and Surender, R. (2004) *Welfare State Change: Towards a Third Way?* Oxford: Oxford University Press.

Lincoln, Y.S. and Guba, E.G. (2000) 'The Only Generalisation Is that There Is No Generalisation.' In R. Gomm, M. Hammersley and P. Foster (eds) *Case Study Method*. London: Sage.

Lippmann, W. (1992) *Public Opinion*. New York: Macmillan.

Lister, R. (2006) 'Children (but not women) first: New Labour, child welfare and gender.' *Critical Social Policy 26*, 2, 315–335.

Littlechild, B. (2008) 'Child protection social work: risks of fears and fears of risks – impossible tasks from impossible goals?' *Social Policy & Administration 42*, 6, 662–675.

London Borough of Brent (1985) *A Child in Trust: Report of the Panel of Inquiry Investigating the Circumstances Surrounding the Death of Jasmine Beckford*. Brent: London Borough of Brent.

London Borough of Greenwich (1987) *A Child in Mind: Protection of Children in a Responsible Society: The Report of the Commission of Inquiry into the Circumstances Surrounding the Death of Kimberley Carlile*. Greenwich: London Borough of Greenwich.

Lownsborough, H., and O'Leary, D. (2005) *The Leadership Imperative: Reforming Children's Services from the Ground up.* London: Demos.

Lund, B. (2002) *State Welfare: Social Justice or Social Exclusion.* London: Sage.

Macdonald, G. and Macdonald, K. (2010) 'Safeguarding: a case for intelligent risk management.' *British Journal of Social Work 40*, 4, 1174–1191.

MacInnes, T., Parekh, A. and Kenway, P. (2010) *London's Poverty Profile: Reporting on the Recession.* London: New Policy Institute.

MacNicol, J. (2010) *New Labour's Anti-Poverty Strategy 1997–2010.* Available at www. sciencespo.fr/ceri/sites/sciencespo.fr.ceri/files/art_jm_0.pdf, accessed on 22 March 2016.

Maluccio, A.N., Fein, E. and Olmstead, K.A. (1986) *Permanency Planning for Children: Concepts and Methods.* New York: Routledge/Chapman and Hall.

Mann, K. (2009) 'Remembering and rethinking the social divisions of welfare: 50 years on.' *Journal of Social Politics 38*, 1, 1–18.

Margetts, H.Z., John, P., Hale, S.A. and Reissfelder, S. (2013) *Leadership without Leaders? Starters and Followers in Online Collective Action.* Presentation to 'Collective Action' ECPR Conference, Rejkavik. Available at http://paperroom.ipsa.org/papers/paper_16025.pdf, accessed on 22 March 2016.

Masson, J. (2008) 'The state as parent: the reluctant parent? The problem of parents as last resort.' *Journal of Law and Society 35*, 52–74.

Masson, J., Pearce, J. and Bader, K. (2008) *Care Profiling Study.* London: Ministry of Justice.

Masson, J.M. (1984) *The Assault on Truth: Freud's Suppression of the Seduction Theory.* Harmondsworth: Penguin.

Mauthner, M.L. (2002) *Ethics in Qualitative Research.* London: Sage.

Maxwell, J.A. (2008) 'The Value of a Realist Understanding of Causality for Qualitative Research.' In N. Denzin and M.D. Giardina (eds) *Qualitative Research and the Politics of Evidence.* Walnut Creek, CA: Left Coast Press.

Maxwell, J.A. (2012) *A Realist Approach for Qualitative Research.* Los Angeles, London, New Delhi, Singapore, Washington D.C.: Sage.

Mazzoleni, G. (2008) *Media Logic.* Available at www.communicationencyclopedia. com/public/search?query=Mazzoleni, accessed on 22 March 2016.

McIntosh, M. (1988) 'Family secrets as public drama.' *Feminist Review Special Issue 28 (Spring)*, 6–15.

Menzies Lyth, I. (1988/1960) *Containing Anxiety in Institutions. Selected Essays, Vol. 1.* London: Free Association.

Mills, N. (2001) 'The new culture of apology.' *Dissent 48*, 113–116.

Milner, J. (2001) *Women and Social Work.* Basingstoke: Palgrave Macmillan.

Money-Kyrle, R. (2015/1961) *Man's Picture of His World and Three Papers.* London: Karnac.

Morris, C. (1984) *The Permanency Principle in Child Care Social Work*. Norwich: Social Work Monographs.

Motz, A. (2008) *The Psychology of Female Violence: Crimes against the Body*. East Sussex: Routledge.

Munro, E. (1996) 'Avoidable and unavoidable mistakes in child protection work.' *British Journal of Social Work 26*, 6, 793–808.

Munro, E. (2004) 'The Impact of Child Abuse Inquiries since 1990.' In N. Stanley and J. Manthorpe (eds) *The Age of the Inquiry: Learning and Blaming in Health and Social Care*. London: Routledge.

Munro, E. (2005) 'A systems approach to investigating child abuse deaths.' *British Journal of Social Work 35*, 4, 531–546.

Munro, E. (2010) 'Learning to reduce risk in child protection.' *British Journal of Social Work 40*, 4, 1135–1151.

Munro, E. and Hubbard, A. (2011) 'A systems approach to evaluating organisational change in children's social care.' *British Journal of Social Work 41*, 4, 726–743.

Munro, W. (2011) *The Search for Objectivity in Measuring Social Work Outcomes*. Available at www.communitycare.co.uk/2011/12/02/the-search-for-objectivity-in-measuring-social-work-outcomes, accessed on 22 March 2016.

Murray, C. and Hernstein, R. (1994) *The Bell Curve*. New York: Simon and Schuster.

Nava, M. (1988) 'Cleveland and the press: outrage and anxiety in the reporting of child sexual abuse.' *Feminist Review Special Issue 28 (Spring)*, 103–121.

Neubaum, G., Rosner, L., Rösenthal-von der Pütten, A.M. and Krämer, N.C. (2014) 'Psychosocial functions of social media usage in a disaster situation: a multi-methodological approach.' *Computers in Human Behaviour 34*, 28–38.

Neuman, W.L. (2011) *Social Research Methods: Qualitative and Quantitative Approaches* (7th edition). Boston, MA: Pearson.

Newman, J. (2001) *Modernising Governance*. London: Sage.

Newman, J. (2004) 'Constructing accountability, network governance and managerial agency.' *Public Policy and Administration 19*, 4, 17–33.

Newman, J. (2010) 'Civicness and the Paradoxes of Contemporary Governance.' In T. Blanden, P. Dekker and A. Evers (eds) *Civicness in the Governance and Delivery of Social Services*. Baden Baden: Nomos.

Obama, B. (2006) *The Audacity of Hope: Thoughts on Reclaiming the American Dream*. New York: Crown Publishers.

Ofsted (2003) *Haringey Inspection Report*. Available on application to Ofsted at enquiries@ofsted.gov.uk.

Ofsted (2005) *Haringey Annual Performance Assessment*. Available on application to Ofsted at enquiries@ofsted.gov.uk.

Ofsted (2006) *Haringey Joint Area Review 2006*. Available on application to Ofsted at enquiries@ofsted.gov.uk.

Ofsted (2007a) *Haringey Annual Performance Assessment*. Available on application to Ofsted at enquiries@ofsted.gov.uk.

Ofsted (2007b) *The Annual Report of Her Majesty's Chief Inspector 2006/7*. Available on application to Ofsted at enquiries@ofsted.gov.uk.

Ofsted (2008a) *The Haringey Joint Area Review 2008*. Available on application to Ofsted at enquiries@ofsted.gov.uk.

Ofsted (2008b) *Learning Lessons, Taking Action: Ofsted's Evaluations of Serious Case Reviews. April 2007–March 2008*. Available on application to Ofsted at enquiries@ofsted.gov.uk.

Ofsted (2008c) *London Borough of Haringey Fostering Service*. Available on application to Ofsted at enquiries@ofsted.gov.uk.

Ofsted (2008d) *London Borough of Haringey Private Fostering Arrangements Service*. Available on application to Ofsted at enquiries@ofsted.gov.uk.

Ofsted (2008e) *Haringey Annual Performance Assessment 2008*. Available on application to Ofsted at enquiries@ofsted.gov.uk.

Ofsted (2009) *Learning Lessons from Serious Case Reviews: 2008–2009*. Available on application to Ofsted at enquiries@ofsted.gov.uk.

Ofsted (2010) *Learning Lessons from Serious Case Reviews: 2009–2010*. Available on application to Ofsted at enquiries@ofsted.gov.uk.

Parker, R. (1997) 'The Production and Purposes of Maternal Ambivalence.' In W. Hollway and B. Featherstone (eds) *Mothering and Ambivalence*. London: Routledge.

Parton, N. (1985) *The Politics of Child Abuse*. London: Macmillan.

Parton, N. (1986) 'The Beckford Report: a critical appraisal.' *British Journal of Social Work 16*, 5, 511–530.

Parton, N. (1991) *Governing the Family: Child Care, Child Protection and the State*. London: Macmillan.

Parton, N. (1998) 'Risk, advanced liberalism and child welfare: the need to rediscover uncertainty and ambiguity.' *British Journal of Social Work 28*, 1, 5–27.

Parton, N. (2001) 'Risk and Professional Judgment.' In L. Cull and J. Roche (eds) *The Law and Social Work: Contemporary Issues for Practice*. Basingstoke: Palgrave Macmillan.

Parton, N. (2004) 'From Maria Colwell to Victoria Climbié, reflections on possible inquiries into child abuse a generation apart.' *Child Abuse Review 13*, 2, 80–94.

Parton, N. (2006) *Safeguarding Children: Early Intervention and Surveillance in a Late Modern Society*. London: Palgrave Macmillan.

Parton, N. (2010) The Increasing Complexity of 'Working Together to Safeguard Children'. Available at http://eprints.hud.ac.uk/9906/3/The_Increasing_Complexity_of_Working_Together_to_Safeguard_Children_in_EnglandJune101RevisedOct10.pdf, accessed on 22 March 2016.

Parton, N. (2011) 'Child protection and safeguarding in England: changing and competing conceptions of risk and their implications for social work.' *British Journal of Social Work 41*, 5, 854–875.

Parton, N. (2014) *The Politics of Child Protection: Contemporary Developments and Future Directions.* Hampshire: Palgrave Macmillan.

Parton, N. and Frost, N. (2009) *Understanding Children's Social Care: Politics, Policy and Practice.* London, California, New Delhi, Singapore: Sage.

Payne, M. (2005) *The Origins of Social Work: Continuity and Change.* Hampshire: Palgrave Macmillan.

Perri, 6., Radstone, S., Squire, C. and Treacher, A. (2007) *Public Emotions.* Hampshire and New York: Palgrave Macmillan.

Petts, J., Horlick-Jones, J.T. and Murdock, G. (2001) *Social Amplification of Risk: The Media and the Public.* Sudbury: HSE Books.

Porter, T. and Gavin H. (2010) 'Infanticide and neonaticide: a review of 40 years of research literature on incidence and cause.' *Trauma, Violence and Abuse 11,* 3, 99–112.

Postman, N. (1994) *The Disappearance of Childhood.* New York: Vintage Books.

Powell, F. (2001) *The Politics of Social Work.* London: Sage.

Powell, F. and Scanlon, M. (2015) *Dark Secrets of Childhood.* Bristol: Policy Press.

Powell, M. (2000) *New Labour, New Welfare State?* (Second edition). Bristol: Policy Press.

Powell, M. (2002) *Evaluating New Labour's Welfare Reforms.* Bristol: Policy Press.

Powell, M., Bauld L. and Clarke, K. (eds) (2005) *Social Policy Review 17: Analysis and Debate in Social Policy.* Bristol: Policy Press.

Power, M. (2007) *Organised Uncertainty: Designing a World of Risk Management.* Oxford: OUP.

Prior, L. (2003) *Using Documents in Social Research.* London: Sage.

Prout, A. (2005) *The Future of Childhood: Towards the Interdisciplinary Study of Childhood.* London: Routledge Falmer.

Radford, L., Corral, S., Bradley, C., Fisher, H., Bassett, C., Howat, N. and Collishaw, S. (2008) *Child Abuse and Neglect in the UK Today.* London: NSPCC. Available from www.nspcc.org.uk/globalassets/documents/research-reports/child-abuse-neglect-uk-today-research-report.pdf, accessed on 31 May 2016.

Reamer, F.G. (2006) *Social Work Values and Ethics* (Third edition). New York, West Sussex: Columbia University Press.

Reavey, P. and Warner, S. (eds) (2003) *New Feminist Stories of Child Sexual Abuse: Sexual Scripts and Dangerous Dialogues.* London: Routledge.

Reder, P. and Duncan, S. (2004) 'From Colwell to Climbié: Inquiring into Fatal Child Abuse.' In N. Stanley and J. Manthorpe (eds) *The Age of the Inquiry, Learning and Blaming in Health and Social Care.* London: Brunner-Routledge.

Richards, B. (2007) *Emotional Governance: Politics, Media and Terror.* Hampshire and New York: Palgrave Macmillan.

Riley, D. (2005) *Impersonal Passion, Language as Affect.* Duke University Press.

Ritzer, G. (2008) *Sociological Theory* (Seventh edition). New York: McGraw-Hill.

Riviere, J. (1952) 'Developments in Psycho-Analysis.' In M. Klein, P. Heimann, S. Isaacs and R. Riviere (eds) *Developments in Psycho-analysis.* London: Hogarth Press.

Rosen, L.N. and Etlin, M. (1996) *The Hostage Child: Sex Abuse Allegations in Custody Disputes.* Bloomington: Indiana University Press.

Roseneil, S. (2009) 'Haunting in an age of individualisation: subjectivity, relationality and the traces of the lives of others.' *European Societies 11*, 3, 411–430.

Roseneil, S. and Mann, K. (1996) 'Unpalatable Choices and Inadequate Families: Lone Mothers and the Underclass Debate.' In E. Bortolaia-Silva (ed.) *Good Enough Mothering? Feminist Perspectives on Lone Motherhood.* London and New York: Routledge.

Roth, E.T. (2010) 'The Moral Construction of Risk.' In S. Hitlin and S. Vaisey (eds) *Handbook of Sociology of Morality.* New York: Springer Science and Business Media.

Ruch, G. (2007) 'Reflective practice in contemporary child care social work: the role of containment.' *British Journal of Social Work 37*, 2, 659–680.

Ruch, G., Turney, D. and Ward, A. (2010) *Relationship-Based Social Work.* London: Jessica Kingsley Publishers.

Rustin, M. (2004) 'Learning from the Victoria Climbié Inquiry.' *Journal of Social Work Practice 18*, 1, 9–18.

Rustin, M. (2005) 'Conceptual analysis of critical moments in Victoria's life.' *Child and Family Social Work 10*, 11–19.

Rustin, M. (2007) 'Private Solutions to Public Problems? Psychoanalysis and the Emotions.' In Perri 6, S. Radstone, C. Squire and A. Treacher (eds) *Public Emotions.* Hampshire: Palgrave Macmillan.

Ryan Report (2009) *The Commission to Inquire into Child Abuse (CICA).* Available from www.childabusecommission.ie/publications/index.html, accessed on 22 March 2016.

Schlesinger, P. and Tumber, H. (1994) *Reporting Crime: The Media Politics of Criminal Justice.* Oxford: Clarendon.

Schlosberg, J. (2013) *Power Beyond Scrutiny: Media, Justice and Accountability.* London: Pluto.

Schudson, M. (2003) *The Sociology of News.* New York: Norton.

Secretary of State for Social Services (1974) *Report of the Committee of Inquiry into the Care and Supervision Provided in Relation to Maria Colwell.* London: HMSO.

Secretary of State for Social Services (1988) *Report of the Inquiry into Child Abuse in Cleveland.* London: HMSO.

Seebohm, F. (1968) *Report of the Committee on Local Authority and Allied Personal Social Services.* CM 3703. London: HMSO.

Segal, H. (1973) *Introduction to the Work of Melanie Klein.* London: Hogarth Press.

Segal, H. (1988) *Introduction to the Work of Melanie Klein.* London: Hogarth Press.

Seu, I.B. (2013) *Passivity Generation, Human Rights and Everyday Morality.* Hampshire, New York: Palgrave Macmillan.

Shenassa, C.R. (2001) *The Scapegoat Mechanism in Human Group Processes.* Cincinatti, OH: The Union Institute Graduate College.

Sibert Report (2008) *Review of Dr Sabah Al-Zayyat's Involvement in Child A [Baby P] Case.* By Professor Sibert and Dr Hodes, available from Great Ormond Street Hospital, Great Ormond Street, London WC1N 3JH.

Sidebotham, P., Brandon, M., Powell, C., Solebo, C., Koistenen, J. and Ellis, C. (2010) *Learning from Serious Case Reviews: Report of a Research Study of Learning Lessons Nationally from Serious Case Reviews.* London: DfE.

Smith, E. (1997) *Integrity and Change, Mental Health in the Marketplace.* London and New York: Routledge.

Stainton-Rogers, W. (2001) 'Constructing Childhood: Constructing Child Concern.' In P. Foley, J. Roche and S. Tucker (eds) *Children in Society.* Milton Keynes: The Open University.

Stake, R.E. (2000) 'The Case Study Method in Social Inquiry.' In R. Gomm, M. Hammersley and P. Foster (eds) *Case Study Method.* London: Sage.

Stanley, N. and Manthorpe, J. (eds) (2004) *The Age of the Inquiry, Learning and Blaming in Health and Social Care.* London: Routledge.

Stanley, S. (2001) 'Disembodiment is a cyberspace myth: discourse and the self in real space.' *Cyberpsychology and Behaviour 4*, 1, 77–93.

Steiner, J. (1993) *Psychic Retreats.* London and New York: Tavistock/Routledge.

Stokes, J. and Schmidt, G. (2011) 'Race, poverty and child protection decision making.' *British Journal of Social Work 41*, 6, 1105–1121.

Stroud, J. (2008) 'A psychosocial analysis of child homicide.' *Critical Social Policy 28*, 482–505.

Stroud, J. and Pritchard, C. (2001) 'Child homicide, psychiatric disorder and dangerousness: a review and an empirical approach.' *British Journal of Social Work 31*, 2, 249–269.

Sturken, M. and Cartwright, L. (2001) *Practices of Looking: An Introduction to Visual Culture.* New York: Oxford University Press.

Syed, M. (2015) *Black Box Thinking.* New York and Harmondsworth: Portfolio/Penguin.

Taft, L. (2000) 'Apology subverted: the commodification of apology.' *Yale Law Journal 109*, 5, 1135–2000.

Taylor, J. and Daniel, B. (eds) (2005) *Child Neglect – Practice Issues for Health and Social Care.* London: Jessica Kingsley Publishers.

The Bichard Inquiry Report (2004) Available at http://media.education.gov.uk/assets/files/pdf/b/bichard%20inquiry%20report.pdf, accessed on 22 March 2016.

The Francis Report (2013) *Report of the Mid Staffordshire NHS Foundation Trust Public Inquiry: Executive Summary.* London: TSO. Available at http://webarchive.nationalarchives.gov.uk/20150407084003/http://www.midstaffspublicinquiry.com/sites/default/files/report/Executive%20summary.pdf, accessed on 7 June 2016.

The Orkney Report (1992) *The Report of the Inquiry into the Removal of Children from Orkney 1991.* Available at www.gov.uk/government/publications/inquiry-into-the-removal-of-children-from-orkney-in-february-1991, accessed on 22 March 2016.

Thompson, D.F. (1980) 'Moral responsibility of public officials: the problem of many hands.' *American Political Science Review 74*, 4, 905–916.

Trowler, I. (2015) 'Chief social worker: "Very difficult" to secure convictions from Cameron's jail proposals,' Community Care, 9 March 2015. Available at www.communitycare.co.uk/2015/03/09/chief-social-worker-difficult-secure-convictions-camerons-jail-proposals, accessed on 22 March 2016.

Turner, B.S. (ed.) (2009) The *New Blackwell Companion to Social Theory* (Third edition). Oxford: Blackwell.

Walker, M. (1997) 'Working with Abused Clients in an Institutional Setting.' In E. Smith (ed.) *Integrity and Change, Mental Health in the Marketplace.* London and New York: Routledge.

Walsh, D. and Evans, K. (2014) 'Critical realism: an important theoretical perspective for midwifery research.' *Midwifery 30*, e1–e6.

Warner, J. (2013a) '"Heads must roll?" Emotional politics, the press and the death of Baby P.' *British Journal of Social Work 44*, 6, 1637–1653.

Warner, J. (2013b) 'Social work, class politics and risk in the moral panic over Baby P.' *Health, Risk and Society 15*, 3, 217–233.

Warner, J. (2015) *The Emotional Politics of Social Work and Child Protection.* Bristol: Policy Press.

Weaver, R.K. (1986) 'The politics of blame-avoidance.' *Journal of Public Policy 6*, 4, 371–398.

Webb, S.A. (2007) *Social Workers in a Risk Society: Social and Political Perspective.* Basingstoke: Palgrave Macmillan.

Webster, F. (2001a) 'A new politics?' In F. Webster (ed.) *Culture and Politics in the Information Age.* London and New York: Routledge.

Webster, F. (ed.) (2001b) *Culture and Politics in the Information Age.* London and new York: Routledge.

Welch, M. (2006) *Scapegoats of Sept 11th: Hate Crimes and State Crimes in the War on Terror.* New Brunswick, NJ: Rutgers University Press.

Welch, M. (2007) 'Moral Panic, Denial And Human Rights: Scanning the Spectrum Moral Underclass Discourse from Overreaction to Underreaction.' In D. Downes, P. Rock, C. Chinkin and C. Gearty (eds) *Crime, Social Control and Human Rights, from Moral Panics to States of Denial, Essays in Honour of Stanley Cohen.* Cullompton: Willan.

White, S., Wastell, D., Broadbent, K., and Hall, C. (2010) 'When policy o'erleaps itself: the 'tragic tale' of the Integrated Children's System.' *Critical Social Policy* 30, 405.

Whitfield, D. (2007) *New Labour's Attack on Public Services.* Nottingham: Spokesman Books.

Whittier, N. (2009) *The Politics of Child Sexual Abuse: Emotions, Social Movements and the State.* New York and Oxford: OUP.

WHO (World Health Organisation) (2008) *Health For All Database.* Copenhagen: Regional Office for Europe.

Williams, F. (2004) 'What matters is who works: Why every child matters to New Labour. Commentary on the DfES Green Paper 'Every Child Matters'.' *Critical Social Policy 24*, 3, 406–427.

Williams, F. (2005) 'New Labour's Family Policy.' In M. Powell, L. Bauld and K. Clarke (eds) *Social Policy Review 17: Analysis and Debate in Social Policy.* Bristol: Policy Press.

Winnicott, D.W. (1964) *The Child the Family and the Outside World.* London: Pelican.

Women's Budget Group (2005) *Women's and Children's Poverty: Making the Links.* Available at www.wbg.org.uk/documents/WBGWomensandchildrenspoverty.pdf, accessed on 22 March 2016.

Young, R.M. (1995) *Psychoanalysis and/of the Internet.* Available at www.human-nature.com/rmyoung/papers/paper36.html, accessed on 22 March 2016.

Young, R.M. (1996) *Primitive Processes on the Internet.* Available at www.human-nature.com/rmyoung/papers/prim.html, accessed on 22 March 2016.

Zelizer, V.A. (1985) *Pricing the Priceless Child.* Princeton, NJ: Princeton University Press.

Zinn, J.O. (ed.) (2008) *Social Theories of Risk and Uncertainty: An Introduction.* Oxford, Malden and Australia: Blackwell.

Notes

Introduction

1. Article available from www.communitycare.co.uk/blogs/social-work-blog/2009/01/community-care-calls-on-sun-to-2.

2. The Royal Courts of Justice, The Queen on application of Sharon Shoesmith v Ofsted, Secretary of State for Children, Schools and Families, and London Borough of Haringey, Judgment of the Administrative Court, 23 April 2010 is available at www.familylaw.co.uk/system/uploads/attachments/0000/2670/shoesmith-full-judgment.pdf, referred to in footnotes as the High Court Judgment 23/04/10. The Appeal Court judgment, 27 May 2011, is available at www.bailii.org/ew/cases/EWCA/Civ/2011/642.html.

3. Appeal Court Judgment, paragraph 135.

4. Full speech by Rebekah Brooks available at www.theguardian.com/media/2009/jan/27/rebekahwade-sun.

5. Information available at www.theguardian.com/uk-news/2014/feb/27/brooks-regrets-page-3-attack-clare-short-phone-hacking-trial.

6. Interview with BBC1 available at http://news.bbc.co.uk/1/hi/uk/7745497.stm.

7. Available at http://webarchive.nationalarchives.gov.uk/20130401151655/http://www.education.gov.uk/researchandstatistics/statistics/statistics-by-topic/childrenandfamilies/lookedafterchildren.

Chapter 1

8. *The cost of culpability*, available at www.theguardian.com/society/2002/mar/18/3.

9. *Fears of Climbié inquiry 'injustice'*, available at www.theguardian.com/society/2001/dec/13/1.

10. Ibid.

11. Ibid.

Chapter 2

12. *'The woman who could have stopped Orkney satanic abuse scandal,'* available at www.bbc.co.uk/news/uk-scotland-23958348.

13. *Climbié inquiry chief under fire*, available at www.theguardian.com/society/2001/jan/19/socialcare.

Chapter 4

14. *Profile: Dr David Kelly*, available at http://news.bbc.co.uk/1/hi/uk_politics/3076869.stm.

15. *Derek Lewis's dismissal illustrates the urgent need to re-examine the respective roles of those in day-to-day control and their political masters*, available at www.lawgazette.co.uk/news/yes-minister-no-minister-derek-lewis-dismissed-illustrates-the-urgent-need-to-re-examine-the-respective-roles-of-those-in-day-to-day-control-and-their-political-masters/20132.fullarticle.

16. *Ed Balls accused over SATs fiasco by ex-QCA head*, available at www.guardian.co.uk/education/2009/apr/23/sats-ed-balls-ken-boston.

17. See High Court Judgment 23/04/08 paragraph 49.

Chapter 5

18. Details at www.bbc.co.uk/programmes/b04n6sm0.

19. BBC Five Live, News at Five, Tuesday 11 November 2008.

20. High Court Judgment 23/04/10 paragraph 114.

21. High Court Judgment 23/04/10, paragraphs 94, 95, 101 and 117.

22. See references to these briefings in the High Court Judgment 23/04/10, paragraphs 94, 95, 101 and 117.

23. Information available at www.bbc.co.uk/news/uk-32928540.

24. Available to view at http://news.bbc.co.uk/1/hi/uk_politics/7725514.stm

25. High Court Judgment 23/04/10, paragraphs 94 and 95.

26. High Court Judgment 23/04/10, paragraphs 133 and 134.

27. Available at http://news.bbc.co.uk/1/hi/7730419.stm.

28. For a description of the three Facebook groups, see Appendix 3.

29. High Court Judgment 23/04/10, paragraphs 131 and 134.

30. Quoted during the High Court case and reprinted in the *Guardian* at www. theguardian.com/society/2009/oct/07/baby-p-sharon-shoesmith-emails.

31. Detail available at http://news.bbc.co.uk/1/hi/england/london/7730817. stm.

32. See www.mirror.co.uk/news/uk-news/whistleblower-baby-p-warning-358193.

33. See Hansard 20 November 2008, Column 376.

34. High Court Judgment paragraph 310.

35. For example, videos at www.youtube.com/watch?v=zxmAnxKUzJY and www.youtube.com/watch?v=_XrKBZ2B9jo.

Chapter 6

36. Minutes of meeting between senior DCSF staff and senior Ofsted officials, 20/11/08 in which the requirements that Ed Balls had were communicated in terms of him wanting closure of 'the public enclosure'.

37. A transcript of my contemporaneous record of this feedback is referred to in the High Court Judgment at paragraph 237.

38. See High Court Judgment 23/04/10 paragraphs 131 and 134.

39. This meeting is referred to in the High Court Judgment 23/04/10 paragraph 300.

40. See High Court Judgment 23/04/10 paragraphs 20–22.

41. See High Court Judgment 23/04/10 paragraph 173.

42. Minutes of meetings between senior civil servants and Ofsted officials on Tuesday 18 and Thursday 20 November 2008.

43. Email from David Bell to Jeanette Pugh on 19/11/08 23:24.

44. The 38 SCRs consisted of 20 published in Ofsted (2008b) and covered the timescale April 2007–March 2008; the remaining SCRs were included (with others) in Ofsted (2009). The SCR for Peter Connelly was in Ofsted (2009).

45. See High Court Judgment 23/04/10 paragraph 244.

46. See High Court Judgment 23/04/10 paragraph 260.

47. See High Court Judgment 23/04/10 paragraph 260.

48. See High Court Judgment 23/04/10 paragraphs 302–303.

49. See High Court Judgment 23/04/10 paragraph 306.

50. See High Court Judgment 23/04/10 paragraph 348.

51. See www.theguardian.com/society/2009/jan/26/haringey-social-workers-baby-p.

52. See High Court Judgment 23/04/10 paragraph 328.

53. See High Court Judgment 23/04/10 paragraph 215.

54. See High Court Judgment 23/04/10 paragraph 216.

55. See www.haringeylscb.org/baby-peter-serious-case-review-statement-chairman-graham-badman.

56. See http://news.bbc.co.uk/1/hi/england/london/8616597.stm.

57. See http://news.bbc.co.uk/1/hi/england/7993069.stm.

58. 'Inquest into the Death of Peter Connelly Reports/Inquiries/Disciplinary Proceedings' MPS 18/10/10, available from coroners@justice.gsi.gov.uk.

59. 'In a Matter Touching the Death of Peter John Wood Connelly', available from coroners@justice.gsi.gov.uk.

60. Available from coroners@justice.gsi.gov.uk.

Chapter 7

61. Available at www.gov.uk/government/uploads/system/uploads/attachment_data/file/455736/CM9128_Web.pdf.

Appendix 3

62. *Belfast Telegraph, Children and Young People Now, Community Care, Daily Express, Daily Mail, Daily Mirror, Daily Star, Daily Sport, Daily Telegraph, Evening Standard, Financial Times, Guardian, Ham and High, Health Service Journal, Independent, Inside Housing, Local Government Chronicle, London Lite, London Paper, Metro, Morning Star, Municipal Journal, News of the World, Nursery World, Observer, PR Week, Public Finance, People, Spectator, Sun, Sunday Express, Sunday Mirror, Sunday Telegraph, Sunday Times, The Times, Voice, Universe.*

63. *Belfast Telegraph, Daily Express, Daily Mail, Daily Mirror, Daily Star, Daily Telegraph, Evening Standard, Guardian, Independent, London Lite, Metro, News of the World, Observer, Sun, Sunday Express, Sunday Mirror, Sunday Telegraph, Sunday Times, The Times.*

64. Available at www.google.co.uk/search?q=Facebook+users+by+gender+2008.

65. In 2008 the majority of Facebook users were in the age group 18–34 but this is not broken down by gender. The statistics for gender in 2010 showed that 54 per cent were women although the overall number of users had grown substantially.

Subject Index

accountability
  media role in 91–4
  in Children's Services 119–23, 128
Ahmed, Sara
  on 'circulation of affect' 86–9
Annual Performance Assessments (APAs)
    37–8, 112–13, 187

Baby P *see* Connelly, Peter
Badman, Graham 200, 205
Balls, Ed
  announces removal of Sharon Shoesmith
    16, 193
  and Judicial Review of Shoesmith's removal
    17
  declines to meet Sharon Shoesmith 23
  and inspection of Haringey Children's
    Services 38, 143, 181, 186–7, 188–9,
    192–3
  forces Ken Boston to resign 122
  response to death of Peter Connelly 137,
    142–3, 155–8, 162, 177
  defended by Gordon Brown 141
  public reaction to 159–60
  media reaction to 169
  relationship with media 180, 182–5, 191
  meeting with George Meehan 186
  and cultural trope of Peter Connelly 196
  and second Serious Case Review 199–200,
    203
Barker, Steven
  trial of 13, 131

  sentencing of 14, 172, 176, 205
BBC 146–8
Beckford, Jasmine 53, 56–60
Belfast Telegraph 162, 171
Bell, David 137–8, 156, 187, 1889
Bell, Stuart 61
Bell Curve, The (Murray and Hernstein) 106
Birmingham Children's Hospital 125–6
Black Box Thinking (Syed) 212
Blair, Tony 64, 90–1, 102
Blakelock, Keith 32–3, 36
blame
  psychosocial perspectives of 83–4
  avoidance of 121–2
  social workers as carriers of 191
Boston, Ken 122
Brent Council 34
British Association of Social Workers (BASW)
    219–20, 221
Brooks, Rebekah 17–18, 127, 153, 154, 174,
    182–3
Brown, Gordon 102
  response to death of Peter Connelly 15,
    141–2, 155–6, 174, 177, 196
  record as Prime Minister 123–8
  attacked by media 151
Bulger, James 53, 64–5, 154
Burstow, Paul 67
Bush, George W. 94–5
Butler, Ian 17
Butler–Sloss Inquiry 62–3

Cameron, David 127–8, 182
  response to death of Peter Connelly 15,
      140–2, 143–7, 156, 169, 174, 177–8, 196
  relationship with media 127, 152–5
  article in *Evening Standard* 143–7, 153
  supported by media 151
  letter in *The Sun* 151–5, 178
Capita 36, 37
cascade activation model 95–6, 180, 182–3
child abuse
  sequestration of information about 45–6
  and idealisation of motherhood 46–9
  growing awareness of 50–1
  government inquires into 53, 60–4, 66
  predication and prevention of 58–9
  characteristics of high-profile cases 69–70
  psychosocial perspectives of 81–3
  and response to paedophilia 98–9
  effect on of 'Every Child Matters' 113–16
  and risk management 114–18
Child Abuse Investigation Team (CAIT)
  awareness of Peter Connelly 14
  in Haringey child protection services 31
  reaction to death of Peter Connelly 132
child deaths
  sequestration of information about 45–6
  and idealisation of motherhood 46–9
child poverty 1244
child protection services
  in Haringey 31
  after Cleveland child sexual abuse case 63
  and 1989 Children Act 63
  problems of 116
child sexual abuse
  in Cleveland 53, 60–4
  and James Bulger 65
  role of media on victims 98–9
childhood attachment
  in Kleinian theory 75–7
children
  historic notions of 41–2
  development of welfare services for 42–3
  post-war notions of 43
Children Act (1948) 55
Children Act (1975) 55
Children Act (1989) 63–4
Children Act (2004)
  as response to Victoria Climbié 35, 103, 108
  and 'Every Child Matters' 109
  and inspection of Children's Services 112
  and accountability 121
children in care
  rise in after Peter Connelly's death on 18–19
  in Haringey 19, 30
  rise in during Labour government 124–5

Children and Families Act (2014) 55
Children and Social Work Bill (2016) 220
Children's Charter (1889) 42–3
Children's Services
  created under 'Every Child Matters' 108
  governance of 111
  partnership working in 111–12
  inspection of 112–13
  accountability in 119–23, 128
Children's Trusts 108–9, 121
'circulation of affect' 86–9, 99–100
  on first day after trial 135
  on second day after trial 138–9
Clark, Sally 50
Clarke, Kenneth 61–2
Cleveland child sexual abuse 53, 60–4, 122
Climbié, Victoria 28, 33–4
  and Laming Inquiry 34–6, 53, 66–9, 81–2,
      102–3, 135, 218–19
  legislation after 35
  psychosocial perspectives of 80–1
Clyde Inquiry 66
College of Social Work 219, 220
Collins, Jane 125-6, 132-3, 134
Colwell, Maria 17, 53, 54–6, 178
Commission for Social Care Inspection (CSCI)
  168
Community Care 15, 214
Comprehensive Performance Assessment
  (CPA) 113
Connelly, Peter
  death of 13, 14
  in popular culture 18
  impact of death on social care services
      18–19
  and familial child homicide 28, 29
  and 'Every Child Matters' 116
  Serious Case Review into 126, 138, 141, 142,
      143, 156–7, 170–1, 181, 187–8, 192,
      199–203, 206
  reaction to death on first day after trial
      131–8
  reaction to death on second day after trial
      138–50
  reaction to death on third day after trial
      150–61
  reaction to death on fourth day after trial
      162–7
  reaction to death on fifth and sixth day after
      trial 167–75
  as cultural trope 196–207
  lack of inquest into death 206–7
  factors in response to death 208–9
Connelly, Tracey
  trial of 13, 131, 205

Connelly, Tracy *cont.*
  sentencing of 14
  release from prison 16
  attacked in media 169–70, 172
  questions about 211–12
Corbyn, Jeremy 32
Corporate Manslaughter and Corporate
    Homicide Act (2007) 216
cot deaths 50, 51
Coughlan, John 188
Coulson, Andy 127, 153–4
critical realism 20–1
cultural congruence/incongruence 96–7
'cultural relativism' 34, 56

Daily Express 140, 151, 162, 168, 178
Daily Mail 33, 139, 151, 162, 168, 169, 170
Daily Mirror 151, 167, 168
Daily Star 151
Daily Telegraph 139–40, 146, 147, 151, 157, 167,
    169, 170
Davies, Nick 183
Defamation Act (2014) 85
demographics of Haringey 29–30
denial
  in psychosocial perspectives 79–83, 194–5
  of familial child homicide 177–9
Department for Children, Schools and Familes
    (DCSF) 136–8, 187, 189, 192
Devlin, Tim 62
documentary evidence 21–2, 236–7
Domestic Violence Crime and Victims Act
    (DVCVA 2004)
  description of 13
  data on familial child homicide 27, 28
Drakeford, Mark 17
Duncan Smith, Iain 169

Ealing Council 34
Easton, Mark 146–8
Enfield Council 34
Ennals, Paul 134–5
ethics of book 22–4
Evening Standard 135, 139, 152, 158, 162, 164,
    168–9, 178
  David Cameron's article in 143–7, 153
Every Child Matters
  as response to Victoria Climbié 35, 103, 108
  and Children's Services 108, 111–13
  social care policies in 108–9
  impact of 113–23, 128
  as flagship policy 143

failure
  nature of 212–13

familial child homicide
  and moral panic 17
  prevalence of 26–9, 51–2, 59–60, 177, 178
  as taboo 40
  government inquires into 53–60, 66–9
  realities of denied 177–9
  nature of 191
  and cultural trope 196
Featherstone, Lynne 136, 156–7, 169, 182
Foskett, Mr Justice 193
Freedom of Information Act (2000) 27
Freud, Sigmund 73–4

General Medical Council (GMC) 50
Gilbert, Christine 52, 187, 189, 197–8
Goddard Inquiry 51
Gove, Michael 147, 157, 158, 169
Grant, Bernie 33, 36
Great Ormond Street Hospital
  awareness of Peter Connelly 14
  paediatrician attacked by media 15, 16, 135
  in Haringey child protection services 31
  reaction to death of Peter Connelly 131,
    132, 135–6
  in Sibert Report 200
  in Peter Connelly's Serious Case Review 203

*Great Ormond Street Hospital – Too Important to
    Fail* (TV documentary) 18
Greenland, Cyril 57, 58
Guardian, The
  and death of Victoria Climbié 34, 67, 69
  on Bernie Grant 36
  and death of James Bulger 64
  and 2008 financial crisis 126, 127
  on death of Peter Connelly 139, 146, 167,
    168, 169
  on child abuse 178
  interview with Christine Gilbert 197–8

Haringey Council
  reaction to death of Peter Connelly 15,
    185–6
  emergency inspection by Ofsted 16, 143,
    181, 185–94, 196–9
  and Judicial Review of Shoesmith's removal
    17
  impact of Peter Connelly's death on 19
  demographics of 29–30
  poverty in 30
  work of Children's Services 30–1
  children in care 30–1
  child protection services in 31
  'loony left' reputation 32
  media attacks on 33

Haringey Council *cont.*
  and Victoria Climbié 33–4, 35–6
  improvements in Children's Services 36–8,
    133
  vulnerability of 38–9
  and Personal Social Services Performance
    Assessment Framework 110
  on first day after trial 131–5, 136, 137–8
  on second day after trial 139–43, 145–6, 149
  on third day after trial 150, 152, 158–9
  on fourth day after trial 163–4
  on fifth and sixth day after trial 168, 170–1
Health Care Commission
  response to death of Peter Connolly 15
Her Majesty's Inspectorate of Constabulary
  (HMIC)
  response to death of Peter Connolly 15
Heywood, Jeremy 188
Higgs, Marietta 61, 62, 122
Howard, Michael 64, 122
Hughes, Beverley 143, 185
Hunt, Jeremy 125

Johnson, Alan 125
Joint Area Reviews (JARs) 37–8, 112–13, 143,
  156, 181, 185–6, 187, 188, 192
Joseph, Keith 54, 106

Independent, The 134, 138–9, 163, 169, 171
Integrated Children's System (ICS) 110–11,
  114–15, 120
Introduction to the Work of Melanie Klein (Segal)
  77

Kelly, David 122
Key Concepts of Psychoanalysis (Frosh) 74
Klein, Melanie 73
  theories of 74–7, 84
  and reaction to death of Peter Connolly 150
Kober, Claire 158
Kouao, Thérèse 33, 34

Labour Party in government
  familial child homicide under 28–9
  and Victoria Climbié 35–6, 66–7, 102–3
  social work under 44
  relationship with media 90–1
  and paedophilia scare 98
  family and child protection policies 103–8
  and policies in 'Every Child Matters' 108–9
  and impact of 'Every Child Matters' 113–23
  difficulties under Gordon Brown 123–8
Laming Inquiry 34–6, 53, 66–9, 81–2, 102, 135,
  218–19
Lammy, David 157

Leveson Inquiry 127, 154–5
Lewis, Derek 122
Local Safeguarding Children Boards (LSCBs)
  108–9, 131–2, 190, 200
London Lite 139, 170, 175
Loughton, Tim 23, 200, 203
Lynch, Patricia 218–19

Mail on Sunday, The 33
Major, John 64
Manning, Carl 33
media
  reaction to death of Peter Connolly 15–16,
    133–4, 135, 138–40, 150–5, 162–4,
    167–72
  attacks on Haringey Council 33–4, 163–4
  and death of Maria Colwell 54
  and death of Jasmine Beckford 59
  relationship with politicians 89–91, 100,
    182–5
  psychosocial perspectives of 89–94, 99–100
  role in accountability 91–4
  and public engagement 94–7
  role of on victims of child sexual abuse
    98–9
  and Leveson Inquiry 127
Meehan, George 16, 158, 171, 185, 186
metonymy 87–8, 136
Metropolitan Police Service
  investigations into conduct over Peter
    Connolly 200–5
  in Peter Connolly's Serious Case Review 203
Mid-Staffordshire NHS Foundation Trust 125
moral underclass 105–6, 107–8, 128, 135,
  169–70
motherhood
  idealisation of 46–9, 70–1
  and death of James Bulger 64
  and 'gendered denial' 70–1
  in Kleinian theory 75–6
  and Tracey Connolly 170
MPS Response to the Death of Baby P 201–2
Munschausen Syndrome by proxy 50, 51, 82
Murdoch, Rupert 127

National Health Service 125–6
'natural love' 56–7
New Statesman 123
News at Ten 145–7
News of the World
  attacks Great Ormond Street paediatrician
    15
  publishes list of 'paedophiles' 97
  and phone-hacking scandal 154
  attacks Tracey Connolly 170
  attacks Ofsted 171

demands maximum sentences 172
North Middlesex University Hospital 31, 34
NSPCC
    and familial child homicide 27, 28, 52
    and Victoria Climbié 34
    early history of 42, 43
    exaggerates child abuse figures 45–6, 50
    establishes Battered Child Research Unit 51

Observer, The 62, 123, 178
O'Donovan, Ita 185–6
Office of National Statistics 26–7, 28
Ofsted
    response to death of Peter Connelly 15
    emergency inspection of Haringey Council
        16, 143, 181, 185–94, 196–9
    and Judicial Review of Sharon Shoesmith's
        removal 17
    declines to meet Sharon Shoesmith 23
    data on familial child homicide 27, 28
    inspections of Haringey's Children's
        Services 37, 38, 133
    takes over inspections of Children's Services
        112–13, 119–20
    evaluation of Peter Connelly's Serious Case
        Review 157
    attacked in media 171, 182
    evaluation of Peter Connelly's Serious Case
        Review 202
Orkney satanic abuse 53, 66
'otherness'
    in psychosocial perspectives 77–9
    and 'circulation of affect' 88
    and paedophilia scare 98
Owen, Jason
    trial of 13, 131
    sentencing of 14, 172, 205

paedophilia
    scare in Portsmouth 97–8
Panorama 18, 64, 137
Payne, Sarah 97, 154
Personal Social Services Performance
    Assessment Framework (PSSPAF) 109–11
politicians
    relationship with media 89–91, 100, 182–5
    and public engagement 94–7
    avoidance of blame 121–2
Politics of Child Abuse, The (Parton) 17
Psychic Retreats (Steiner) 79
psychoanalysis
    in psychosocial perspectives 73–7
psychosocial perspectives
    and post–Kleinian thinkers 72–3
    psychoanalysis in 73–7
    sense of 'other' in 77–9

denial in 79–83, 194–5
and social media 84–6
and 'circulation of affect' 86–9, 99–100
relationship between media and politicians
    89–91, 100
role of media in accountability 91–4
and public engagement 94–7
public responses
    on second day after trial 147–50
    on third day after trial 159–61
    on fourth day after trial 164–7
    on fifth day after trial 172–5
    planned protest 175–7
Pugh, Jeanette 126, 137–8, 156, 177, 187, 188–9

Richardson, Sue 61
risk management 114–18, 128
'rule of optimism' 56–7

Santry, Liz 16, 158–9, 160, 185
Savage, Wendy 122
scapegoating
    psychosocial perspectives of 83–4
Seebohm Report 44
Serious Case Reviews
    under 'Every Child Matters' 109
    description of 118–19
    into Peter Connelly 126, 138, 141, 142, 143,
        170–1, 181, 187–8, 192, 199–203, 206
    purpose of 212
Sheerman, Barry 157
Shoesmith, Sharon
    attacked in media 15–16, 184
    dismissed from post 16, 193
    Judicial Review of dismissal 16–17, 189,
        193, 198
    and ethics of book 22–4
    improvements at Haringey Council under
        36–7
    on first day after trial 132–4, 137
    on second day after trial 138–9, 140, 141,
        144, 145–7, 149
    on third day after trial 150, 152, 158–9
    on fourth day after trial 162–3, 164–5, 167
    invited to resign 185–6
    mentioned by Ed Balls on television 192–3
    recommendations 221–4
Sibert Report 200, 201
Singer, Henry 18
Single Central Records (SCRs) 113
social care services
    impact of Peter Connelly's death on 18–19
    and 'Every Child Matters' 108–9
    and Personal Social Services Performance
        Assessment Framework 109–11
    and notion of risk 114

social media
    reaction after death of Peter Connelly 17,
        148–9, 159–61, 165–7, 172–5
    psychosocial perspectives of 84–6
social workers
    attacked by *The Sun* 17
    post-war developments in 43–5
    as gendered profession 48–9
    and Jasmine Beckford Inquiry 56–7
    media attacks on 70
    psychosocial perspectives of 82
    and risk management 117–18
    on first day after trial 132–6, 137, 138
    on second day of trial 139–40, 144–5
    on fourth day of trial 162–3, 166–7
    on fifth and sixth days after trial 168, 170,
        173, 174–5
    as carriers of blame 191
    as cultural trope 194–7, 209–11
    and proposed crime of 'wilful neglect'
        213–18
    comparison with Germany 216–17
    fragmentation of profession 219–20
Southall, David 50, 51, 82–3
Stevenson, Olive 54–5
Story of Baby P, The – Setting the Record Straight
    (Jones) 18
Sun, The
    reaction after death of Peter Connelly 15,
        17–18, 133–4, 140, 147, 152–3, 162–4,
        165, 167–8
    and 'Beautiful Baby Campaign' petition 15,
        152–3, 155, 163, 165, 167–8, 178, 180,
        182, 183, 184, 190–1, 193

attack on social workers 17
attacks on Haringey Council 33, 163–4
campaign after James Bulger death 62, 154
develops 'Broken Britain' theme 123–4, 169
David Cameron's letter in 151–5, 178
attacks Tracey Connelly 170
relationship with Ed Ball 182–5, 191
calls for Sharon Shoesmith to resign 184
Sunday Express 168, 169, 170
Sunday People 167, 168
Sunday Times 64, 134, 178
Syndicate, The 18

Times, The 54, 126, 139, 151, 168, 170, 169,
    172, 218
Trowler, Isabelle 214

Untold Story of Baby P, The (TV documentary)
    18, 132, 187

Venables, Jon 65

Wakefield Express 162
Walker, Andrew 206–7
Whittington Hospital 31
'wilful neglect' 213–18
Willmore, Ian 36
World Health Organisation (WHO) 27

Young, Stuart 134

Author Index

Ahmed, S. 38, 72, 73, 86, 87, 88, 134, 136, 1195
Altheide, D.L. 21
Ariès, P. 41
Ashenden, S. 44
Atmore, C. 47, 60, 62
Audit Commission 37, 38, 121

Bader, K. 115
Bailey, R. 45
Baldwin, N. 107
Bauld, L. 113
Bauman, Z. 85, 117
Bazalgette, L. 55
Beattie, G. 85
Beck, U. 113, 117, 119, 157
Behlmer, G. 42
Behn, R.D. 120
Bennett, W.L. 93, 155
Bion, W. 78
Bird, J. 84, 85
Blair, T. 91, 104
Bovens, M. 92, 119, 120, 122
Bowlby, J. 43
Brake, M. 45
Brandon, M. 114, 118, 178
British Association of Social Workers (BASW)
    52
Broadhurst, K. 115
Butler, I. 17, 54
Butler-Sloss, Lady Justice 53, 62
Bynner, J. 107

CAFCASS 18, 19
Campbell, B. 60, 61, 62
Care Quality Commission (CQC) 205
Carlile, K. 59
Carsten, R. 120
Cartwright, D. 138
Centre for Public Scrutiny 123
Chodorow, N.J. 47
Civin, M. 84, 85
Clapton, G. 42
Clarke, K. 111
Cohen, S. 79, 191, 194, 198
Conn, L. 47
Contratto, S. 47
Cooke, H.F. 83
Cooper, A. 68, 80, 81, 82, 115, 150, 191
Cooper, D. 32, 33
Corby, B. 41, 58
Corbyn, J. 33
Coughlan, John 142
Crawford, C. 47
Cree, V. 42, 46
Cruddas, J. 123
CSCI 109
Cunningham, H. 42
Cutler, J. 84

Dally, A. 47
Daly, M. 112
Davies, N. 127, 183
Davis, A. 73, 89–90, 91, 92, 100, 142, 148, 151,
    154

Daycare Trust 124
DeMause, L. 41
DEMOS 108
Department for Education and Skills (DfES) 35, 103, 109, 143
Department of Health (DH) 35, 59, 68
Department of Health and Social Security (DHSS) 53, 54, 55, 63
Dickens, J. 44, 45
Dingwall, R. 57
Doig, A. 58
Douglas, M. 83, 106, 117, 165, 186
Drakeford, M. 17, 54
Driver, S. 103, 106
Duncan, S. 49
Dykman, J. 84

Edelman, L. 40
Eekelaar, J. 57
Elliot, A. 119
Elliot, F. 154
Ellis, C. 23, 122
Entman, R. 73, 94, 95, 96, 97, 100, 136, 150, 182
Esser, F.120
Etlin, M. 47
Evans, J. 21, 73, 97, 98, 99, 100, 174, 176

Fan, D. 120
Fawcett, B. 105
Featherstone, B. 49, 104, 105
Fein, E. 55
Ferguson, H. 42, 43, 46, 52, 112, 115, 116
Fitzgibbon, W. 17, 114
Francis Report 125
Freeman, M. 61, 65
Freud, S. 47, 73, 74
Frosh, S. 74
Furedi, F. 22

Game, C. 32
Giddens, A. 46, 103, 104, 114, 117, 119
Gilbert, C. 52
Girard, R. 83
Goddard, C. 105
Goldson, B. 40
Gordon, K. 47, 60
Greenland, C. 57
Griffiths, D. 50
Gyford, J. 32

Hanning, J. 154
Hannon, C. 55
Hansard 33, 62, 125, 136, 140, 157, 184
Harris, J. 43

Hart, P.T. 92
Hattersley, R. 123
Haydon, D. 64
Hernstein, R. 106
Hills, J. 112, 124
Hinshelwood, R.D. 73, 161
HM Government 35, 107, 109
HM Treasury 106
Hoggett, P. 78, 79, 82, 85, 105, 161
Holland, S. 85
Hollway, W. 117
Home Office 104
Hood, C. 120
Horlick-Jones, T. 115
Hunt, A. 117

Iphofen, R. 22

Jackson, L.A. 41, 47
James, A. 41
Jefferson, T. 117
Jeffrey, V. 83
Jenks, C. 41
Johnston, R. 107
Jones, R. 17, 18, 54

Kempe, C.H. 50, 57
Kenway, P. 124
Kitzinger, J. 47, 98, 99, 100, 135
Kuhn, R. 91

Laming Report 34, 35, 53, 81, 103, 108, 112, 116, 121
Latour, B. 115
Law, J. 115
Leach, S. 32
Leveson Inquiry 154, 183
Levitas, R. 105
Lewis, J. 103
Lippmann, W. 138
Lister, R. 105
Littlechild, B. 114
London Borough of Brent 53, 56, 58
London Borough of Greenwich 59
Lownsborough, H. 108
Lund, B. 103

Macdonald, G. 115, 117, 118
Macdonald, K. 115, 117, 118
MacInnes, T. 124
Maluccio, A.N. 55
Mann, K. 64, 169
Manthorpe, J. 154
Martell, L. 103, 106

Masson, J. 115
Mauthner, M.L. 22
Mazzoleni, G. 94
McIntosh, M. 47, 48
Menzies Lyth, I. 82
Mills, N. 158, 159
Milner, J. 48
Money-Kyrle, R. 81
Morris, C. 55
Motz, A. 48
Moynihan, F.J. 50
Munro, E. 45, 115
Murray, C. 57, 106

Nava, M. 47, 60, 61, 62
Neubaum, G. 86, 161
Newman, J. 203, 110, 111, 112, 221
NSPCC 27

Ofsted 27, 28, 38, 57, 112, 187, 188, 190, 192
O'Leary, D. 108
Olmstead, K.A. 55
Orkney Report 53

Parekh, A. 124
Parker, R. 47
Parton, N. 15, 17, 43, 44, 45, 50, 51, 54, 55, 56, 57, 58, 59, 63, 112
Pattie, C. 107
Payne, M. 45, 112
Pearce, J. 115
Postman, N. 41
Powell, M. 43, 50, 51, 103, 111, 112
Prior, L. 21
Prout, A. 41

Radford, L. 107
Reder, P. 49
Richards, B. 53, 100
Roberts, V. 58
Rosen, L.N. 47
Roseneil, N. 64, 169
Roth, E.T. 116
Ruch, G. 115
Rustin, M. 67, 68, 80-1, 115, 191
Ryan Report 48

Scanlon, M. 50, 51
Schillemans, T. 92
Schmidt, G. 107
Scholsberg, J. 73, 92-4, 100, 135, 138, 156, 163
Scraton, P. 64
Seebohm, F. 44
Sefton, T. 124
Segal, H. 76, 77
Seu, B. 79-80, 122
Shemmings, D. 41
Sibert Report 200
Smith, E. 42
Spencer, N.J. 107
Stainton-Rogers, W. 41
Stanley, N. 154
Steiner, J. 49, 79, 194
Stewart, K. 124
Stokes, J. 107
Stroud, J. 212
Sturken, M. 138
Surender, R. 103
Syed, M. 212

Taft, L. 158
Trickett, J. 123
Trowler, I. 214
Turney, D. 115

Waldfogel, J. 112
Walker, M. 48, 97, 99
Walsh, D. 21
Ward, A. 115
Warner, J. 118, 144, 150, 170, 192
Welch, M. 83, 84
Wilkins, D. 41
Williams, F. 105
Winnicott, D. 43
Woman's Budget Group 105
Wood, C. 55

Zelizer, V.A. 41, 43
Zinn, J.O. 114

Sharon Shoesmith worked for children for almost 40 years in a career which included her role as Director of Children's Services in the London Borough of Haringey, and a nationwide role as one of Her Majesty's Inspectors. She now works as a researcher, writer and public speaker in areas related to education and social care. Sharon also works as a volunteer with Macmillan Cancer Care at University College Hospital. In 2015, she completed a PhD in Psychosocial Studies at the University of London, Birkbeck College, upon which this book is based.